DAVID LEWIS
(1750–1798)
and
JOANNAH TRUNDLE
(1754–1810)
from
Frederick County, Maryland
to
Harrison County, (West) Virginia

Some Ancestors and Descendants

Doris Jean Post Poinsett

"A people that take no pride in the noble
achievements of remote ancestors will
never achieve anything worthy to be
remembered with pride by remote
descendants." —*Macaulay*

HERITAGE BOOKS
2016

HERITAGE BOOKS

AN IMPRINT OF HERITAGE BOOKS, INC.

Books, CDs, and more—Worldwide

For our listing of thousands of titles see our website
at
www.HeritageBooks.com

Published 2016 by
HERITAGE BOOKS, INC.
Publishing Division
5810 Ruatan Street
Berwyn Heights, Md. 20740

Heritage Books by the author:

*David Lewis (1750–1798) and Joannah Trundle (1754–1810) from
Frederick County, Maryland to Harrison County, (West) Virginia:
Some Ancestors and Descendants*

*John/Jean Poinset (- by 1739) of Burlington, New Jersey, Pierre Poinset L'aîné (-1699)
of Charles Town, South Carolina and Some of Their Descendants*

*CD: John/Jean Poinset (- by 1739) of Burlington, New Jersey, Pierre Poinset L'aîné (-1699)
of Charles Town, South Carolina and Some of Their Descendants*

Valentin Pfost/Post, 1740–1800 of Hardy County, (West) Virginia and Some of His Descendants

International Standard Book Numbers
Paperbound: 978-0-7884-6337-2
Clothbound: 978-0-7884-2214-0

Dedicated to the memory of

*Clara Ercle (Strader) Post,
granddaughter of Elmore Dow Lewis
and his first wife, Sarah (Post) Lewis*

PREFACE

Two early settlers living in the Province of Maryland around 1700 were Jonathan Lewis and John Trundle I. This is an attempt to provide information about some of their descendants. The title contains the name of David Lewis and Joannah Trundle, one descendant of each settler.

This work is divided into two parts to cover descendants of the two settlers and their known wives. The first part is limited to the first four generations of descendants of Jonathan and Mary (---) Lewis and the second part is limited to the first four generations of descendants of John I and Mary (---) Thorley Trundle. Female lines have been extended for only one generation out of the surname. Within those limitations descendants through great-great-grandchildren for whom records were found have been included.

Certainly there must have been descendants within those limitations for whom no information was found. Also a few connections were made through preponderance of the evidence rather than through a record of proof.

The time allowed for research and compilation of information did not permit the inclusion of any descendants in generations not already mentioned. Those interested in a probable connection to this Lewis family or this Trundle family should be able to determine whether there is a connection by researching more recent generations back to the period covered in this work.

Doris Jean Post Poinsett

CONTENTS

PART ONE

LEWIS FAMILIES

PART TWO

TRUNDLE FAMILIES

aft. .... after
ahp .... author has photocopy
Apr. .... April
AR .... Arkansas
Aug. .... August
b. .... born
bef. .... before
bet. .... between
Bn. .... Battalion
bp. .... baptized
bur. .... buried
ca. .... *(circa)* about
Capt. .... Captain
Cem. .... Cemetery
Co. .... Company, County
Col. .... Colonel
comp. .... compiler(s)
d. .... died
DAR .... National Society Daughters of the American Revolution
dau. .... daughter
DC .... District of Columbia
dec. .... deceased
Dec. .... December
Dist. .... District
d/o .... daughter of
DRHC .... Patricia B. Hickman, *Harrison County, West Virginia Death Records 1853-1903* (Bowie, MD, 1991)
ed. .... editor(s), edition
Eng. .... England
Esq. .... Esquire
et al. .... (*et alia*), and others
f. (ff., plural) .... folio(s)
Feb. .... February
Gen. .... General
Gent .... Gentleman
Gov. .... Governor
HCWV 1850 .... *1850 Census of Harrison County WV* (n.p., n.d.)
HCWV 1860 .... *1860 Census of Harrison County WV* (n.p., 1986)
Hon. .... Honorable
husb. .... husband
ibid. .... (*ibidem*), in the same place
IN .... Indiana
Jan. .... January
Jr. .... Junior
jurat .... (*juratum*), certificate added to an affidavit
KY .... Kentucky
lbs. .... pounds
LCWV 1850 .... *1850 Census of Lewis County WV* (n.p., n.d.)
LCWV 1860 .... *1860 Census of Lewis County West Virginia* (n.p., 1985)
LCWV 1870 .... *1870 Census of Lewis County West Virginia* (n.p., 1987)
m. .... married
MA .... Massachusetts
Mar. .... March
MCHS .... Montgomery County Historical Society

LIST OF ABBREVIATIONS

MD	....	Maryland
MR	....	Marriage Record
MRHC	....	*Harrison County Marriages 1785-1894* (n.p., 1985)
MRLC	....	Wes Cochran *et al.*, *Lewis County Marriages 1817-1880* (n.p., n.d.)
MRUC	....	*Upshur County WV Marriages 1851-1896* (n.p., 1992)
MSA	....	Maryland State Archives
MSS	....	Manuscript(s)
NARA	....	National Archives and Records Administration
NC	....	North Carolina
NJ	....	New Jersey
n.d.	....	no date
no.	....	number
Nov.	....	November
n.p.	....	no publisher
n. pag.	....	no pagination
Oct.	....	October
OH	....	Ohio
p. (pp., plural)	...	pages(s)
PA	....	Pennsylvania
PO	....	Post Office
poss.	....	possible, possibly
PPTB	....	Personal Property Tax Books, Virginia State Library, Richmond, VA
prob.	....	probable, probably
repr.	....	reprint
Rd.	....	Road
Rev.	....	Reverend
Rt.	....	Right
Sep.	....	September
s/o	....	son of
Soc.	....	Society
Sr.	....	Senior
St.	....	Saint, Street
stg.	....	sterling
TN	....	Tennessee
Twp.	....	Township
US	....	United States
UT	....	Utah
v.	....	volume(s)
VA	....	Virginia
vs.	....	versus
w/o	....	wife of, widow of
(W)V	....	State abbreviation for that part of Virginia which was to become a part of West Virginia 20 June 1863
WV	....	West Virginia
WV 1880	....	William A. Marsh, *1880 Census of West Virginia* (Parsons, WV & Baltimore, MD; 1979 & later)

LIST OF ILLUSTRATIONS

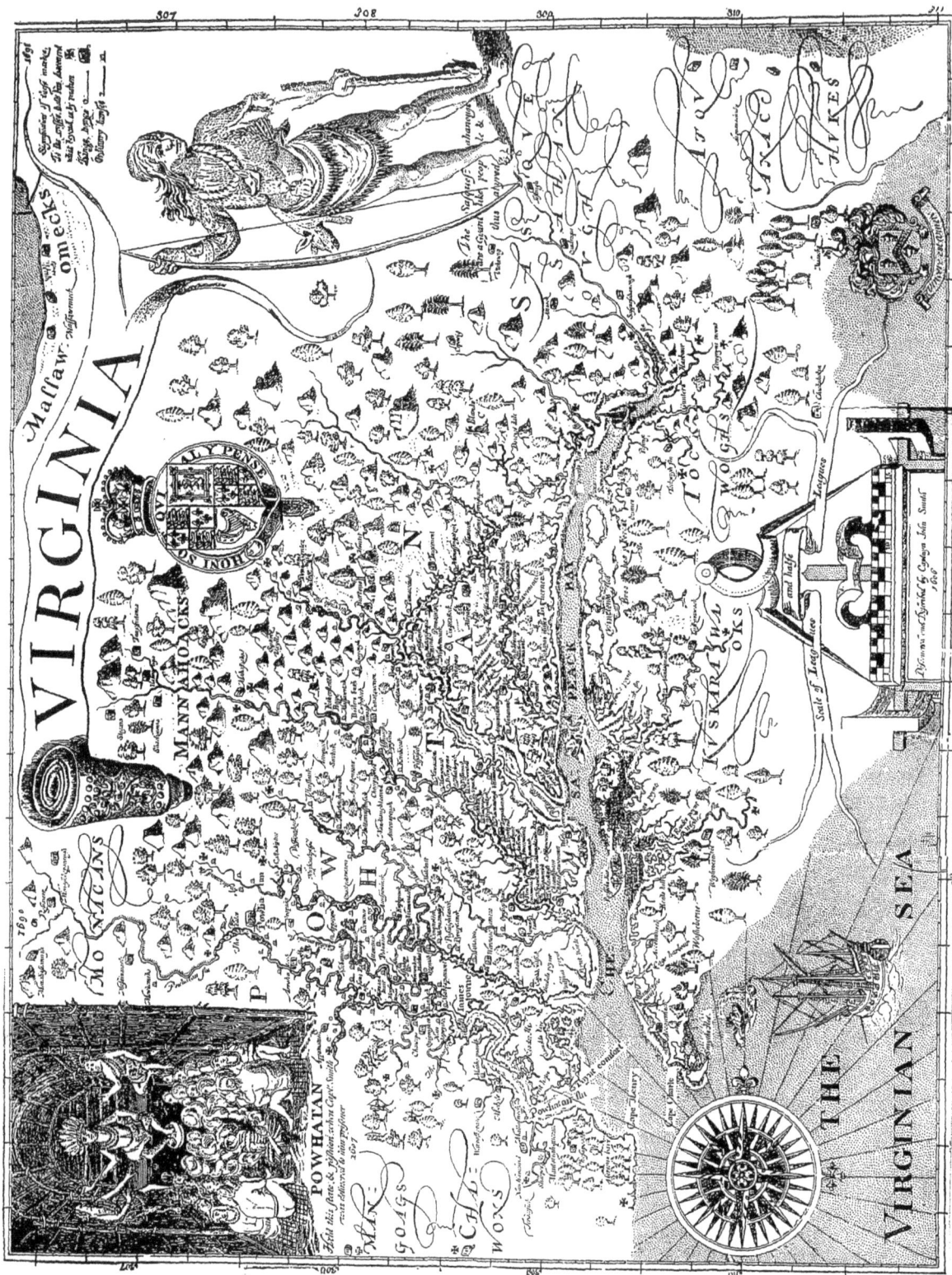

Ill. 1 - Captain John Smith Map of Chesapeake Bay. Reproduced from J. Thomas Scharf, *History of Maryland*... (Hatboro, PA, 1967 repr. 1879 ed.), v. 1, p. 6.

INTRODUCTION

Purpose

The purpose of this work is to provide information about some ancestors and descendants of David Lewis, born in 1750, and his wife, Joannah Trundle, born in 1754. This couple is said to have come from Monocacy, Maryland to Harrison County, (West) Virginia (Bernard L. Butcher, ed., *Genealogical and Personal History of the Upper Monongahela Valley* [New York, 1912], v. 2, pp. 437-439). The provider of that information published in 1912 appears to have been Ernest Daniel Lewis, a great-grandson of the couple, who was at that time a practicing attorney in Clarksburg, West Virginia. This present work provides some descendants of Jonathan Lewis and John Trundle I, the two progenitors, but is generally limited to those born into the fifth generation with the surname of Lewis or Trundle and those born into female lines for one generation out of those surnames. This allows for some lateral line ancestors, as well as some later lateral line relatives of both David Lewis and Joannah Trundle.

Information was assembled for the interest of present and future generations of descendants and related families, with special emphasis on citing sources of primary evidence to prove bloodlines. This work is intended only as a guide and should not be considered an authoritative source. The allotted time limited the amount of data that was collected, verified, and assembled. Data for any part of this work may have been faulty and were subject to further error during processing. Anyone who is interested in the family is encouraged to check original records further if available.

Maryland

The reader may appreciate this work more fully if he knows something of the geography and governing jurisdictions where Jonathan Lewis, John Trundle I, and all of their early descendants settled and lived. Their children were all born along the banks of the streams emptying into the Chesapeake Bay. This was in the Province of Maryland, chartered in 1632 as a proprietary colony of the Crown of England. Jonathan Lewis lived in Prince George's County, formed in 1696 from Calvert and Charles Counties, and John Trundle I lived in Anne Arundel County, formed in 1650 as an original county. It was not until 1691 that Annapolis was made the seat of government.

Land Grants

Some of the earliest records of the proprietary colony concerned land grants. The Conditions of Plantation under the proprietary form of government offered certain amounts of land to those who furnished their own transportation or who provided for the passage of others to Maryland. Records of land patents, first handled by the Governor and Council, began in 1633 about a year before the first settlers arrived.

INTRODUCTION

By 1637, generally an applicant presented his claim to the Secretary of the Province. The Secretary would issue a warrant to the Surveyor who was "to lay out and survey the specified quantity of land... and return the certificate of survey to the Secretary's office. The certificate named the person for whom the survey was made, described the boundaries of the land, and gave the total acreage of the tract. If the certificate was made out in proper form and there were no conflicting claims, a patent was issued granting the land described... to the applicant." A grant of land was given a name which often contained a family surname as in *Trundles Folley* and others noted in this work.

Counties and Hundreds

Prior to 1650 two areas of Maryland were treated as counties. The western shore was called St. Mary's County and the eastern shore was called Kent County. During those early provincial times before counties were officially formed there were no towns but there was a division of local government known as the hundred. The early hundreds were formed from important settlements. The hundred, initially composed of approximately 100 heads of family, was the militia district and the district for the assessment of taxes. The head officer was a justice of peace and under him was a constable. In 1650 upon the official formation of counties the Maryland hundred became a division within the county with a high constable, commander of the militia, tobacco viewers, overseer of roads, and assessor of taxes. The boundaries of the hundred frequently varied and as the population increased there were divisions and new hundreds were formed. The hundred system remained until 1824 when it was abolished and replaced with electoral districts.

A map of Maryland during early statehood was found and a portion of that map has been reproduced and appears below in this introduction. The map was for the time of the ratification of the constitution and is from 1780 and 1794 originals in the Library of Congress in Washington, and was issued by the United States Constitution Sesquicentennial Commission. It includes places of interest mentioned in the text of this work that should be of interest to Lewis and Trundle descendants. The following can be noted: (1) the Church (apparently St. Barnabas) in Prince George's County on Collington Branch between Bowie and Upper Marlborough; (2) Herring Bay, Anne Arundel County which is fed by Herring Creek, though that creek is not noted on this map; (3) Bennets Creek, Montgomery County; (4) Monocacy River, Frederick County.

Following is a chronological list of all 23 counties and one independent city in the State of Maryland with the year of formation and, when applicable, the county or counties from which each was formed:

St. Mary's	-	1637	-	Original County
Kent	-	by 1642	-	Original County
Anne Arundel	-	1650	-	Original County
Calvert	-	1654	-	Original County
Charles	-	1658	-	Original County
Baltimore	-	by 1659/60	-	Original County

Ill. 2 - Part of Maryland, from 1780 and 1794 originals in the Library of Congress in Washington, DC. Reproduced from collections of the Library of Congress, Geography and Map Division.

INTRODUCTION

Talbot	- by 1661/62	-	Original County
Somerset	- 1666	-	Original County
Dorchester	- 1669	-	Somerset and Talbot
Cecil	- 1674	-	Baltimore and Kent
Prince George's	- 1696	-	Calvert and Charles
Queen Anne's	- 1706	-	Dorchester, Kent, and Talbot
Worcester	- 1742	-	Somerset
Frederick	- 1748	-	Baltimore and Prince George's
Caroline	- 1773	-	Dorchester and Queen Anne's
Harford	- 1773	-	Baltimore
Montgomery	- 1776	-	Frederick
Washington	- 1776	-	Frederick
Allegany	- 1789	-	Washington
Carroll	- 1837	-	Baltimore and Frederick
Baltimore City	- 1851	-	Baltimore County
Howard	- 1851	-	Anne Arundel
Wicomico	- 1867	-	Somerset and Worcester
Garrett	- 1872	-	Allegany

Parishes

Although Maryland was known for its religious tolerance, the act of assembly of 1692 established the Anglican Church as the Church of Maryland and determined the parish boundaries. Many records from Anglican parish registers of the late seventeenth century, and later, are extant and have been published. These parish registers include some families in Prince George's and Anne Arundel counties and are mostly birth or baptismal records. Birth dates for children of Jonathan Lewis appear in the register of Queen Anne Parish, Prince George's County. A birth date for the son of John Trundle I appears in the register of St. James Parish, Anne Arundel County.

Colonial Records

The early records found were recorded in Maryland. There are several types of court or court like records such as land grants, deeds, wills, and estates, as well as other types of records found less frequently. Court records of the counties of Prince George's and Anne Arundel that were kept during colonial times were found at the Maryland State Archives in Annapolis. Court records of Frederick County for 1748 and later, were found at the county courthouse in the city of Frederick. Court records of Montgomery County, formed in 1776 after the colonial period, were found at the county courthouse in Rockville.

Photocopies of nearly all pertinent court documents were obtained from either the original or microfilm. In this way they could be studied and transcribed as necessary. Several of those transcribed documents have been published herein. Court copies are usually filed in huge record volumes. Most records found were in good condition but the

INTRODUCTION

volumes are clumsy to handle and close binding sometimes makes it impossible for clerks to photocopy the document completely from edge to edge. This may also have been a problem for some records at the time of microfilming, resulting in microfilm which is incomplete. In addition the ink on a few original documents is faded to the extent that any type of reproduction is difficult.

Colonial handwriting is often difficult to transcribe. Documents were written according to Colonial or early Maryland law and included words and phrases of the period. Often personal names were not capitalized but other nouns and adjectives were. Spelling was phonetic and often varied within one document written by the same clerk. In fact names continued to be spelled in many ways throughout the nineteenth century.

Later Records

On 4 July 1776 with *The unanimous Declaration of the thirteen united States of America,* Maryland, as one of those states became involved in the Revolutionary War. Many records related to that war have been published and provide names of interest. By 1778 one Lewis descendant had moved to North Carolina and around 1796 another Lewis descendant had moved to (West) Virginia. Shortly after 1800 some Trundle descendants moved to Kentucky. Records of counties in those states confirm these moves.

Beginning with 1790 decennial Federal Census records of counties contain names of heads of families and provide some clues as to family composition. It was not until 1850 that all members of a household were listed by name.

When counties required marriage licenses they were recorded at courthouses. Most of those marriage records have survived and have been published. Most descendants owned land resulting in numerous county deeds and assessment records. The time allowed for this work did not permit a detailed review of most later deeds that involve members of the later generations. In addition most later deeds involving female lines out of the surnames of Lewis and Trundle were not reviewed.

Some cemetery records that name later generations have been published. Vital records for some later generations were found in family Bibles.

Primary and Secondary Evidence

Perhaps one can understand the problems that have faced most researchers of any surname as common as Lewis. But another problem in researching this work was that the only names given to early Trundle males in Maryland seem to have been either John or Thomas. It was only when one descendant had a third male sibling born into the fourth generation that this pattern changed.

When information was found in an original record or facsimile thereof it was considered primary evidence. Types of original records have been covered above. When original records were not reasonably accessible, published works which are less reliable, were referenced as secondary evidence. Many public records, especially census and

INTRODUCTION

marriage records of counties in Maryland and other states, have been published in recent years. Some church and cemetery records have also been published.

A few Lewis and Trundle descendants were included in contemporary biographies published in earlier local histories of the various states and counties where they lived. There are also a few published genealogies for branches of the Lewis and Trundle families and connecting families.

In addition to information from published works, some descendants or connecting family members provided information. This was usually for later generations of their branches.

It is reasonable to expect some error from all types of information sources. Corrections to data are welcome and should be sent to the author along with a source of proof.

Acknowledgments

I am obligated to so many. First and foremost I am grateful to my Creator who has given me the ability, and graciously spared me long enough to assemble a third work in genealogy.

During the course of this work many archivists, court clerks, and librarians were instrumental in directing me to important sources of information. Other individuals contributed information and most of those individuals have been recognized in notes within this work.

My thanks are due to archivists at the Maryland State Archives who were especially helpful, enabling me to find documents, acquire copies, and publish some of those earliest records in the pages that follow. I am grateful to librarians at the Library of Congress, particularly those of the Geography and Map Division, who helped me locate early maps that could be reproduced. Jane Sween, Patricia Abelard Andersen, and other librarians at the Montgomery County Historical Society Library (Maryland), were very helpful when they assisted me in finding works of interest. Francis P. O'Neill, librarian at the Maryland Historical Society, helped me to make the most of a limited amount of time while in Baltimore. David R. Houchin provided copies of court documents from Harrison County, (West) Virginia. Dr. Noel W. Tenney made it possible to include the photo on the dedication page. Dr. Elaine Foster willingly answered questions related to editing. I am grateful to Benjamin Franklin Poinsett who accompanied me to distant research sites, helped with heavy court record volumes, provided necessary technical support in solving computer problems, and assisted me in so very many other ways.

Doris Jean Post Poinsett

WORKS REFERENCED:

Boyd, T.H.S. *The History of Montgomery County, Maryland from the Earliest Settlement in 1650 to 1879*. Clarksburg, MD, 1880, 2d ed.

Brown, Helen W. *Index to Register of Queen Anne Parish, 1686-1777*. DAR, 1960.

INTRODUCTION

Brumbaugh, Gaius Marcus. *Maryland Records: Colonial Revolutionary, County, and Church from Original Sources*. v. 1, Baltimore, 1985 repr. 1928 ed.

Hall of Records. *Instructions to Our New Researchers*. Annapolis, 1983.

"Maryland Rent Rolls: Baltimore and Anne Arundel Counties, 1700-1707, 1705-1724," A Consolidation of Articles from the *Maryland Historical Magazine*. Baltimore, 1976.

Scharf, J. Thomas. *History of Maryland*. v. 1, Hatboro, PA, 1967 repr. 1879 ed.

Skordas, Gust. *The Early Settlers of Maryland*. Baltimore, 1968.

Wright, F. Edward. *Anne Arundel County Church Records of the 17th and 18th Centuries*. Westminster, MD, 1989.

PART ONE

LEWIS FAMILIES

*"I was glad when they said
unto me, Let us go into the
house of the Lord." Ps.122.1*

Ill. 3, 4 - Entrance sign and view of St. Barnabas Church, Leeland, Prince George's Co., MD. Photos by Benjamin Franklin Poinsett, 22 May 1999.

CHAPTER ONE

JONATHAN LEWIS, THE PROGENITOR

1. **JONATHAN**[1] **LEWIS** was living in Prince George's Co., MD on 11 Sep. 1706 when he and his wife, **MARY**, had a son, Thomas, born there.[1] They were probably living in Queen Anne Parish in the vicinity of St. Barnabas Church (Anglican) located in a place now called Leeland.[2] In 1706 the rector of the then Chapel of Ease that preceded St. Barnabas was Robert Owen[3] and apparently Jonathan and Mary (---) Lewis were parishioners there.[4] Church registers show that by 8 July 1720 eight children had been born to this couple.[5] From 1708 to 1717 the rector was Jonathan White and he was followed by Jacob Henderson from 1717 to 1751.[6]

Jonathan Lewis was probably born *ca.* 1684 and one seminal work has him as a son of one Thomas Lewis but the limited source information provided seems to leave that unproved.[7] No records dated before 1706 were found for this Jonathan Lewis, but the fact that his first known son was named Thomas Lewis, makes it seem reasonable that Jonathan's father was also a Thomas Lewis. The name, Thomas Lewis, was common in Maryland before 1700.[8] Nothing significant was found to connect Jonathan to the suggested Thomas Lewis. At that time, there were also Lewis families across the Potomac River in Virginia.[9] Presently, the identity of the father of this Jonathan Lewis seems inconclusive.

Circa 1705 Jonathan Lewis married Mary ---. Apparently, from 1706 to 1720 they lived in the area now known as Leeland, Prince George's Co., MD.[10] In 1719 his name appeared in a list of taxables of Collington Hundred, Prince George's Co.[11] which before 1696 was a part of Calvert Co., MD.[12] Jonathan Lewis died *ca.* 1721/22, likely under the age of 40. On 7 July 1722 in Prince George's Co., MD there was a bond.

> 7 July 1722
> Bond of Joseph Belt Tho[s] Clagett Edward Sprigg bound unto R[t] Hon[ble] ye Lord P[r] of this Province
>   Sum of Thirty pounds Ster: Money
>   Seventh day of July 1722
> All and Singular Rights Creditts of Jonathan Lewis deced doe make or cause to be made a true and pfect Inventory of all & Singular the goods Chattles Credits of ye S[d] deced...

---

[1] Helen W. Brown, comp., *Prince George's County, Maryland, Indexes of Church Registers 1686-1885* (1979), v. 1, p. 321.

[2] In 1704 Queen Anne Parish was created from the northern portion of St. Paul's Parish. The first parish church of Queen Anne Parish was a frame building which had been a Chapel of Ease in St. Paul's Parish for some time prior to 1704. The Chapel of Ease was replaced by a brick building begun in 1708 and finished in 1715. Part of the present building of St. Barnabas Church on this site was begun in 1771 and finished in 1776 (ibid., v. 1, p. 281; 1999 rector, Reverend Mr. Harris).

[3] Constance Pelzer Ackerson, *Holy Trinity - Collington Her People and Their Church* (1978), p. 150.

[4] Brown, v. 1, p. 321.

[5] Ibid.

[6] Ackerson, p. 150.

[7] Michael L. Cook, *Pioneer Lewis Families* (Evansville, IN, 1984), v. 4, pp. 992-996. This multi-volume work should be studied by anyone researching Lewis families in America before 1700.

[8] Robert J.C.K. Lewis, *Lewis Patriarchs of Early Virginia and Maryland* (Bowie, MD, 1998, 3d ed.), pp. 127-128, 132-135, 143-147.

[9] Ibid., pp. 48-125.

[10] Brown, v. 1, p. 321.

[11] Publications of the Hall of Records Commission No. 1, *Calendar of Maryland State Papers, No. 1 The Black Books, State of Maryland* (Baltimore, 1967), #163, pp. 160-161.

[12] Louise Joyner Hienton, *Prince George's Heritage* (Baltimore, 1972), pp. 7-8.

to be Exhibited into the prorogation Court of Annapolis at or before the Seventh day of October next

Jo⁸. Belt   (seal)
Tho: Clagett   (seal)
Ed: Sprigg   (seal)

In presence of us
Richard greene
Tho⁸ Brooke J^r13

There was an inventory of

yᵉ goods & chattels of Jonathan Lewis Late of prince geo: county... taken 13 february 1724¹⁴

There were cows, heifer, mare, colt, young horse, etc., for a total value of £6.2.0. Inventory received 24 Nov. 1725 was made by E^d Holmes and Samuel Brashears.¹⁵ On 29 June 1726 an account of Joseph Belt, administrator of Jonathan Lewis, shows £16.11.7 paid with an overpayment of £7.7.¹⁶ It took nearly four years to settle the estate of Jonathan Lewis.

He left a widow and as many as seven children. His widow, Mary (---) Lewis, must have remarried shortly after the death of her husband. In Mar. 1723 there was the following:

LEWIS, David:-
LEWIS, Jonathan:- Mary Beckett in her proper person in Court here binds her Sons Jonathan Lewis & David Lewis both (being twins) Five years old the 7 of October last unto William Mordant untill they arrive to the age of 21 years - Whereupon he the said William Mordant in Court here Engages to Learn the said Jonathan and David to read and write and to give each of them a decent suit of Apparell at the Expiration of their time ·¹⁷

Earlier, in 1719, the name of William Moredent appeared in a list of taxables in West Branch Hundred, Prince George's Co.¹⁸ On 31 Mar. 1741 William Mordant made his will which was as follows:

In the name of god amen I William Mordant of Prince georges County being Sick of body but of Perfect mind and memory do make and constitute this to be my last will and testament and do Dispose of my worldly Estate which it hath pleased god to Bless me w^th (?) in the following manner Viz⁺. Item I will and bequeath unto my god Daughter Elir^a (?) Burgess my chest of Drawers and Large Looking glass w^th (?) is now in possession of (?) Edwd Diggs
Item I will and bequeath unto Sarah Harvie all my Deceased wifes wearing apparrell and all the remainder part of my Estate I Devise it may be Equally Divided Between Sarah Harvie Jonathan Lewis and ~~David~~ David Lewis and do constitute and appoint Ignatius Diggs to be my Exe^tr of this my last will and testament given und^r my hand and Seal this 31st day of march 1741 ___
Seal^d. Sign^d and Declar^d   Wm Mordant

─────────────────────────

¹³ MSA, Bond Box 5, Folder 50, Prince George's Co., MD, abstracted 13 June 1998. Col. Joseph Belt m. (1) Hester/Ester Beall d/o Col. Ninian Beall (Elizabeth B. Heterick, *Five Families "Beall" of Maryland, Their Intermarriages and Descendants...*, section for "Colonel Ninian Beall," pp. 1-6; Ackerson, pp. 61-62; Brown, v. 1, pp. 286-287). He m. (2) Margery (Wight) Sprigg (MSS, Belt folder, MCHS). The Belts were parishioners at St. Barnabas where births of some of their children are recorded in church registers (Brown, v. 1, pp. 286-287). In 1719 Joseph Belt was a taxable in Collington Hundred (Publications of the Hall of Records).
¹⁴ MSA, Inventory Box 6, Folder 20, Prince George's Co., MD, abstracted 13 June 1998, difficult to read.
¹⁵ Ibid.
¹⁶ MSA, Account Liber 7, f. 443, Prince George's Co., MD, transcribed 13 June 1998.
¹⁷ Dorothy H. Smith, *Orphans and Infants of Prince Georges County, Maryland 1696-1750* (Annapolis, 1976), pp. 66-67. David & Jonathan Lewis b. 7 Oct. 1718 to Jonathan & Mary Lewis (Brown, v. 1, p. 321).
¹⁸ Publications of the Hall of Records, #161, p. 23.

in the presents of all
     his
John O O Osborn
     mark
Peter P Parker
     his mark
Robert Ridell
April 20th   Then came John Osborn & Peter Parker two subscribing
1741   Evidence to the foregoing will and being Duly Sworn Declare they saw sa^d: Wm Mordant
the Deces^d Testator sign the foregoing will and heard him publish & Declare the same to be his last
will and Testament and at the time of his so doing he was of Sound & Disposing memory to the
best of their apprehension and in his presence & at his request they Subscribed the same as
evidences and they believed the other subscribing evidence saw and heard the same as they did
Sworn before
                    Pet^r Dent D^ty Cle (?) of Pr. Geo. County[19]

On 26 Apr. 1741 John Hepburn, Ignatius Diggs, Basil Waring, and George Parker were
bound four hundred pounds to settle the estate of William Mordant, deceased. This was
in presence of Tho: Dawson and Pet^r Dent.[20] There was an inventory 15 July 1741 that,
as a legatee, young Jonathan Lewis signed by mark. John Hepburn was one of the
executors and the estate was valued at £194.6.9.[21]

Mary (---) Lewis seems to have married Humphrey Beckett by Mar. 1722 and had at
least four more children. Humphrey and Mary (---) Lewis Beckett had the following
children born near now Leeland, Prince George's Co., MD: Benjamin, b. 18 Dec. 1722;
Humphrey, b. 18 Dec. 1722 (twin of Benjamin); dau. b. *ca.* 1726,[22] prob. Johanna;[23]
Joseph, b. 4 Apr. 1729.[24] Indeed, Mary (---) Lewis Beckett must have been a healthy and
strong woman to have survived the birth of 12 children.

Earlier, on 30 Apr. 1706, one Humphrey Beckett, planter of Prince George's Co. for
3,000 pounds of tobacco acquired a 31 acre portion of *First Purchase*, part of a tract of
land called *Cattail Meadows*. This land was acquired from Elizabeth Anderson, wife of
the late Robert Anderson, and Robert Anderson, planter, son of the late Robert
Anderson.[25] Humphrey Beckett signed by mark when he sold this 31 acre parcel of land
on 11 July 1719 for £50 to Mahitabell Pierpont, James Holland, and Larking Pierpont of
Prince George's Co.[26] By 4 August 1736 this Humphrey Beckett was aged 63 according to
his own deposition about this same land.[27] On 11 Sep. 1711 Humphrey Beckett
witnessed by mark an indenture from Michael Ashford of Stafford Co., VA to John
Bradford, merchant of Prince George's Co.[28] On 2 July 1723 Humphrey Beckett was
witness to another indenture, Benj. Clark, Gent of Virginia to Robt Tyler, Gent of Prince

[19] MSA, Will Box 6, Folder 11, Prince George's Co., MD, transcribed 1 June 1999. William Mordant m. 22 Dec. 1715 Anne Arundel Co., MD, Ann Watts (Brown, v. 1, p. 327).
[20] MSA, Bond Box 11, Folder 61, Prince George's Co., MD, abstracted 1 June 1999.
[21] MSA, Inventory Box 12, Folder 21, Prince George's Co., MD, abstracted 1 June 1999.
[22] Brown, v. 1, p. 286.
[23] One Johanna Beckett (*ca.* 1725-1770) m. Hugh Tomlinson Sr. (*ca.* 1720-1765) (MSS, Tomlinson folder, MCHS).
[24] Brown, v. 1, p. 286.
[25] Prince George's Co., MD, Deed Liber C, f. 239, cited in Elise Greenup Jourdan, *The Land Records of Prince George's County, Maryland 1702 to 1709* (Annapolis), p. 66.
[26] Ibid., Deed Liber F, Old Series 6.i, ff. 232/819, cited in Elise Greenup Jourdan, *The Land Records of Prince George's County, Maryland 1717 to 1726* (Knoxville, TN, 1991), p. 22.
[27] Harry Wright Newman, *Mareen Duvall of Middle Plantation* (Washington, 1952), p. 165.
[28] Prince George's Co., MD, Deed Liber F, f. 95, cited in Elise Greenup Jourdan, *The Land Records of Prince George's County, Maryland 1710 to 1717* (Knoxville, TN, 1990), p. 11.

George's Co.[29] The 1706 and later Humphrey Beckett of Prince George's Co. was likely the Humphrey Beckett who married Mary (---) Lewis. Perhaps he had lived in Virginia some time before 1706.

It seems likely the Humphrey Beckett who married Mary (---) Lewis was the same Humphrey Beckett who was a son of an earlier Humphrey Beckett. Also, one John Beckett who was a son of Ester/Hester (---) Beckett Abrahams was likely a younger son of the earlier Humphrey Beckett. If so, the two sons may have been only half-brothers. The earlier Humphrey Beckett probably died some years before 14 Aug. 1712. Ester/Hester (---) Beckett Abrahams was the wife of Hugh Abrahams who died *ca.* 1713. Previously, she may have been a wife of the earlier Humphrey Beckett.[30] In 1733 both a Humphrey Beckett and a John Beckett were listed in Patuxent Hundred, Prince George's Co., MD.[31]

In summary, **JONATHAN LEWIS**, b. prob. *ca.* 1684 MD; d. *ca.* 1721/22 near now Leeland, Prince George's Co., MD; m. *ca.* 1705 prob. MD, **MARY** ---, b. *ca.* 1685 prob. MD; d. aft. 4 Apr. 1729 prob. Prince George's Co., MD. **MARY (---) LEWIS** m. (2) prob. by Mar. 1722 Prince George's Co., MD, **HUMPHREY BECKETT**, b. *ca.* 1673 prob. VA or MD; d. prob. aft. 4 Aug. 1736 Prince George's Co., MD.

Children of Jonathan and Mary (---) Lewis, all born in the vicinity of now Leeland, Prince George's Co., MD:

	i.	Thomas[2], b. 11 Sep. 1706.
	ii.	William, b. 13 Oct. 1708.
	iii.	Jonathan, b. 29 Aug. 1711; d. by 7 Oct. 1718.
	iv.	John, b. 30 Nov. 1713.
2.	v.	Daniel, b. 6 Oct. 1715.
3.	vi.	David, b. 7 Oct. 1718.[32]
	vii.	Jonathan, b. 7 Oct. 1718 (twin of David).[33] When Jonathan Lewis was five years old his mother, Mary (---) Lewis Beckett, had him bound to William Mordant.[34] On 31 Mar. 1741 when William Mordant made his will in Prince George's Co., he named Jonathan Lewis, making Jonathan a legatee to his somewhat sizable estate.[35] Jonathan was then a young man 22 years of age. By 1770 he probably lived in Frederick Co., a part that in 1776 became part of Montgomery Co. On 12 Dec. 1770 one Jonathan Lewis reported stray livestock at his place in Frederick Co.[36] In 1777 the name of one Jonathan Lewis appears with two taxables in a Linganore Hundred, Montgomery Co.,

[29] Ibid., Deed Liber F, Old Series 6.1, f. 467, cited in Elise Greenup Jourdan, *The Land Records of Prince George's County, Maryland 1717 to 1726* (Knoxville, TN, 1991), p. 71.

[30] Jane Baldwin Cotton, comp., *The Maryland Calendar of Wills...1703 to 1713* (Baltimore, 1968), v. 3, p. 249, will of Hugh Abrahams, 14 Aug. 1712, proved 12 May 1713. John Beckett m. (1) 18 Nov. 1723 Prince George's Co., MD, Mary Nicholls (Brown, v. 1, p. 286); John Becket m. (2) 17 Nov. 1724 Prince George's Co., MD, Ann Drayne (ibid., p. 285).

[31] Publications of the Hall of Records, #266, pp. 38-39. There was a Humphrey Becket who was a pensioned Revolutionary War soldier for service with the Maryland Line (*Prince George's County Genealogical Society Bulletin* [1984], v. 15, p. 80). This soldier must have been someone b. aft. 1722, thus not the s/o Humphrey & Mary (---) Lewis Beckett. Houses of Assembly, the name of one John Beckett was in a petition for release from imprisonment for debt; recommendation of the county court for clemency; certification of the clerk, dated 3 Apr. 1762 (Publications of the Hall of Records, #1182, p. 83).

[32] Brown, v. 1, p. 321.

[33] Ibid.

[34] Smith.

[35] MSA, Will Box 6, Folder 11; MSA, Inventory Box 12, Folder 21.

[36] F. Edward Wright, *Early Lists of Frederick Countians 1765-1775* (Silver Spring, MD, 1986), p. 5.

MD tax list,[37] suggesting he may have had a son. There was surely a younger Jonathan Lewis who on 5 June 1778 enlisted as a private in the First Regiment of the Continental Service and was discharged 1 Nov. 1780.[38] This younger Jonathan Lewis was likely the same Jonathan Lewis who was listed as a private with the Maryland Line between 1 Aug. 1780 and 15 Nov. 1783.[39]

viii.   Mary, b. 28 Sep. 1720.[40]

---

[37] Eleanor M.V. Cook, "1777 Tax List of Montgomery County," *Maryland Genealogical Society Bulletin* (1990), v. 31, pp. 8-9.

[38] *Archives of Maryland, Muster Rolls and Other Records of Service of Maryland Troops in the American Revolution 1775-1783* (Baltimore, 1972), v. 18, pp. 131-132.

[39] Ibid., pp. 522- 543. Records indicate the discharge date of the first service overlaps the beginning date of the second service, but it seems unlikely this means there were two Jonathan Lewises serving during this period.

[40] Brown, v. 1, p. 321; Michael L. Cook, v. 4, p. 996 has a son Jeremiah b. 1722, but Mary (---) Lewis had m. Humphrey Beckett by 1722. Their twin sons, Benjamin & Humphrey Beckett, b. 18 Dec. 1722 (Brown, v. 1, p. 286).

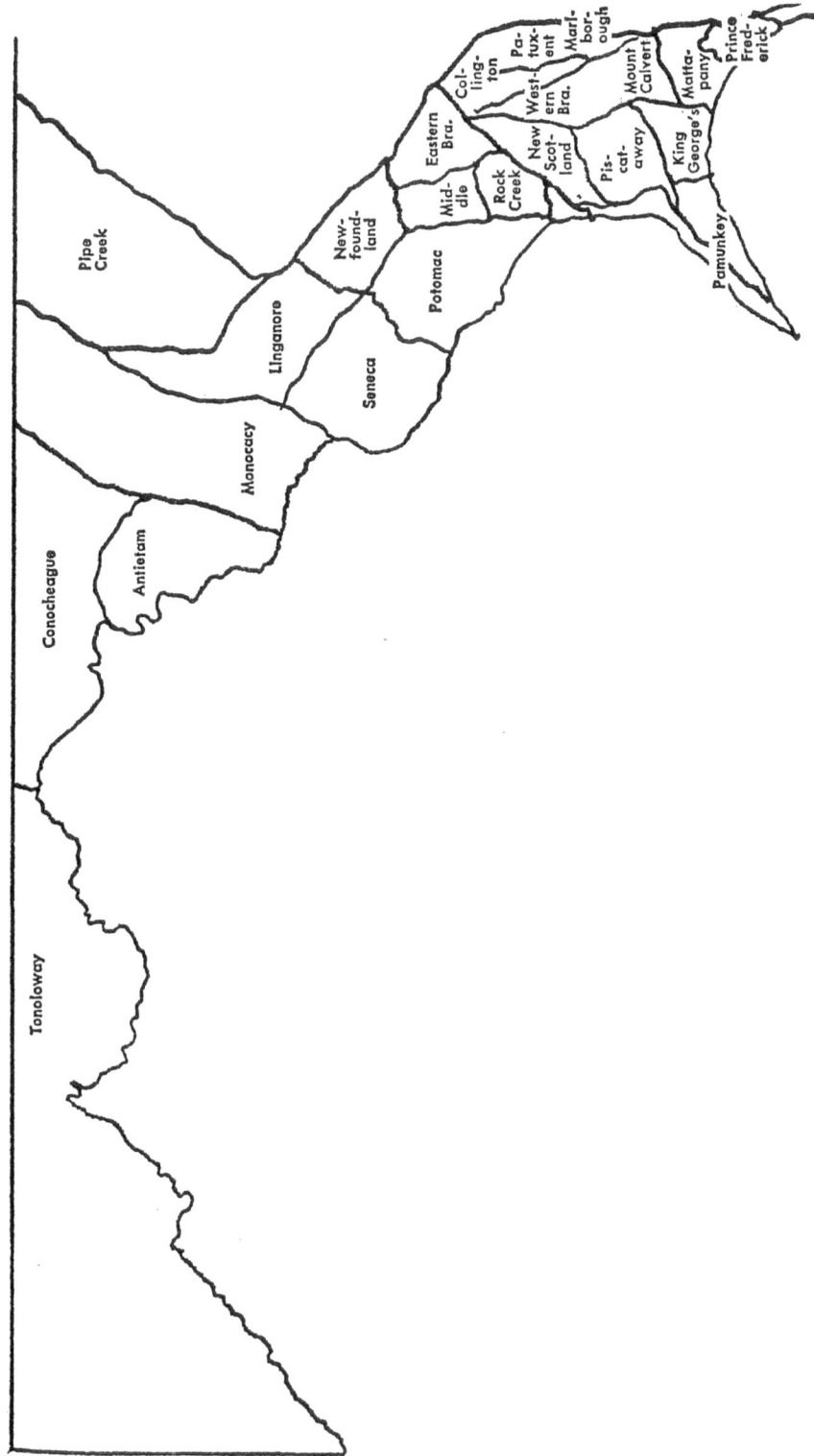

Ill. 5 - Hundreds of Prince George's Co., MD from 1745 to 1748. Reproduced from Louise Joyner Hienton, *Prince George's Heritage* (Baltimore, 1972), p. 45.

CHAPTER TWO

LEWIS, SECOND GENERATION

2. **DANIEL**[2] **LEWIS** (*Jonathan*[1]) (see 1), b. 6 Oct. 1715 near now Leeland, Prince George's Co., MD;[1] d. bet. 1783[2] & 11 June 1787[3] Bennett Creek, Montgomery Co., MD;[4] m. by 1761[5] prob. Prince George's Co., MD, **MARGARET ?BEALL**, b. poss. *ca.* 1732 Prince George's Co., MD;[6] d. prob. *ca.* 1793 Bennett Creek, Montgomery Co., MD;[7] d/o John (s/o Robert) & prob. Elisabeth (---) Beall.[8]

Daniel Lewis probably lived in the home of his parents, Jonathan and Mary (---) Lewis, until 1721/22 when his father died. This seems to have been near now Leeland, Prince George's Co., MD. At that time Daniel was a lad of only six years of age. Shortly, his mother married Humphrey Beckett and he likely grew to manhood in the home of Humphrey and Mary (---) Lewis Beckett, probably in the same area of Maryland.

In 1748 Daniel Lewis was a soldier in the Maryland Militia. He served with Capt. George Beall's Troop of Horse, Prince George's Co., MD.[9] In that same year Frederick Co., MD was formed from Baltimore and Prince George's Co. Little else is known of Daniel Lewis as a young man, but surely he had married Margaret Beall by 1761, perhaps much earlier. The 1761 will of John Beall, son of Robert, named a daughter, Margaret, who must have been the wife of Daniel Lewis at the time of that will. Because Daniel's first known child, Jeremiah, was born in 1745[10] and his last known child, Drusilla, was born in 1775,[11] it is reasonable to think Daniel Lewis had been married before. One researcher says Daniel married Margaret Edwards, but left open the possibility that he could have married Margaret Beall later.[12] An effort to verify that a Margaret Edwards was a wife of Daniel Lewis failed. The will of John Beall was as follows:

> In the Name of God Amen I John Beall son of Robert of prince Georges County in the province of maryland being in good health and perfect memory blessed be to god therefore do this twenty third day of December in the year of our Lord one thousand Seven hundred and Sixty one do make and publish this my Last Will and Testament in manner and form following

---

[1] Helen W. Brown, comp., *Prince George's County, Maryland, Indexes of Church Registers 1686-1885* (1979), v. 1, p. 321.

[2] Eleanor M.V. Cook, *1783 Maryland General Assessment of Montgomery County, Maryland and 1782 Maryland General Assessment Upper Potomac Hundred* (1997), p. 41.

[3] Montgomery Co., MD, Will Liber 1, ff. 190-191.

[4] Ibid., Will Liber B, ff. 220-221, author has photocopy of original; ibid., Deed Liber A, ff. 394-396, ahp.

[5] MSA, Will Box 10, Folder 48, Prince George's Co., MD, original, transcribed 23 Feb. 1999; Watkins family Bible, "Copied personally by contributor, Mrs. Harry Gutridge. Present owner of Bible [1930-1932] is Mr. Bates Watkins of Montgomery County, Md. Original owner was Nicholas Watkins, Born Nov. 1, 1763," in Helen Harman & Mrs. Elmer E. Curry, *Report of Committee on Genealogical Research, District of Columbia Daughters of the American Revolution,* (1930-1932), v. 5, pp. 4-7 has Jeremiah Lewis, s/o Daniel, b. 30 Mar. 1745.

[6] MSA.

[7] *Heads of Families at the First Census of the United States... 1790 Maryland* (Washington, 1907), p. 90; Montgomery Co., MD, Deed Liber E, ff. 524-527, ahp.

[8] MSA.

[9] Murtie June Clark, *Colonial Soldiers of the South 1732-1774* (Baltimore, 1983), p. 23.

[10] Montgomery Co., MD, Will Liber B, ff. 220-221, author has photocopy of original; ibid., Will Liber 3, ff. 198-200; Watkins family Bible.

[11] Montgomery Co., MD, Will Liber B, ff. 220-221; gravestone, old family burying ground, David Trundle's near Barnesville Dist., Dickerson Station, Montgomery Co., MD, cited in Helen W. Ridgely, *Historic Graves of Maryland and the District of Columbia* (Baltimore, 1967), p. 181.

[12] Information, courtesy of Jackson H. Day, e-mail, 24 Feb. 1999 has Daniel m. to a Margaret Edwards but provides no source.

Imps I Commend my Soul into the hands of Almighty God who it me and my body to the Earth from whece it Came in hope of as Joyful Resurrection (?) the Merits of my Lord and Savior Jesus Christ and as for that worldly Estate wherewith it has pleased god to bless me with I dispose there of as follows.

first I give to my Son Robert Beall that tract of Land Coled yᵉ addition of godfathers gift wear on he Lives

Item I give to my Son James Beall all the old tract of Land Coled Godfathers Gift to him and his Ears

Item I give to my son Menmon Beall that parcel of land I bought of Thomas Plummer to him and his Ears and Asines

Item I give to Son John Beall Sixty Ares of Land coled Elizabeths choses that he lives on to him and his Ears and Asines for Ever and like I give to my son John forty fore acres of Land Coled Ceamzen to him and his Ears and Asines for Ever

Item I give to my son losson Beall one (?) and that land cold the mil land wher Richard Scadges feads to him and his Ears and asines and I give to my son lossen that seventy (?) acres of Land that he lives on Cold Addison to him & his Ears and Asines for Ever

Item I give to my son Shadrak Beall one hundred Acres of Land Coled Chands to him & his Ears & asines for Ever and Like wise I give to my son Shadrak Seventy fore acors of Land to him & his Ears & asins for Ever

Item I give to my Son Frances Beall all that tract of Land I now live on Cold the James and marry to him and his Ears and asines for Ever after the Deseas of his mother and likewise I give to my Son frances a tract of Land Coled plumers Jack to him and his Ears and asins for Ever and Likewise I give to my Son fransses a tract of Land Coled worthe nothing to him and his Ears and asins for Ever

Item I give to my two Sons Robert and John Beall all that part of the James and Mary that Wm Huse Live on to be Ecolle Divided to them and thear Ears and Asins for Ever

Item I give to my Daughter fife pounds Curence to hir and hir Ears and Asins

Item I give to my daughter Margare that part of the Mil Land I had of Dannel Lous if he make good the Right to me or hir if not the Land whear on he now lives to hir and hir Ears and asins for Ever and likewise twenty acors of that Mil Land I leave to my Son Losson Joyn to that of Louses and Likewise I give my Daughter Margery the best feather Bed and furniture to it her chases and Like I give hir the mare and Saddel (?) now Cools hirs and fore hed of Cattel at her Choes and fore hed of Sheep the Same

Item I give to my Daughter Elisabeth fife pounds Currence

Item I give to my Son Robert fifteen pounds Currence to be pad to my grandaughter Nace Woodward to be good to hir at the age of Sixteen or the Day of Marriage

Item I give all the Rest of my Estate to my Loving wife after my Just Debts are pade all back Rents and other Debts to me hir Rite and properties

Item I do appoint my Loving wife Elisabeth Beall full and Soul executor of this my last will and Testament

In Testimony where of I have hereto Set my hand and Seall the day and year within Written

Signed sealed acknowledged
and declared in the presence of us
and or mentioned being Requested by the
Testator & witnesses
    hir
Mary X Woodward
    mark
Wm Magruder Selby
William mullikin Juner
Joh. Mullikin the son of William

                his
John EB Beall Son of Robert (seal)
      mark

Maryland Prince Geo. County Ist On the 24ᵗʰ day of Janury Anno Dom 1767 came Wᵐ Magruder Selby Wᵐ Mullican Junior & John Mullican son of Wᵐ & made oath on the holy Evangelists of Almighty God, that The did see John Beall son of Robert sign & seal the above instrument of writing & publish the same as his last Will & testament, that at the time of his so doing he was to

the best of their apperehention of sound memory & of a disposing mind, when in his fore (?) & at his request they did subscribe the same as Witnesses, when Mary Woodward did the same
     Sworn before me day & year affs[d]
       G Scott D Camry Pr. geo.[13]

Daniel Lewis had a daughter named Margaret[14] and seems to have had a daughter named Elisabeth,[15] possibly named for her maternal grandmother, Elisabeth (---) Beall.[16] One researcher said she was Elisabeth Cameron but had no source for that information.[17] Nothing was found for an Elisabeth Cameron as the wife of John Beall. Daniel Lewis is known to have had two sons, almost certainly a third son, and possibly a fourth son. Three of those Lewises had daughters named Margaret. The three were: Jeremiah, born 1745;[18] David, born 1750;[19] and Daniel Jr., born 1755.[20] Apparently Daniel Lewis was living in Frederick Co., MD by 1755.[21] The land on which he was living in 1761, according to the will of John Beall, seems to have been called *Mill Land* in Frederick Co. On 11 Sep. 1769, after the death of John Beall, there was a deed of 108 acres of land to Daniel Lewis from Robert Beall, son of John. Robert Beall must have been the brother-in-law of Daniel Lewis. This deed may have been in compliance with the will of John Beall and was part of a tract called *John and Elizabeth* being part of a tract called *Three Bealls Manor*. The deed was as follows:

At the Request of Daniel Lewis the following Deed was Recorded september 25th. 1769 To wit. This Indenture Made this Eleventh Day of Septem[r]. in the year of Our lord One thousand seven hundred and sixty Nine Between Robert Beall son of John of Prince Georges County in the province of Maryland planter of the One part and Daniel Lewis of Frederick County in the s[d]. Province planter of the Other part witnesseth that the s[d]. Robert Beall son of John for and in Consideration of the sum of Fifty pounds Current Money of Maryland to me in hand paid the Receipt whereof I do hereby acknowledge doth grant bargain and make Over unto Daniel Lewis his heirs and assigns all that tract a parcell of land Called John and Elizabeth being part of a tract of land Called Three Bealls Mannour situate lying and being in Frederick County Beginning at a stake near a bounded white Oak being the beginning Tree of the Original Tract and standing South three Perches and an half from s[d]. Tree and Running Hence North fifty five degrees and an half Degree & west twenty and three Perches then north forty degrees East One hundred and seventeen perches then North twenty seven degrees East forty four perches then south forty Eight Degrees East Ninety Perches then south twelve degrees East One hundred and fifty Perches then with a straight line to the beginning stake Containing and laid out for One hundred and Eight acres of land more or less Together with

[13] MSA

[14] Montgomery Co., MD, Will Liber B, ff., 220-221; Frederick Sheely Weiser, ed. & translator, *Records of Marriages and Burials in the Monocacy Church in Frederick County, Maryland and in the Evangelical Lutheran Congregation in the City of Frederick, Maryland 1743-1811* (Washington, 1972), pp. 40-41.

[15] Ibid., pp. 36-40.

[16] MSA.

[17] Information, courtesy of Mr. Day.

[18] Montgomery Co., MD, Will Liber B, ff. 220-221; ibid., Will Liber 3, ff. 198-200; Watkins family Bible.

[19] Montgomery Co., MD, Will Liber B, ff. 220-221; Lewis family Bible, possession of Edgar Lewis, Johnstown, Harrison Co., WV (1982), may have been the Bible of Jonathan Lewis (b. 1793), family records transcribed and provided, courtesy of Noel Kent Dawson, Springfield, VA.

[20] *Montgomery Co., Md. Oath of Fidelity & Tax Lists - 1778*, pp. 3-4, presented by Mrs. Lilly C. Stone through the Janet Montgomery Chapter, DAR (1949) has his name as Daniel Lewis Junr. with his mark "X;" NARA, Revolutionary War Pension, roll 1555, S4531, No. 9559, his pension application of 1832, Iredell Co., NC has his name as Daniel Lewis, b. 1755 Frederick Co., now Montgomery Co., MD, signed Daniel Lewis with his mark "X." He was not named in the will of Daniel Lewis (Sr.) though he must have been his son. Iredell Co., NC, Will Book 2, p. 159, cited in Lois M. P. Schneider, *Inventory of the Estate Papers of Iredell County, North Carolina 1788-1915* (Troutman, NC, 1987), p. 59; Mary Elinor Lazenby, *Lazenby, Some Account of Families in the United States Which Bear the Name* (Washington, 1942, 2d ed.), p. 43 gives this Daniel Lewis a dau., Margaret.

[21] NARA.

all houses Edifices gardens orchards woods underwoods profits Commodities advantages and appurtenances whatsoever to the said parcell of land belonging or in any ways appertaining and all the Estate right and title Claims and demand whatsoever of him the s^d. Robert Beall son of John of in and to the s^d. land and premises and Every part thereof to have and to hold the s^d. land and premises above mentioned and Every part and parcel thereof with the appurtenances unto the s^d. Daniel Lewis his heirs and assigns to the Only Proper use and behoof of the s^d. Daniel Lewis his heirs and assigns for Ever and the said Robert Beall son of John for himself and his heirs the s^d. tract or parcell of land against him and his heirs to the s^d. Daniel Lewis and his heirs or assigns shall and will warrant and for Ever defend by these presents and further he the said Robert Beall son of John his heirs and all and Every of them Lawfully Claiming any Esate Title or Interest in and to the premises above in and by these presents bargained and sold or any part thereof by from or under him them or any of them shall and will from time to time and at all times hereafter upon the Reasonable request and at the proper Costs and Charges in the law of the said Daniel Lewis his heirs or assigns make do seal and Execute all and Every which further and other lawfull and reasonable act and acts Device and Devices Conveyance and Conveyances in the law whatsoever for the further and better granting and Confirming and assuring of the land and premises affors^d. unto the said Daniel Lewis his heirs and assigns at by the s^d. Daniel Lewis his heirs or assigns or his Or their Councel learned in the law shall be Reasonably advised Devised and Required in witness whereof the party first Mentioned in this Indenture hath hereunto put his name and affixed his seal the day and Year first above written.........
(signed sealed and delivered in presence of)................. Ro^t. Beall son of John).... (Seal)
NB. the word fifty in the third line was Underlined before the sealing and Delivery of these presents.............................
David Lynn. Andrew Heugh......................
On the Back of which Deed was the following Indorsement To wit.........
Received sept^r. ye 11th. 1769 from Daniel Lewis the sum of Fifty pounds Current Money of Maryland being the full Consideration for the land and premises above Mentioned witness my hand.............
(testes) David Lynn, Andrew Heugh.........................Ro^t. Beall son of John).............
Fred^k. County on the 11th. day of September 1769 Came Robert Beall son of John before me the subscribers two of his Lordships Justices for the County affors^d. and acknowledged the above Indenture to be his act and Deed and the land and Premises therein Mentioned to be the right and Estate of the above named Daniel Lewiss his heirs and assigns for Ever...David Lynn Andrew Heugh).............
Recv^d. sept^r. 25 1769 of Daniel Lewis Four Shillings & four pence sterling an alienation fine on the above land by Order of Daniel of s^d. Thomas Jenifer Esqr. his lordships agent..........Christ^r. Edelen[22]

One may note the mention of orchards in this deed. An early twentieth century work states in reference to descendants of this Daniel Lewis:

> In this family there have been several nurserymen and fruit experts, known to the horticultural world for the fine quality of fruit they have produced after scientific methods of culture.[23]

In 1776 Montgomery Co. was formed from Frederick Co. and in 1777 Daniel Lewis Senr. was taxed in Lower Part of Newfoundland Hundred, Montgomery Co., MD. Apparently he was the one taxable in his household.[24] This was during the Revolutionary War. The following year, on 26 Feb. 1778, the name of Daniel Lewis Sr. appears in a list of all "Free Male Persons Names in Lower Newfoundland Hundred above eighteen years old," taken in by George Small, Constable.[25] Also in the list was the name of Daniel

[22] Frederick Co., MD, Deed Liber M, ff. 492-493, ahp.
[23] Bernard L. Butcher, ed., *Genealogical and Personal History of the Upper Monongahela Valley* (New York, 1912), v. 2, p. 437.
[24] Eleanor M.V. Cook, "1777 Tax List of Montgomery County," *Maryland Genealogical Society Bulletin* (1990), v. 31, p. 5.
[25] *Montgomery Co., Md. Oath of Fidelity & Tax Lists - 1778*, pp. 67-68.

Lewis Jr.[26] who seems to have been his son. In the same year, perhaps March 1778, both signed the Oath of Fidelity to the State of Maryland from Montgomery Co. Their names appear with their marks, as Daniel Lewis with his mark "DL" and Daniel Lewis Junr. with his mark "X" in the list delivered to the Court by Edward Burgess.[27] The Oath:

> 'I do sware I do not hold myself bound to yield any Allegience or obedience to the King of Great Britain his heirs or Successors and that I will be true and faithful to the State of Maryland and will to the utmost of my power, Support maintain and defend the Freedom and Independence thereof and the Government as now established against all open enemies and secret and traterous Conspriaces and will use my utmost endeavours to disclose and make known to the Governor or some one of the Judges or Justices thereof all Treasons or Treaterous Consperaces, attempts or Combinations against this State or the Government therof which may come to my Knowledge so help me God.'[28]

On 1 Jan. 1779 Daniel Lewis sold the 108 acres called *John and Elizabeth*, part of a tract of land called *Three Bealls Manor*, then in Montgomery Co., for £759 to Thomas Trundle III whose name appeared as Thomas Trundell Jr. Thomas Trundle III may have been a son-in-law of Daniel Lewis. The signature of Daniel Lewis was by his mark, "D," and was witnessed by Charles Jones and Richard Thompson.[29] In that deed the name of the wife of Daniel Lewis is given as Margaret. She appeared "according to the form of the Act of Assembly in such cases" stated as follows:

> On the Day and year within written came before us two of the Justices of the Law for Montgomery County Daniel Lewis party to the within Deed who acknowledged the same to be his Act and Deed and the Land and premises therein mentioned to be the right property and Estate of the within named Thomas Trundell junior his heirs and Assigns forever and according to the Form of the Act of Assembly in such cases made and provided At the same time came Margaret the Wife of the said Daniel Lewis and being by us privately Examined apart and out of the hearing of her said Husband relinquished her right of Dower to the within Land and premises and declared the same to be the right property and estate of the said Thomas Trundell junior his heirs and Assigns forever and that she made this acknowledgment freely and willingly without threats from her said Husband or fear of his displeasure and according to the form of the Act of Assembly in such cases made and provided
> Acknowledged before us Charles Jones Richard Thompson[30]

In the same year, on 22 Oct. 1779, Daniel Lewis acquired from Alexander Beall for £300, two parcels of land on "Hether Bennetts Creek" of Montgomery Co.: 305 acres called *Trouble Enough*, partly on Maple Branch of Hether Bennetts Creek, and 14 acres called *Close Tract*. The deed was as follows:

> At the Request of Daniel Lewis the following Deed was Recorded November the 12th: 1779 (to wit) This Indenture made this twelfth Day of November in the year of our Lord one thousand seven hundred and seventy nine between Alexander Beall of Mongomery County and States of Maryland planter of the one part and Daniel Lewis of the County and States aforesaid of the other part witnesseth that the said Alexander Beall for and in consideration of the Sum of three hundred pounds Current Money to him in hand paid by the said Daniel Lewis the receipt whereof the said

---

[26] Ibid.
[27] Ibid., pp. 3-4. One work has confused Daniel Lewis Sr. with Daniel Lewis Jr. by making Daniel Lewis Sr. a private in Capt. Edward Burgess' Co. and having him married to Margery Waters (Henry C. Paden Jr., *Revolutionary Patriots of Montgomery County, Maryland 1776-1783* [Westminster, MD, 1996], p. 200).
[28] Gaius Marcus Brumbaugh & Margaret Roberts Hodges, *Revolutionary Records of Maryland* (Baltimore, 1967), p. 1.
[29] Montgomery Co., MD, Deed Liber A, ff. 219-220, ahp.
[30] Ibid., f. 220.

Alexander Beall doth acknowledge and himself therewith fully satisfied and content and thereof and of and from every part and parcel thereof doth fully and clearly absolutely acquit exonerate and discharge the said Daniel Lewis his heirs Executors Administrators and Assigns and every of them for ever the said Alexander Beall hath bargained sold aliened enfeoffed conveyed confirmed and made over and by these presents doth bargain sell alien enfeoff convey confirm and make over unto the said Daniel Lewis his heirs and Assigns for ever All that Tract or parcel of Land called Trouble enough lying and being in Mongomery County aforesaid beginning at a bounded White Oak standing on the South side of Maple branch a draft of hether Bennetts Creek and running thence South twenty two Degrees West sixty perches then South sixty eight Degrees East twenty perches North fifty three Degrees East nine prs. then South sixty eight Degrees East nine perches then North fifty three Degrees East seventy two perches then North thirty seven Degrees East sixty six perches then North seventeen Degrees East thirty two perches then North twenty one Degrees West twenty perches then with a straight line to the beginning of the seventh line of the Original then with the said lines North forty seven Degrees West sixty perches then North sixty three Degrees West forty eight perches then to the and of the twenty forth line of Trouble Enough then South eighty five Degrees West to the out lines of Hazard then reverse with the said lines to the bounded (?) of Hazard then with a straight line to the eight perch on the sixteeth line of Trouble enough then South twenty seven Degrees West one hundred and twelve perches then South forty Degrees East sixteen perches then North twenty seven Degrees East sixty perches then South sixty nine Degrees and one quarter of an Degree East one hundred and forty perches then North sixty eight Degrees East one hundred and fifty eight perches then a straight line to the beginning Tree containing and now laid out for Three hundred and five Acres be the same more or less also one other Tract of Land lying and being in the County and State aforesaid called the Close Tract beginning at a bounded White Oak standing near a Creek called Hether Bennetts Creek and runing thence North thirty seven Degrees West twenty perches then North fifty six Degrees West twenty perches then South seventy nine Degrees West thirty six perches then North seventy seven Degrees West eighteen perches then South three Degrees East twenty perches then South seventy two Degrees East forty perches then by straight Line to the beginning Tree containing and laid out for forten Acres be the same more or less together with all and singular the rights profits benefits privileges and Advantages thereunto belonging or in any ways appertaining the grave yard only excepted to have and to hold all and singular the above mentioned Land and premises and every part and parcel thereof with the Appurtenances thereunto belonging on aforesaid unto him the said Daniel Lewis his heirs and Assigns to the only proper use and behoof of him the said Daniel Lewis his heirs and Assigns for ever and to no other use intent or purpose whatsoever and the said Alexander Beall for himself his heirs Executors and Administrators and every of them doth hereby covenant promise grant and agree to and with the said Daniel Lewis his heirs and Assigns that he the said Alexander Beall at and before Ensealing and delivery of these presents stands lawfully preserved and seized of the above mentioned Land and premises and every part and parcel thereof by a good perfect and absolute Estate of Inheritance in fee simple free and clear from all incumbrances whatsoever to the date of these presents and that he hath in himself good right full power and lawful Authority to sell and dispose thereof in manner and form as aforesaid And further the said Alexander Beall for himself his heirs Executors and Administrators doth covenant and promise to warrant and defend the said Daniel Lewis his heirs and Assigns in a quiet and peaceable free possession of all and singular the herein mentioned Land and premises again himself the said Alexander Beall his heirs Executors and Administrators and against all other persons whatsoever claiming and to claim any right title interest property claim or demand whatsoever by from or under him the said Alexander Beall his heirs Executors or Administrators by from or under any other person or persons whatsoever by virtue of these presents   In Witness whereof the said Alexander Beall hath hereunto set his Hand and affixed his Seal the day and Year first above written.

Charles Jones Will Deakins Junr.   Alexander Beall   {Seal}

On the Back of which Deed were the following and (?) (?) (to wit)

November 12th: 1779 Received the full and just sum of three hundred pound Current Money it being the full Consideration Money within mentioned Witness my Hand - Alexander Beall Charles Jones Will Deakins Junr.

Mongomery County Nov[r]. 12th. 1779. then came the within named Alexander Beall before us two of the Justices of the Peace for the County and States aforesaid and acknowledged the within mentioned Land and premises to be the right of the within named Daniel Lewis his heirs and Assigns forever Also Elisabeth Beall the wife of the said Alexander Beall being privately examined by us the Subscribers acknowledged her Right of Dower to the within Land and premises to be the right of the within named Daniel Lewis his heirs and Assigns forever and that she made the same acknowledgment without threats (?) (?) from her said Husband or for fear of his displeasure according to the direction of an Act of Assembly in that case mad and provided.

Taken and Acknowledeg before us. Charles Jones Will Deakins Jun[r].[31]

Trouble Enough and *Close Tract* were to become part of his final estate. It seems likely his home would have been on the smaller *Close Tract* that contained a graveyard apparently connected to the Alexander Beall family. On 9 Oct. 1780 Daniel Lewis leased 50 acres on Maple Branch, part of *Trouble Enough,* to Loyd Ward who was to plant and care for an orchard of 50 apple trees. The lease was as follows:

At the request of Loyd Ward the following Lease was received October 22[d]: 1780. (to wit) This Indenture made this 9th. day of October seventeen hundred and eighty between Loyd Ward of Montgomery County and Province of Maryland farmer of the one part and Daniel Lewis of the same County and Province of the other part Witnesseth that for and in consideration of this covenant hereafter mentioned and contained in the part and behalf of the said Loyd Ward his heirs Executors or Administrators to be paid kept and performed he the said Daniel Lewis hath demised granted and to perform better and by these presents doth demise grant and let unto the said Loyd Ward his heirs Executors or Administrators part of that tract of land situate lying and being in the County and Province aforesaid on Maple Branch being part of the tract called Trouble enough containing fifty Acres of land to have and to hold the said piece or parcel of land meant mentioned or intended to be unto him the said Loyd Ward his heirs Executors and Administrators from the date hereof for and during the time of twelve years to be compleat yielding and paying thereon the sum of three Pounds in the old way to be paid in grain wheat of two shillings p[r]. Bushel Corn at 2/. and Rye at 3/ p[r]. Bushel per year after the first 3 years is expired the first rent to be paid the first day of September in the year of our Lord 1784 and then to pay the above sum yearly the last rent to come due y[e]. 1st. day of Sept[r]. in the year of our Lord 1792 farther the said Daniel Lewis is to find 50. Apple trees and deliver the said Loyd Ward is to plant the said 50. Apple trees and keep then in good order and if a Tree or more should die he shall plant others in their room further the said Loyd Ward is to make no wilful waste of Timber more than for the new & vary use of the plantation fencing and building the said Daniel Lewis doth firmly bind himself his heirs Executors Administrators and Assigns in the covenant and contract aforesaid according to the true intent and meaning of these presents. In Witness whereof the partes above mentioned have unchangeably set their hands and Seals the day and year above written

Signed Sealed and delivered
in the presence of # # #

Jonathan Browning Jun[r]. Margaret X Lewis
            her   mark

Daniel D Lewis
  his   mark   Seal

Loyd X Ward
 his   mark[32]   Seal

Shortly, on 12 Dec. 1780 there was a bond between Daniel Lewis and his son, Jeremiah, which had to do with 150 acres of the same tract of land called *Trouble Enough*. The bond was as follows:

[31] Ibid., ff. 394-396, ahp.
[32] Ibid., f. 570, ahp.

At the Request of Jeremiah Lewis the following Bond was Recorded this (?) Day of June 1787. to wit: Know all men by these presents that - I Daniel Lewis of Montgomery County and states of Maryland am held and firmly bound unto Jeremiah Lewis of this same place in the full and Just - sum of two Thousand pound Old contenantel Currency to be paid unto the said Jeremiah Lewis his Lawfull Money heirs Executors administrators or assigns to the which payment well and Truly to be made and (?) I bind myself my heirs Executors and administrators in the whole and for the whole Jointly and severally firmly by these presents vested with my seal and dated this twelfth day of December one Thousand seven hundred and Eighty

The Condition of this Obligation is such that if the above bound Daniel Lewis his heirs Executors or administrators or either of them do and shall well and Truly make over or cause to be made over by a good and sufficient Deed of conveyance in fee simple unto Jeremiah Lewis his heirs or assigns forever part of a Tract of Land called Trouble Enough begining at the end of the twenty third line and then with the first line of the beginning at the first original bound to and with the Lines Express[t]. in a deed given by a Deed from Alexander Beall to the said Daniel Lewis unto the end of the Twelfth Line of the said Land and thence with a straight Line to the first beginning to Contain in and about one hundred and fifty acres of land more or Less and that or before the Twentyeth (Day of may Next Ensuing the date hereof - then this Obligation to be void and of none effect otherwise to remain in full force and virtue in Law   his

Signed sealed and delivered   Samuel Baker   Daniel   D   Lewis   {Seal}
in the presents of Test ----------- Alexander Beall   mark[33]

With the lease and bond of 1780 covering 200 acres of *Trouble Enough*, it seems likely the health of Daniel Lewis may have begun to fail soon after 1779 when he had acquired that tract. Further, on 4 Sep. 1781 Daniel Lewis made his will. It was as follows:

The Sate of Maryland in the Name of god amen I Daniel lewes of montgumery County Do make and ordain this my last will and testement in manner following I give and bequeth my Soul to god that made it in hopes of Eternil life only through the merits of and interssion of my Blesed lord and sav[ior] and Redemer Jesus Christ and my Body to the earth buaried by my excuters herafter named Item I give and bequeath unto my son Jaremiah lewes part of a tract of land Calld trouble enought a greable to a Bond given him in the year of our lord one thousand Seven hundred and eighty and also a nother tract of land Calld the Claose tract laying on Bennets Creek Run containing ten accers more or less Item I give and bequeath to my Daughter margret lewes one Bay mare Item I give and bequath unto my Daughter drusiller lewes one sorrel gildin Item I give and bequath unto my son David lewes one hiffer Item I give and bequath unto my[loving]wife margret lewes the whole Residue of my estate lasly I Do Cons (?) and appoint my son Jaremiah Lewes my Sole excataor of this my (?) last will and testement and I do hereby Revoke and make void all former by me made Ratifying and affirming this only to be my last will and testement in wittness wherof I have here unto Set my hand and affixd my Seal this forth Day of September anno Domin 1781 Signd Seald and Delivred in presents of

Alexander Beall   his   {Seale}
John Beall   Daniel   D   lewes
                                           mark[34]

Daniel Lewis likely lived more than five years after he made his will, recorded 11 June 1787.[35] It appears to have been Margaret (?Beall) Lewis, wife of Daniel Lewis, who was witness to the lease of 1780, rather than his daughter named Margaret, who would have been too young for that legal transaction. In 1783 the name of Daniel Lewis appears in "A List of Paupers in Linganore and Sugar Loaf Hundreds." There were then

[33] Ibid., Deed Liber C, f. 539, ahp.
[34] Ibid., Will Liber B, ff. 220-221, author has photocopy of original.
[35] Ibid., Will Liber 1, ff. 190-191.

Ill. 6 - Will of Daniel Lewis, on file in Montgomery Co., MD.

five white persons in his household, allowing for his wife, Margaret, and three unmarried daughters: Margaret, Drusilla, and probably Elisabeth who was almost certainly another daughter. Daniel must have disposed of all of his taxable property by 1783.[36]

On 15 Feb. 1785 Margreth Louis, daughter of Daniel Lewis, married Archibald Browning at the Frederick, Maryland Evangelical Lutheran Church. Witnesses were: Jonathan Browning, father of Archibald; Parsell Hervey and wife, Elisabeth; John Trandel, and James Castor.[37] A few months before, on 28 Dec. 1784, Elisabeth Louis married Parsell Hervey, both of "Benets-Crick." They were married at the same Evangelical Lutheran Church and witnesses were: Jonathan and Archibald Browning, Jeremia and Margreth Louis, and Alexander Beal.[38] Jeremia and Margreth Louis were surely either Elisabeth's brother and mother or her brother and sister. Elisabeth was not mentioned in the will of Daniel Lewis.[39]

Daniel Lewis was a planter and he seems to have grown apple trees and perhaps other fruit trees. Apparently he was unable to read and write, usually signing his name with his mark, "D." Daniel and his wife, Margaret (?Beall) Lewis, may have been members of, or worshipped at, the Evangelical Lutheran Church in Frederick, MD. Their known daughter, Margaret, and likely daughter, Elisabeth, were married there. It is said that Lewisdale, Montgomery Co., MD was named for this family. Lewisdale is located in northern Montgomery Co. at Lewisdale Rd. and Prices Distillery Rd. Orchards can still be seen in this part of the county. Daniel Lewis seems to have died in 1787 at the age of 71.

Margaret (?Beall) Lewis survived her husband and after he died she probably continued to live in what had been their home. In 1790 Margaret (?Beall) Lewis appears to be living alone in Montgomery Co. very near her likely step-son, Jeremiah Lewis.[40] She probably died *ca.* 1793. Daniel Lewis must have had an earlier wife. He is known to have had four children, but it seems almost certain there were at least six, possibly eight.

Children of Daniel Lewis and a probable earlier wife, likely all born in Prince George's Co., MD or, after 1748, Frederick Co., MD:

4. i. Jeremiah[3], b. 30 Mar. 1745.

    ii. Poss. Rachel, b. 30 Mar. 1748;[41] d. 1822 Bourbon Co., KY;[42] m. (1) *ca.* 1769 prob. Frederick Co., MD, **THOMAS TRUNDLE III**, b. 16 Jan. 1746/47[43] (see Trundle Families, Chapter Eight, No. 6); m. (2) by 8 Oct. 1813 prob. Bourbon Co., KY, **JAMES MATSON**.[44]

5. iii. David, b. 23 Sep. 1750.

---

[36] Eleanor M.V. Cook, *1783 Maryland General Assessment.*

[37] Weiser, pp. 40-41. Records were translated from the German and names retained some of that German spelling.

[38] Weiser, pp. 36-40.

[39] Montgomery Co., MD, Will Liber B, ff. 220-221.

[40] *Heads of Families.*

[41] DAR membership papers of Anita Claire Willison #462691, descendant of Thomas III. If Rachel Lewis was not a d/o Daniel Lewis, then it is likely she was a d/o one of Daniel's brothers.

[42] Ibid.; Montgomery Co., MD, Deed Liber Q, ff. 442-443, ahp.

[43] DAR membership papers of Anita Claire Willison.

[44] Montgomery Co., MD, Deed Liber Q, ff. 442-443, ahp.

Children of Daniel and Margaret (?Beall) Lewis, probably all born in Frederick Co., MD:

6.   iv.   Prob. Daniel Jr., b. 1755.

     v.   Poss. Stephen, b. poss. *ca.* 1760. In 1790 one Stephen Lewis was head of a family in Montgomery Co., MD. In his household were: one white male 16 years and upward, one white male under 16, and three white females. He seemed to be living very near the following: Margaret (?Beall) Lewis, widow of Daniel Lewis; Jeremiah Lewis, known son of Daniel Lewis; and Nicholas Watkins, known son-in-law of Jeremiah Lewis.[45] On 27 Jan. 1794 there was a deed from Stephen Lewis to Jeremiah Lewis for the tracts called *Trouble Enough* and *Close Tract*. The deed was probably necessary as a result of the death of Margaret (?Beall) Lewis whose name appears in the deed. The deed signed by Stephen Lewis may also have been necessary to comply with the will of Daniel Lewis.[46] In 1800 Stephen Lewis was head of a family in Montgomery Co., MD. In his household were: three white males under ten, one white male at least 16 but under 26, one white male at least 26 but under 45, one white female under ten, and one white female at least 26 but under 45.[47] By 1810 his household had grown to: one white male under ten, two white males at least ten but under 16, two white males at least 16 but under 26, one white male at least 26 but under 45, one white male 45 or over, two white females under ten, two white females at least 16 but under 26, one white female 45 or over, two free persons of color, and 14 slaves.[48] In 1820, and as late as 1840 the name of Stephen Lewis was recorded as head of a family in Montgomery Co., MD.[49] He seems to have been married with several children.

    vi.   Prob. Elisabeth, m. 28 Dec. 1784 Evangelical Lutheran Church, Frederick, MD, **PARSELL HERVEY**.[50] Elisabeth Lewis was surely the daughter of Daniel and Margaret (?Beall) Lewis and was probably named for her maternal grandmother, Elisabeth (---) Beall. Though she was not named in the 1781 will of Daniel Lewis, she was likely one of five white persons in the household of Daniel Lewis in 1783 when he was living in Linganore or Sugar Loaf Hundred, Montgomery Co., MD.[51] In the 1784 record of her marriage to Parsell Hervey, her name appears as Elisabeth Louis and both she and her husband were of "Benets-Crick." Witnesses to the marriage record were: Jonathan and Archibald Browning; Jeremia and Margreth Lewis, surely either her brother and mother or, possibly, her brother and sister; and Alexander Beall.[52] On 15 Feb. 1785 Parsell Hervey and wife, Elisabeth, were

[45] *Heads of Families.*

[46] Montgomery Co., MD, Deed Liber E, ff. 525-527, ahp, published herein.

[47] Ibid., NARA, 1800 census, roll 11, p. 36 or 216.

[48] Ibid., 1810 census, roll 14, p. 361.

[49] Ronald Vern Jackson & Gary Ronald Teeples, ed., *Maryland 1820 Census Index* (Bountiful, UT), p. 67; ibid., *Maryland 1840 Census Index* (Bountiful, UT, 1977), p. 89. More research is needed to determine how, or whether Stephen Lewis was related to Daniel Lewis.

[50] Weiser, pp. 36-40.

[51] Eleanor M.V. Cook, *1783 Maryland General Assessment.*

[52] Weiser, pp. 36-40.

witnesses when almost certainly her sister, Margreth Louis, identified as a daughter of Daniel Lewis, married Archibald Browning. Some of the church records retained the German spelling in translation.[53] On 13 Mar. 1787, Parsel Harvey was a witness to the marriage of Rachel Louis, his likely half niece-in-law, to Nicolas Watkins at the Evangelical Lutheran Church, Frederick, MD.[54] Nothing more was found for Parsell and Elisabeth (Lewis) Hervey in Maryland but they may have migrated, likely westward to another state, where the surname would likely appear as Harvey.

vii.   Margaret, d. poss. by 1809 Montgomery Co., MD;[55] m. 15 Feb. 1785 Evangelical Lutheran Church, Frederick, MD, **ARCHIBALD BROWNING**,[56] b. 10 Apr. 1753; d. 22 Aug. 1837 Bourneville, Ross Co., OH;[57] s/o Jonathan Browning.[58] Archibald Browning m. poss. (1) 2 Oct. 1774 Middletown, Frederick Co., MD, Sarah Johnson;[59] m. poss. (3) Eleanor Browning.[60] Margaret Lewis was the known daughter of Daniel Lewis and was probably named for her mother, Margaret (?Beall) Lewis. According to the 1781 will of Daniel Lewis, his daughter, Margaret, was to have one bay mare.[61] In 1783 she must have been one of five white persons living with Daniel Lewis in Linganore or Sugar Loaf Hundred, Montgomery Co., MD.[62] When she married Archibald Browning in 1785 witnesses were: Jonathan Browning; Parsell Hervey and wife, Elisabeth; John Trandel; and James Castor.[63] In 1790 Archibald Browning was living in Montgomery Co. probably with his wife, Margaret, two sons, and one daughter.[64] At least two of the children were likely from his earlier marriage to Sarah Johnson. In 1800 one Archibald Browning was head of a family in Montgomery Co., MD. In his household were: one white male under ten, one white male at least 26 but under 45, and one white female at least 26 but under 45.[65] Margaret (Lewis) Browning probably died by 1809. In 1810 Archibald Browning appears to be living in Montgomery Co., MD near Jeremiah Lewis, his former half brother-in-law. Living in the Browning household were: one white male 45 or over, two white females under ten, one white female at least 26 but under 45, and four slaves.[66] One Archd. Browning lived there in 1820.[67] Archibald Browning is believed to have married a third time to Eleanor Browning and later moved to Bourneville, Ross Co., OH where he died in 1837. Possible children of Archibald and Margaret (Lewis) Browning, born in Montgomery Co., MD:

[53] Ibid., pp. 40-41.
[54] Ibid., pp. 51-52.
[55] William Neal Hurley Jr., *Our Maryland Heritage, Book Twelve, Browning Families* (Bowie, MD, 1998), pp. 46-48.
[56] Weiser, 40-41.
[57] Hurley, p. 46.
[58] Weiser, pp. 40-41.
[59] Hurley, p. 46.
[60] Ibid., p. 46-47.
[61] Montgomery Co., MD, Will Liber B, ff. 220-221.
[62] Eleanor M.V. Cook, *1783 Maryland General Assessment.*
[63] Weiser, pp. 40-41.
[64] *Heads of Families.*
[65] Montgomery Co., MD, NARA, 1800 census, roll 11, p. 50 or 230.
[66] Ibid., 1810 census, roll 14, p. 318 or 931.
[67] Gary W. Parks, comp., *Index to the 1820 Census of Maryland and Washington, D.C.* (Baltimore, 1986), p. 33.

Baker, b. 29 Mar. 1787, d. young; Wesley, b. 15 Aug. 1795; Sarah Ann, b. 5 May 1805.[68]

viii. Drusilla, b. 22 Nov. 1775; d. 23 Sep. 1855 Montgomery Co., MD, bur. old family burying ground, David Trundle's, near Barnesville Dist., Dickerson Station, Montgomery Co., MD;[69] m. 18 Jan. 1797 Frederick Co., MD, **DAVID TRUNDLE**[70] (see Trundle Families, Chapter Eight, No. 7, i), b. 21 June 1773 Frederick Co., MD; d. 8 Mar. 1846 Montgomery Co., MD, bur. beside wife;[71] s/o John IV & Ruth (Lewis) Trundle.[72] Drusilla Lewis was the known daughter of Daniel Lewis and probably Margaret (?Beall) Lewis.[73] Her given name appears as Drusiller in the 1781 will of Daniel Lewis. She was to have one sorrel "gildin."[74] In 1783 she must have been one of five white persons living with Daniel Lewis in Linganore or Sugar Loaf Hundred, Montgomery Co., MD.[75] By 1790 her probable mother, Margaret (?Beall) Lewis, was living alone in Montgomery Co. suggesting Drusilla Lewis must have been living elsewhere.[76] On 18 Jan. 1797 she married David Trundle, said to have been her first cousin,[77] though more precisely, he was her first cousin once removed. In 1800 David Trundle was head of a family in Montgomery Co., MD. In his household were: one white male at least 26 but under 45, two white females at least 26 but under 45, and three slaves.[78] David Trundle was living very near several of his married siblings in 1810. In his household then were: one white male probably at least 26 but under 45, one white female under ten, one white female at least 26 but under 45, six free persons of color, and nine slaves.[79] When Ruth (Lewis) Trundle made her will, 3 Feb. 1810, she named her son, David Trundle, as executor. Further, he was to bring up her granddaughter, Drusilla Lewis Trundle Wilcoxen, whose mother, Letha (Trundle) Wilcoxen, had died.[80] Drusilla Lewis Trundle Wilcoxen was likely the female child living with David and Drusilla (Lewis) Trundle in 1810.[81] David Trundle died 8 Mar. 1846 at the age of 72. Drusilla (Lewis) Trundle survived her husband and died 23 Sep. 1855 at the age of 79. Though David and Drusilla (Lewis) Trundle had no children, it is said they reared 18 orphans and part orphans of the family.[82]

---

[68] Hurley, pp. 46-48.

[69] Gravestone, apparently on the property that had belonged to David Trundle, her husband, cited in Ridgely.

[70] Robert Barnes, comp., *Maryland Marriages 1778-1800* (Baltimore, 1978), p. 231.

[71] Gravestone, cited in Ridgely.

[72] Montgomery Co., MD, Will Liber G, ff. 149-151, ahp; ibid., Will Liber 2, p. 240.

[73] Montgomery Co., MD, Will Liber B, ff. 220-221.

[74] Ibid.

[75] Eleanor M.V. Cook, *1783 Maryland General Assessment.*

[76] *Heads of Families.*

[77] MSS typewritten, Trundle folder, DAR Library, Washington, DC, information gathered mostly in 1901, from Charles H. Trunnell, Georgetown, Washington, DC, pp. 1, 3, 17.

[78] Montgomery Co., MD, NARA, 1800 census, roll 11, p. 35 or 215.

[79] Ibid., 1810 census, roll 14, p. 359 or 970.

[80] Ibid., Will Liber G, ff. 149-151, ahp.

[81] Ibid., 1810 census, roll 14, p. 359 or 970.

[82] MSS, typewritten, Trundle folder, DAR Library, p. 3.

3. DAVID[2] LEWIS (Jonathan[1]) (see 1), b. 7 Oct. 1718 near now Leeland, Prince George's Co., MD, twin of Jonathan;[83] poss. m. by 1752, **DRUSILLA ---**.[84]

David Lewis probably lived in the home of his parents Jonathan and Mary (---) Lewis until 1721/22 when his father died. This seems to have been near now Leeland, Prince George's Co., MD. At that time he was barely three years old. In Mar. 1723 when he was five years old his mother, Mary (---) Lewis Beckett bound him and his twin brother, Jonathan, to William Mordant of Prince George's Co.[85] By that time his mother had married Humphrey Beckett and had had another set of twin boys, this time by Humphrey Beckett.[86]

On 31 Mar. 1741 when William Mordant made his will in Prince George's Co., he named David Lewis as a legatee to his somewhat sizable estate.[87] David was then a young man 22 years of age. He seems to have been the David Lewis who married Drusilla --- by 1752. Other information for this David Lewis was not found, but in later life he probably lived in Frederick or Montgomery Co., MD.

Child of David and Drusilla (---) Lewis, possibly born in Frederick Co., MD:

    i.   Ruth[3], b. 6 Mar. 1753;[88] d. 25 Mar. 1810 Montgomery Co., MD, bur. old family burying ground, David Trundle's, near Barnesville Dist., Dickerson Station, Montgomery Co., MD;[89] m. ca. 1771 prob. Frederick Co., MD, **JOHN TRUNDLE IV**,[90] b. ca. 1748[91] (see Trundle Families, Chapter Eight, No. 7).

---

[83] Brown, v. 1, p. 321.

[84] DAR, membership papers of Florence Michele Remmele #524815, descendant of John & Ruth (Lewis) Trundle, has Ruth Lewis b. 6 Mar. 1753. Pauline Beard Cooney, comp., *History of the Beard - Bedichek - Craven, and Allied Families* (1979), p. 159 gives the parents of this Ruth Lewis as David & Drusilla (---) Lewis.

[85] Dorothy H. Smith, *Orphans and Infants of Prince Georges County, Maryland 1696 - 1750* (Annapolis, 1976), pp. 66-67.

[86] Brown, v. 1, p. 286.

[87] MSA, Will Box 6, Folder 11, Prince George's Co., MD, transcribed 1 June 1999; Inventory Box 12, Folder 21, Prince George's Co., MD, abstracted 1 June 1999.

[88] Gravestone, cited in Ridgely.

[89] Ibid.

[90] DAR membership papers of Florence Michele Remmele; Cooney.

[91] Gaius Marcus Brumbaugh, *Maryland Records, Colonial, Revolutionary, County, and Church from Original Sources* (Baltimore, 1985 repr. 1928 ed.), v. 1, p. 226.

CHAPTER THREE

LEWIS, THIRD GENERATION

4. **JEREMIAH**[3] **LEWIS** (Daniel[2], Jonathan[1]) (see 2), b. 30 Mar. 1745[1] Prince George's Co., MD;[2] d. 22 Nov. 1822[3] Montgomery Co., MD;[4] m. *ca.* 1764 prob. Frederick Co., MD, **JANE**[5] **FITZGERALD**,[6] b. poss. *ca.* 1745 Prince George's Co., MD,[7] d. 9 Mar. 1814[8] Montgomery Co., MD.[9]

Jeremiah Lewis probably grew up in the homes of his father, Daniel Lewis, who likely lived first in Prince George's Co., MD, but by 1755 was living in Frederick Co., MD.[10] His mother seems to have been an earlier wife of Daniel Lewis. *Circa* 1764 Jeremiah married Jane Fitzgerald. On 13 Mar. 1787 their daughter, Rachel, who seems to have been their oldest child, married Nicholas Watkins.[11]

On 2 Feb. 1771 there was a lease between Josias Beall of Prince George's Co. and Jeremiah Lewis of Frederick Co. The lease was for 100 acres of land called *Layhill* in Frederick Co. and belonged to Josias Beall. The lease was as follows:

At the request of Jeremiah Lewis the following Lease was Received March the 19ᵗʰ. 1771 To wit...
This Indenture made the twenty Second Day of February in the year of our Lord seventeen hundred and seventy One Between Josias Beall of Prince Georges county of the one part and Jeremiah Lewis of Frederick county of the other part
Witnesseth that the said Josias Beall for and in Consideration of the yearly Rents and covenants herein after mentioned on the part of the said Jeremiah Lewis to be performed fulfilled and kept hath Demised granted and to farm hath and by these presents doth Demise Grant and to farm......Let unto the said Jeremiah Lewis all that part of a tract of Land belonging to the said Josias Beall lying and being in Frederick county Called Layhill Contained in the courses and bound following Begining at the End of Twentieth Line of the Whole Original tract of Layhill and Runing thence south fifty three Degrees West One hundred and fourteen perches then south seven Degrees West fifty Seven Perches then south sixty Degrees East fifty one perches then north Eighty One Degrees East One hundred and forty four Perches thence to the Begining Containing One hundred acres To have the said Parcel of Land and Premises with the appurtenances benefits and advantages thereunto belonging according to the covenants herein Expressed unto the said Jeremiah Lewis his Executors administrators and assigns from the first Day of December last past for and during and unto the full use and Term of Sixteen years from thence next Ensuing and fully

---

[1] Watkins family Bible, "Copied personally by contributor, Mrs. Harry Gutridge. Present owner of Bible (1930-1932) is Mr. Bates Watkins of Montgomery County, Md. Original owner was Nicholas Watkins, Born Nov. 1, 1763," in Helen Harman & Mrs. Elmer E. Curry, *Report of Committee on Genealogical Research, District of Columbia Daughters of the American Revolution*, (1930-1932), v. 5, pp. 4-7 has Jeremiah Lewis, s/o Daniel, b. 30 Mar. 1745.

[2] MSS, Lewis folder, MCHS, "Family Record" compiled, partly from a Lewis family Bible, and signed by Mrs. Myrtle E. (Lewis) Riggs.

[3] Watkins family Bible.

[4] Montgomery Co., MD, Will Liber 3, ff. 198-200, ahp; MSS, Lewis folder.

[5] Watkins family Bible; MSS, Lewis folder.

[6] Ibid.

[7] Ibid.

[8] Watkins family Bible.

[9] MSS, Lewis folder.

[10] NARA, Revolutionary War Pension, roll 1555, S4531, No. 9559.

[11] Frederick Sheely Weiser, ed. & translator, *Records of Marriages and Burials in the Monocacy Church in Frederick County, Maryland and in the Evangelical Lutheran Congregation in the City of Frederick, Maryland 1743-1811* (Washington, 1972), pp. 51-52; Watkins family Bible. In 1850 one Rachel Watkins, age 84, was living alone in Montgomery Co. (William Neal Hurley Jr., *Montgomery County, Maryland, 1850 Census* [Bowie, MD, 1998], p. 61).

to be compleat and Ended yielding and paying therefore yearly and Every year during the said Term unto the said Josias Beall his heirs Executors administrators or assigns at his or their Dwelling house the yearly Rent of Four shillings Sterling money and One Crop Hogshead of nine hundred and fifty pounds of Inspected Tobacco Clear of cask in Bladensburgh Warehouse at or upon the Tenth Day of June next after the said yearly Rent becomes one and if it shall happen that the said yearly Rent shall be behind and unpaid in part or the whole for the space of Seventy Days next after the said Tenth Day of June yearly or which the same ought to have been paid or aforesaid that then and at all times after it shall and may be Lawfull to and for the said Josias Beall his heirs Executors administrators or assigns into the said Demised Tenement and Premisses or into any part thereof in the name of the whole to Reenter under and the same to have again Repossess and Enjoy or in his and their former Right and Estate and the said Jeremiah Lewis his Executors administrators and assigns thruout and therefrom Expell and put out and for what Rent shall be behind and unpaid to Distrain upon the goods and Chattles of the said Jeremiah Lewis his Executors administrators or assigns any thing herein Contained to the contrary thereof in anywise notwithstanding and the said Jeremiah Lewis for himself his Executors and adminis^trs. and assigns doth covenant and Grant to and with the said Josias Beall his heirs Executors and administrators by these presents that he the said Jeremiah Lewis his Executors administrators and assigns shall and will during the said Term hereby Demised will and truly pay or cause to be paid unto the said Josias Beall his heirs Executors administrators or assigns the said yearly Rent of Four shillings sterling money and^one Crop Hogshead of nine hundred and fifty Pounds of nett Inspected Tobacco Clear of cask at the time and Place and in the manner above mentioned for the payment of the same according to the Reservation thereof as aforesaid and the true intent and meaning of these presents and also that the said Jeremiah Lewis his Executors administrators or assigns shall not Dispose of any timber nor sell nor cut Down or Otherways Destroy any timber Trees growing on the Premisses unless for Clearing Ground and necessary to be used about the Premisses and also that the Said Jeremiah Lewis his Executors administrators and assigns do not nor shall under the yearly Rent aforesaid Employ or work on the said Land any Other or more than One person or Labourer of any kind more than the said Jeremiah Lewis and his children but the said Jeremiah Lewis doth by these presents covenant agree and Oblige himself his heirs Executors administrators and assigns to pay the further additional Rent of Two hundred pounds of nett Crop Tobacco or above for Every such Person to be Employed or worked on the said Land to be yearly paid in manner and time and under the Like Condition with the Rent before Reserved and Expressed also that the said Jeremiah Lewis his Executors administrators or assigns shall and will on or before the first Day of December next Plant one hundred good apple Trees at the least on the said Demised Tenement and keep the same well fenced in and from time to time plant Others in the Room of such as shall happen to Die and further that the said Jeremiah Lewis his Executors administrators or assigns shall not assign or in any wise dispose of or make over any part or Parcel of the Premisses to any person whatever without the consent in Writing under the hand of the said Josias Beall first had and Obtained and also that the said Jeremiah Lewis his Executors administrators and assigns Build upon the said Demised Premisses a Dwelling house at Least sixteen Feet Square and a Tobacco house Forty feet in Length and the usual Dimensions in Breadth (agreeable to Thomas Betts Lease) and lastly that the said Jeremiah Lewis his Executors administrators or assigns shall leave the said Land and Premisses with the Buildings Fencing Orchards and Other Improvements thereon in good sufficient and Tenantable Repair at the Expiration or Other Determination of their Demise and the said Josias Beall for himself his heirs Executors administrators and assigns doth covenant and agree to and with the said Jeremiah Lewis and all Rightfully claiming by Virtue of this Demise that Paying the yearly Rents and Performing all and Every other the covenants herein Expressed shall and may Peaceably hold Occupy and Enjoy the Parcel of Land and Premisses herein Demised without the Let Hindrance or molestation of time the said Josias Beall his heirs or assigns or any claiming or to claim by or under him them or any of them-

In Witness whereof the Parties have hereunto set their hands and seals the Day and year above written   Josiah Beall   (Seal)

Sealed and Delivered in the Presence of Geo: Hardey Junr: Geo: Frazer Hawkins

.... Jeremiah Lewis   (Seal)

On the Back of which Deed was the following Indorsements To wit.....

Prince Geo County Is[t].. Feby. the 22nd: 1771 came the within named Josias Beall and Jeremiah Lewis and Each of them on their parts acknowledged this Instrument as their act and Deed for the use and purport on Each of their Parts therein Expressed before us......

    Geo. Hardey Jun[r]: Geo. Frazer Hawkins

Prince Georges County Is[t].. I hereby Certifie to whom it may or will Concern that messures George Hardey Jun[r]: and Geo Frazer Hawkins Gentlemen before whom the above acknowledgement was taken were at the time of taking the same and still are two of his Lordships the Right Honourable Lord Proprietarys Justices of the Peace for the County aforesaid Legally authorized and assigned to whom one of these is and Ought to be given or well in Justice court as thruout.........................

       ....In Testimony whereof I have hereunto set my hand and affixed

P. Geog[s]: County Seal ...the Publick seal of the County upon this Fifteenth Day of March

       ....seventeen hundred and seventy one......................................

       ....Test.........Tho[s]: Jim See Clk of Prince Georges County[12]

Jeremiah was to plant at least 100 good apple trees, keep them fenced, and replace them as necessary. He seems to have lived on the land called *Layhill* for several years after the lease. On 4 Dec. 1771 he witnessed the will of Nathan Garret of Frederick Co.[13]

In 1776 Montgomery Co. was formed from Frederick Co. and in 1777 Jeremiah Lewis was taxed in Rock Creek Hundred, Montgomery Co., MD with two taxables in his household.[14] This was during the American Revolution and in the same year, 1777, Jere. Lewis of Montgomery Co. was a private, 2d Co., 29th (Lower) Bn., Maryland Militia.[15] In 1778 when he signed the Oath of Fidelity to the State of Maryland from Montgomery Co., his name appeared as Jeremiah Leiws.[16] That same year, 1778, he was again taxed in Rock Creek Hundred, Montgomery Co.[17] He further supported the war against the British by supplying wheat and received a receipt for same 30 Apr. 1781.[18]

On 12 Dec. 1780 there was a bond between Jeremiah and his father, Daniel Lewis, for:

> ...part of a Tract of Land called Trouble Enough... to Contain in and about one hundred and fifty acres of land more or Less...[19]

Daniel Lewis seemed to follow the law of primogeniture. When he made his will 4 Sep. 1781 he left his oldest son, Jeremiah, most of his estate. Jeremiah was to receive part of a tract of land called *Trouble Enough* agreeable to the 1780 bond. In addition he was to receive another tract of land called *Close Tract* lying on Bennets Creek Run containing ten acres more or less.[20] On 28 Dec. 1784 his name appeared as Jeremia Louis when he was a witness to the marriage of his likely sister, Elisabeth Louis, to Parsell Hervey at the Frederick, Maryland Evangelical Lutheran Church.[21] This is the same church where

---

[12] Frederick Co., MD, Deed Liber O, ff. 81-82, ahp.

[13] *Maryland Calendar of Wills, 1767-1772* (Westminster, 1993), v. 14, p.227.

[14] Eleanor M.V. Cook, "1777 Tax List of Montgomery County," *Maryland Genealogical Society Bulletin* (1990), v. 31, pp. 15-16.

[15] S. Eugene Clements & F. Edward Wright, *The Maryland Militia in the Revolutionary War* (1987), p. 198.

[16] *Montgomery Co., Md. Oath of Fidelity & Tax Lists - 1778*, pp. 3-4, presented by Mrs. Lilly C. Stone through The Janet Montgomery Chapter, DAR (1949).

[17] Ibid., pp. 60-61.

[18] Edward C. Papenfuse et al., *An Inventory of Maryland State Papers, Volume 1, The Era of the American Revolution 1775-1789* (Hall of Records, Annapolis, 1977), p. 388.

[19] Montgomery Co., MD, Deed Liber C, f. 539, ahp.

[20] Ibid., Will Liber B, ff. 220-221, author has photocopy of original.

[21] Weiser, pp. 36-40.

his daughter, Rachel, was to marry Nicolas Watkins 13 Mar. 1787.[22] In 1790 Jeremiah Lewis was living in Montgomery Co. In his household were two white males 16 years and upward, three white males under 16, and four white females. His probable step-mother, Margaret (?Beall) Lewis, seemed to be living alone in a household nearby. Also, living nearby was one Stephen Lewis,[23] possibly his half brother and younger son of Daniel and Margaret (?Beall) Lewis. On 27 Jan. 1794 there was another deed for the tracts of land called *Trouble Enough* and *Close Tract*. This deed from Stephen Lewis to Jeremiah Lewis, perhaps as a result of the death of Margaret (?Beall) Lewis, was as follows:

At the Request of Jeremiah Lewis the following Deed was recorded this 27th day of February 1794 to wit This Indenture made this fourteenth day of January In the year of Our Lord One thousand Seven hundred and ninety four between Stephen Lewis of Montgomery County and State of Maryland of the one part and Jeremiah Lewis of the County and State aforesaid of the other part Witnesseth that the said Stephen Lewis for and in consideration of the Sum of seven shillings and Six pence current money of Maryland to him in hand paid by the said Jeremiah Lewis the receipt whereof the said Stephen Lewis doth hereby acknowledge hath given granted bargained sold aliened enfeoffed and confirmed unto the Said Jeremiah Lewis his heirs and Assigns forever all that part of a tract or parcel of land called trouble enough lying and being in the County aforesaid beginning at a bounded white oak the beginning tree of a tract of land called trouble enough and the beginning tree of a tract of land called, the resurvey on long looked for and running thence south twenty two degrees west Sixty perches south sixty eight degrees East twenty perches north fifty three degrees east nine perches south sixty eight degrees east nine perches north fifty three degrees East Seventy two perches north thirty Seven degrees East Sixty six perches north Seventeen degrees East thirty two perches north twenty one degrees west twenty nine perches then south seventy five degrees and one half degree west Seventeen perches to the end of the Twenty first at line of said tract called trouble enough then north forty seven degrees west Sixty perches north sixty three degrees west forty eight perches south eighty five degrees west Sixty four perches south twenty seven degrees west twenty five perches to the fourth line of a tract of land called Hazard then with said line reversed south Seventy degrees east ten perches to the beginning of said line then south twenty Seven degrees west three perches to the end of the fifth line of part of said tract called trouble enough as conveyed by Margaret Lewis and Stephen Lewis to James Sherlock then with the said part south fourteen degrees and three quarters of a degree East One hundred and fifty one perches south twenty three degrees west twenty nine perches to a tract of land called the resurvey on trouble enough in deed then north Sixty eight degrees east eighteen perches to the first line of trouble enough then with said line reversed to the first beginning containing and now laid out for two hundred and ninety three acres and one half acre be the Same more or less Also all that tract of land called closed tract lying and being in the County aforesaid beginning at a bounded White oak standing near a creek called Hethero Bennetts Creek being the beginning tree of said tract called closed tract and running thence north thirty seven degrees west twenty perches north fifty six degrees west twenty perches south Seventy nine degrees west thirty six perches north Seventy seven degrees west eighteen perches south three degrees East twenty perches south Seventy two degrees East forty perches then with a straight line to the first beginning containing ten acres of land be the same more or less together with all and Singular the houses buildings gardens orchards woods fences easements ways waters stones mines minerals improvements privileges advantages and appurtenances whatsoever thereunto belonging or in any (?) thereunto appertaining and also the reversion or reversions remainder or remainders rights issues and profits thereof with all the estate right title interest trust property claim and (?) whatsoever of him the aforesaid Stephen Lewis his heirs executors or administrators or any of them in the premises with the appurtenances as aforesaid To Have and To Hold the said part of a tract called trouble enough and all that tract of land called closed tract as aforesaid unto him the said Jeremiah Lewis his heirs and Assigns to the

[22] Ibid., pp. 51-52.
[23] *Heads of Families at the First Census of the United States... 1790 Maryland* (Washington, 1907), p. 90.

use and behoof of him the Said Jeremiah Lewis his heirs and Assigns forever, And to and for no other use intent or purpose whatsoever, And that the said Stephen Lewis do hereby covenant and agree to and with the said Jeremiah Lewis his heirs and Assigns that he the said Stephen Lewis and his heirs shall and will at all times will warrant and forever defend the aforesaid part of a tract of land called trouble enough and the tract of land called closed tract with the appurtenances as aforesaid to him the said Jeremiah Lewis his heirs and Assigns forever agreeable to the - (?) and intent of the present deed, And that the said Stephen Lewis his heirs executors administrators will at anytime hereafter execute any other deed of Conveyance for the (?) the above mentioned premises to the said Jeremiah Lewis his heirs executors administrators or Assigns In Testamony whereof the said Stephen Lewis hath hereunto Set his hand and affixed his Seal the day and year above written Signed Sealed and delivered in the presence of us   Stephen Lewis
    J Holmes Richd Green
On the Back of which Deed are the following endorsements to wit Received the 14th day of Jany One thousand Seven hundred and ninety four of Jeremiah Lewis the Sum of seven shillings and six pence current money of Maryland being the within consideration in full.
Witness J Holmes Richd Green   Stephen Lewis
State of Maryland Montgomery County to wit   On the 14th day of January One thousand Seven hundred and ninety four then came before us two of the Justices of the peace for the County aforesaid Stephen Lewis and acknowledged the within instrument of writing to be his act and deed and the land premises therein mentioned to be the right and estate of Jeremiah Lewis his heirs and assigns forever according to the true intent and meaning thereof and the act of Assembly in Such cases made and provided,
    Acknowledged before us J Holmes Richd Green[24]

In 1800 Jeremiah Lewis was living in Montgomery Co. In his household were: two white males at least 16 but under 26, one white male 45 or over, one female at least ten but under 16, one white female at least 16 but under 26, one white female 45 or over, and one free person of color.[25] On 20 Apr. 1802 one Mrs. Howard died at his home there.[26] In 1810 he was living in Montgomery Co. In his household were: one white male under ten, one white male at least 26 but under 45, one white male 45 or over, two white females under ten, possibly one white female at least ten but under 16, one white female at least 16 but under 26, one white female 45 or over, one free person of color, and eight slaves. It seems likely a married son or daughter with their young children were living with him in that year of 1810.[27] On 9 Mar. 1814 his wife, Jane (Fitzgerald) Lewis, died there. Just over a year later, on 23 Apr. 1815 in Montgomery Co. Jeremiah Lewis made his will which was as follows:

In the name of god Amen, I Jerimiah Lewis of Montgomery County and State of Maryland being far Advanced in age but in good health and of Sound Disposing mind memory and understanding. Considering the certainty of Death and the uncertainty of the time thereof and being desirous of Setling my worldly affairs and thereby be the better prepared to leave this world when it shall please God to call me. I the said Jeremiah Lewis do therefore make this my last Will and Testament in manner and form following that is to say, First and principally I commit my Soul Into the hands of Almighty God, and my body to the Earth to be buried in A Decent Christian like manner at the Discretion of my Executors herein after named Nothing doubting but at the General Resurrection I shall Receive the same again by the mighty power of God - And as touching my worldly Estate, wherewith it has pleased God to bless me in this life after my Just Debts are all

---

[24] Montgomery Co., MD, Deed Liber E, ff. 525-527, ahp. More research is needed to determine any relationship of Stephen Lewis to Daniel Lewis.
[25] Montgomery Co., MD, NARA, 1800 census, roll 11, p. 44 or 224.
[26] Helen W. Brown, comp., *Prince George's County, Maryland, Indexes of Church Registers 1686-1885* (1979), v. 2, (Part 2, Montgomery Co.), p. 264.
[27] Montgomery Co., MD, NARA, 1810 census, roll 14, p. 318 or 931.

paid I give, Divise, Dispose of the same in the following manner - Item I give and bequeath to by Daughter Rachel Watkins the Feather bed whereon I lay together with the bedsted & furniture thereunto belonging - Item I give and bequeath to my son Jeremiah Lewis half a Doz. Windsor chairs and also to hold my plantation two years clear of rent but it is to be understood if there Should be A crop on hand he is to have the whole of that crop and then & in that case such crop Shall be considered as one of the two years - Item all my personal Estate whatsoever it may consist shall be sold by my Executors hereinafter named on A credit of nine monthly with Interest from day of sale, and the money Arising from the sale thereof to be Equally Divided between my Eight children share and share alike namely Rachel Watkins, Thomas Lewis, Margaret Barber, Levy Lewis, Jane Windsor, Jonathan Lewis, Jeremiah Lewis, and Drusillar Browning. and as my son Levy Lewis Deceased about three years Since it is to be understood that his children is to heir the same part as he might if living - and whereas I am possessed of A tract of Land, which Land my son Jeremiah is to have the profits arising from in the manner before mentioned therefore at the Expiration of his time in said Land, The said tract of Land is to be put up at Public sale by my Executors herein after mentioned and sold on such credit as they may think proper, giving at least twenty days notice by an(?) and the money arising From the sale thereof to be Equally Divided between my Eight children Share and share alike namely Rachel, Thomas, Margaret, Levy, Jane, Jonathan, Jeremiah & Drusillar, But as my son Levy has Deceased as above mentioned his children is to Heir the same part as he might do if living - And Lastly I do hereby constitute and Appoint my son Inlaw Nicholas Watkins and my Son Jeremiah Lewis my Sole Executors of this my last Will and Testament Revoking and annuling all former Wills by me heretofore made Ratifying and Confirming this and none other to be my last Will and Testament In Testimony whereof I have hereunto set my hand and seal the twenty third day of April in the year of our Lord one thousand Eight hundred & Fifteen.

Signed Sealed Published and Declared by Jeremiah Lewis the within named Testator as and For his last Will and Testament in the presence of us, who at his Request and in his presence has Subscribed our names as Witness thereto.

John L. Trundle	his	
Daniel Trundle	Jeremiah Lewis	(Seal)
Levin C Beall	mark	

Montgomery County (?) : on the 31st day of December 1822 came John L. Trundle and Daniel Trundle two of the subscribing witnesses to the within last Will and Testament of Jeremiah Lewis late of said county deceased and severally made oaths on the Holy Evangels of Almighty God that they did see the Testator therein named sign and seal this Will that they heard him publish pronounce and declare the same to be his last Will and Testament, that at the time of his so doing he was to the best of their apprehension of sound and disposing mind memory and understanding that they respectively subscribed their names to this will as Witnesses in the presence and at the request of the Testator in the presence of such other also in the presence of the other subscribing Witness thereto -

Certified by
Solomon Holland Reg.[28]

Jeremiah Lewis was to live more than seven years after he made his will. In 1820 he continued to live in Montgomery Co.[29] and died there 22 Nov. 1822 at age 77.

Jeremiah Lewis was 31 when the American Revolution began and soon became a private in the Maryland Militia. He had apple orchards on his property, just as his father before him, and that must have been an important part of his business. The will of Jeremiah Lewis mentions only crops, so there were likely other crops. Though he signed his will by mark, he had signed his name in full on earlier occasions. Members of

[28] Ibid., Will Liber 3, ff. 198-200, ahp.
[29] Ronald Vern Jackson & Gary Ronald Teeples, ed., *Maryland 1820 Census Index* (Bountiful, UT), p. 66.

his family were married at the Evangelical Lutheran Church in Frederick, MD.[30] He and his wife, Jane (Fitzgerald) Lewis, may have been members of, or worshipped at that church. They lived in the area where his parents had lived, in or near Lewisdale in northern Montgomery Co., MD. Many of their descendants still live in that general area.

Children of Jeremiah and Jane (Fitzgerald) Lewis, probably all born in Frederick Co., MD or, after 1776, Montgomery Co., MD:

i.   Rachel[4], b. *ca.* 1765; d. aft. 1849 prob. Montgomery Co., MD;[31] m. 13 Mar. 1787 Evangelical Lutheran Church, Frederick, MD by Rev. Mr. Crook, **NICHOLAS WATKINS**,[32] b. 1 Nov. 1763 Frederick, Co., MD;[33] d. bet. 25 Oct. 1845 & 3 June 1848 Montgomery Co., MD;[34] s/o Jeremiah & Elizabeth (Waugh) Watkins.[35] Rachel Lewis grew up in the homes of her parents, Jeremiah and Jane (Fitzgerald) Lewis, which were first in Frederick Co. but upon the formation of Montgomery Co. in 1776 became part of the new county. By 1781 their home was probably on *Trouble Enough* or *Close Tract*, two tracts of land acquired in 1779 by her grandfather, Daniel Lewis.[36] She must have been born *ca.* 1765. Of eight children mentioned in the will of Jeremiah Lewis, Rachel was named first in the list of names given, which may indicate she was the oldest of his children. On 13 Mar. 1787 she married Nicholas Watkins and in 1790 they were living very near Jeremiah Lewis in Montgomery Co. in a household with: one white male 16 or over, three white males under 16, and one white female.[37] The name of Nicholas Watkins appears in the census of 1800 for Montgomery Co., MD.[38] By 1810 his household was composed of the following: one white male under ten, one white male at least ten but under 16, three white males at least 16 but under 26, one white male 45 or over, two white females under ten, one white female at least ten but under 16, one white female 45 or over, and ten slaves.[39] In 1820, and as late as 1840, the name of Nicholas Watkins appears among heads of families in Montgomery Co.[40] By 1815 Jeremiah Lewis apparently had enough confidence in his son-in-law, Nicholas Watkins, to appoint Nicholas one of the executors of his will. His daughter, Rachel, was to receive his feather bed with the bedstead and furniture thereunto belonging. On 25 Oct. 1845 Nicholas Watkins Sr. made his will in Montgomery Co. and he seems to have died there *ca.* 1848 at about age 84. Rachel (Lewis) Watkins survived her husband and in 1850 as head of

---

[30] Weiser, pp. 36-41, 51-52.

[31] Hurley.

[32] Weiser, pp. 51-52; Watkins family Bible.

[33] Ibid.

[34] Montgomery Co., MD, Will Liber HH-1, f. 485; ibid., Will Liber 4, f. 463, both cited in Mary Gordon Malloy et al., comp., *Abstracts of Wills, Montgomery County, Maryland, 1826-1875*, p. 167.

[35] Watkins family Bible.

[36] Montgomery Co., MD, Deed Liber A, ff. 394-396, ahp; ibid., Deed Liber C, f. 539, ahp.

[37] *Heads of Families.*

[38] Lowell M. Volkel & Timothy Q. Wilson, comp., *An Index to the 1800 Federal Census of Dorchester, Harford, Montgomery, Prince Georges, and Queen Annes Counties, State of Maryland*, page no. missing from copy..

[39] Montgomery Co., MD, NARA, 1810 census, roll 14, p. 321 or 934.

[40] Gary W. Parks, comp., *Index to the 1820 Census of Maryland and Washington, D.C.* (Baltimore, 1986), p. 255; Ronald Vern Jackson & Gary Ronald Teeples, ed., *Maryland 1840 Census Index* (Bountiful, UT, 1977), p. 153.

household, age 84, was living alone in Clarksburg Dist., Montgomery Co. She then had real estate valued at $2000.[41] Many descendants of this couple still live in that same general area of Maryland.[42] Children of Nicholas and Rachel (Lewis) Watkins, probably all born in Montgomery Co., MD: Jeremiah[5], b. 26 Nov. 1787; Gassaway, b. 1 May 1789; Daniel Lewis, b. 1 Mar. 1791; Stephen, b. 11 Mar. 1793, d. 14 Jul. 1819; Richard, b. 25 Jan. 1795, d. 4 May 1814; Delilah, b. 23 Nov. 1796; Margaret, b. 8 Oct. 1798, d. 23 Nov. 1811; Aleatha, b. 14 Oct. 1800; Nicholas, b. 24 Dec. 1802; Rachel, b. 2 Nov. 1804; Leven, b. 5 Nov. 1806; Deborah, b. 25 Feb. 1809; Elizabeth Hall, b. 29 Jan. 1811.[43]

ii.   Thomas, b. *ca.* 1767; prob. m. (1) 1794 Frederick Co., MD, **MARY ELLIS**;[44] m. prob. (2) 28 Oct. 1813 Montgomery Co., MD, **SARAH LIZEAR**.[45] Thomas Lewis grew up in the homes of his parents, Jeremiah and Jane (Fitzgerald) Lewis, which were first in Frederick Co. but upon the formation of Montgomery Co. in 1776 became part of the new county. By 1781 their home was probably on *Trouble Enough* or *Close Tract*, two tracts of land acquired in 1779 by his grandfather, Daniel Lewis.[46] Of eight children mentioned in the 1815 will of Jeremiah Lewis, Thomas was named second in the list of names given, which may mean he was next to the oldest. He was likely the Thomas Lewis, who in 1794 married Mary Ellis in nearby Frederick Co. He seems to have been living near his father, Jeremiah, in 1800 when his name appeared as head of a family in Montgomery Co. In his household were: one white male under ten, one white male at least 26 but under 45, one white female under ten, and one white female at least 26 but under 45.[47] On 28 Oct. 1813 Thomas Lewis married Sarah Lizear in Montgomery Co. as a later wife. He was named in the 1815 will of Jeremiah Lewis, so he was likely that Thomas Lewis who in 1820 was head of a family in Montgomery Co.[48]

iii.   Margaret, b. *ca.* 1769; d. by 7 June 1832[49] prob. Montgomery Co., MD; m. *ca.* 1798 **REZIN**[50] **BARBER**,[51] b. 8 Sep. 1765 Prince George's Co., MD; s/o John Barber Jr. Rezin Barber m. (2) 7 June 1832 Montgomery Co., MD, Eleanor (Holland) Williams, w/o William Williams.[52] Margaret Lewis grew up in the homes of her parents, Jeremiah and Jane (Fitzgerald) Lewis, which were

---

[41] Hurley.

[42] Information, courtesy of Mrs. Sandy Watkins, Hamstead, MD; author, personal knowledge.

[43] Watkins family Bible; Malloy, will of Nicholas Watkins Sr. gives Delilah Sedgwick, Raechel Hilton, Aleatha Moxley, Elizabeth Hall Brown as daughters. More information for this Watkins family is provided in: William Neal Hurley Jr., *Our Maryland Heritage, Book Fourteen, Lewis Families* (Bowie, MD, 1999); ibid., *...Book Four, Watkins Families*.

[44] John Stanwood Martin, *Genealogical Index to Frederick County, Maryland, the First Hundred Years* (Malvern, PA, 1992), v. 3, L-R, p. 44.

[45] Janet Thompson Manuel, comp., *Marriage Licenses Montgomery County, Maryland, 1798-1898* (Silver Spring, MD, 1987), p. 195.

[46] Montgomery Co., MD, Deed Liber A, ff. 394-396, ahp; ibid., Deed Liber C, f. 539, ahp.

[47] Ibid., NARA, 1800 census, roll 11, p. 44 or 224.

[48] Parks, p. 147. More research is needed for this Thomas Lewis.

[49] Donald James Omans & Nancy West Omans, ed., *Maryland Historic Marriage Register, Montgomery County Marriages, 1798-1875* (Athens, GA, 1987), p. 23

[50] Hurley, *...Lewis Families*, pp. 13-14.

[51] Ibid.; Montgomery Co., MD, Will Liber 3, ff. 198-200, ahp.

[52] Omans; Hurley, *...Lewis Families*, p. 13.

first in Frederick Co. but upon the formation of Montgomery Co. in 1776 became part of the new county. By 1781 their home was probably on *Trouble Enough* or *Close Tract*, two tracts of land acquired in 1779 by her grandfather, Daniel Lewis.[53] Of eight children mentioned in the 1815 will of Jeremiah Lewis she was named third in the list of names that gave her name as Margaret Barber. That seems to make her one of the older children. Perhaps it was *ca.* 1798 that she married Rezin Barber who by 1800 was head of a family in Montgomery Co.[54] By 1810 in his household were: two white males under ten, three white males at least ten but under 16, one white male at least 26 but under 45, one white female under ten, one white female at least 26 but under 45, one free person of color, and nine slaves.[55] In 1820 his name again appears as head of a household in Montgomery Co.[56] Margaret (Lewis) Barber must have died by 7 June 1832 when Rezin Barber remarried. Children of Rezin and Margaret (Lewis) Barber, probably all born in Montgomery Co., MD: William[5], b. *ca.* 1800; Lewis, b. *ca.* 1803; Zadok, b. *ca.* 1805; Wilson, b. *ca.* 1807; Henry, b. *ca.* 1807, apparent twin of Wilson; Hezekiah, b. 4 Dec. 1808; Cordelia, b. *ca.* 1810; Jeremiah, b. *ca.* 1812.[57]

7.   iv.   Levi, b. *ca.* 1771.

     v.   Jane, b. *ca.* 1775;[58] m. 20 Dec. 1803 Montgomery Co., MD, **ZADOCK WINDSOR**,[59] b. *ca.* 1780 MD;[60] s/o Thomas & Catherine (Ward) Windsor.[61] Jane Lewis grew up in the homes of her parents, Jeremiah and Jane (Fitzgerald) Lewis, which were first in Frederick Co. but upon the formation of Montgomery Co. in 1776 became part of the new county. By 1781 their home was probably on *Trouble Enough* or *Close Tract*, two tracts of land acquired in 1779 by her grandfather, Daniel Lewis.[62] Of eight children mentioned in the 1815 will of Jeremiah Lewis she was named fifth in the list of names that gave her name as Jane Windsor. That seems to make her one of the younger children. She was likely named for her mother, Jane (Fitzgerald) Lewis. On 20 Dec. 1803 she married Zadock Windsor in Montgomery Co. and in 1809 he was named in the will of his father, whose name appeared as Thomas Winsor.[63] In 1810 Zadock Windsor was head of a family in Montgomery Co. In his household were: one white male under ten, one white male at least 26 but under 45, two white females under ten, one

---

[53]. Montgomery Co., MD, Deed Liber A, ff. 394-396, ahp; ibid., Deed Liber C, f. 539, ahp

[54] Volkel.

[55] Montgomery Co., MD, NARA, 1810 census, roll 14, p. 322 or 935.

[56] Parks, p. 12.

[57] Hurley, *...Lewis Families*, pp. 13-15 provides the names of these Barber children as well as some later generations. It should be noted that some approximate birth years of children given here have been adjusted for this work and may not agree with the work cited.

[58] Mary Fitzhugh Hitselberger & John Philip Dern, *Bridge in Time, the Complete 1850 Census of Frederick County, Maryland* (Redwood City, CA, 1978), p. 233.

[59] Manuel, p. 194 has his name as Zadok Windsor.

[60] Hitselberger, p. 233.

[61] Montgomery Co., MD, Will Liber G, f. 143, cited in Mary Gordon Malloy et al., comp., *Abstracts of Wills Montgomery County, Maryland, 1776-1825*, p. 154; Hurley, *...Lewis Families*, p. 73 has the w/o Thomas Windsor as Catherine Ward.

[62] Montgomery Co., MD, Deed Liber A, ff. 394-396, ahp; ibid., Deed Liber C, f. 539, ahp.

[63] Ibid., Will Liber G, f. 143, cited in Malloy, p. 154.

white female at least 26 but under 45, one free person of color, and five slaves.[64] In 1820 as Zadock Windsar he was head of a family there.[65] He must have been the same person as Zadock Winsor who by 1840 was head of a household in Frederick Co.[66] In 1850 the family was enumerated in Buckeys Town Dist., Frederick Co., MD where they had real estate valued at $540 and Zadock Windsor, age 69, was a farmer. Jane (Lewis) Windsor was then age 74.[67] At that time there seem to have been four adult children living with them. Children of Zadock and Jane (Lewis) Windsor, probably all born in Montgomery Co., MD: Edmund L.[5], b. *ca.* 1815;[68] Zadock Hanson, b. *ca.* 1817;[69] Arnold Hammond, b. *ca.* 1819;[70] Drusilla, b. *ca.* 1821.[71]

8. vi. Jonathan, b. *ca.* 1778.

9. vii. Jeremiah, b. 8 May 1781.

viii. Drusilla, b. *ca.* 1787; d. aft. 1849 prob. Frederick Co., MD;[72] m. 31 Dec. 1808 Montgomery Co., MD, **JEREMIAH BROWNING**,[73] b. *ca.* 1775 Frederick Co., MD;[74] d. bet. 15 Oct. 1839 & 31 Dec. 1839 Frederick Co., MD;[75] s/o Joshua & Nancy (Farmer) Browning. Jeremiah Browning m. (1) Elizabeth Summers.[76] Drusilla Lewis grew up in the homes of her parents, Jeremiah and Jane (Fitzgerald) Lewis, which were in Montgomery Co. where she was born. By the time she was born they were probably living on *Trouble Enough* or *Close Tract,* two tracts of land acquired in 1779 by her grandfather, Daniel Lewis.[77] Of eight children mentioned in the 1815 will of Jeremiah Lewis she was named last in the list of names that gave her name as Drusillar Browning. That seems to make her the youngest child. On 31 Dec. 1808 she married Jeremiah Browning in Montgomery Co. He was likely the Jeremiah Browning who earlier, in 1800, was head of a family in Frederick Co.,[78] probably with his first wife, Elizabeth. By 1810 he was head of a family in Montgomery Co. In his household were: one white male under ten, one white male at least 26 but under 45, one white female under ten, one white female at least 16 but under 26, and four slaves.[79] On 15 Oct. 1839 Jeremiah Browning of Frederick Co., MD made his will, appointing his wife, Drusilla, and son, Richard, executrix and executor. Witnesses were: Joseph Kemp, Solomon Kemp, and John T. Lewis. Jeremiah had died by 31 Dec. 1839. On

---

[64] Ibid., NARA, 1810 census, roll 14, p. 319 or 932.

[65] Parks, p. 267.

[66] Jackson, *Maryland 1840 Census Index,* p. unclear.

[67] Hitselberger, p. 233.

[68] Ibid.; Hurley, *...Lewis Families,* p. 15 has b. 14 Sep. 1810.

[69] Hitselberger, p. 233; Hurley, *...Lewis Families,* p. 15 has b. 8 July 1812.

[70] Hitselberger, p. 233; Hurley, *...Lewis Families,* p. 15 has b. 7 Mar. 1818.

[71] Hitselberger, p. 233. There must have been some other children who were older.

[72] Hitselberger, p. 274.

[73] Manuel, p. 193.

[74] Hurley, *...Lewis Families,* p. 25.

[75] Frederick Co., MD, Will Docket GM-2, ff. 426-427, ahp.

[76] Hurley, *...Lewis Families,* pp. 25-28.

[77] Montgomery Co., MD, Deed Liber A, ff. 394-396, ahp; ibid., Deed Liber C, f. 539, ahp.

[78] Charlotte A. Volkel et al., comp., *An Index to the 1800 Federal Census of Caroline, Cecil, Charles, Frederick, and Kent Counties, State of Maryland,* page no. missing from copy.

[79] Montgomery Co., MD, NARA, 1810 census, roll 14, p. 321 or 934.

17 Jan. 1840 when Drusilla Browning and Richard Browning renounced their appointments she signed by mark.[80] George Hughes became administrator and submitted a first account 23 Feb. 1841[81] and a final account 1 Mar. 1843.[82] Drusilla (Lewis) Browning survived her husband, Jeremiah Browning, and in 1850 she was living in New Market Dist., Frederick Co., MD where she had real estate valued at $1500. Living with her were two sons whose names appeared as Rufus A. and Thomas, both farmers.[83] Children of Jeremiah and Drusilla (Lewis) Browning, probably all born in either Montgomery or Frederick Co., MD: Loretta[5], b. *ca.* 1810; Silas, b. *ca.* 1812; Louisa Ann, b. poss. 17 Jan. 1815; Matilda, b. 17 Jan. 1815, prob. twin of Louisa Ann; Richard, b. *ca.* 1816; Rufus A., b. *ca.* 1818; Jane E., b. 15 May 1819; Tabitha, b. *ca.* 1822; Meshach, b. *ca.* 1824; Jeremiah Thomas, b. *ca.* 1831.[84]

   5. DAVID[3] LEWIS (Daniel[2], Jonathan[1]) (see 2), b. 23 Sep. 1750[85] Prince George's or Frederick Co., MD;[86] d. bet. 18 Sep. 1798 & early 1799[87] Romine's Mill, Harrison Co., (W)V;[88] m. *ca.* 1771 prob. Frederick Co., MD, **JOANNAH TRUNDLE**,[89] b. bet. 19 Mar. 1754 & Nov. 1754[90] Frederick Co., MD;[91] d. aft. 16 Apr. 1808, prob. by 1810 Harrison Co., (W)V;[92] d/o John III & Ann (---) Trundle[93] (see Trundle Families, Chapter Seven, No. 4, iv). Joannah (Trundle) Lewis m. (2) 18 Aug. 1806 Harrison Co., (W)V, **PATRICK BURNSIDE**.[94]

   David Lewis probably grew up in the homes of his father, Daniel Lewis, who likely lived first in Prince George's Co., MD, but by 1755 was living in Frederick Co., MD.[95] He was probably the son of an earlier wife of Daniel Lewis. *Circa* 1771 David married Joannah Trundle. Their daughter, Ann, was born 17 Nov. 1772.[96] According to the will of John Trundle Sen[r], written 12 Mar. 1771, his daughter, Joanna Trundle, was to receive

[80] Frederick Co., MD, Will Docket GM-2, ff. 426-427, ahp. In his will Jeremiah named 11 children including Joab Browning, a son by his first wife, & daughters, Loretta Molesworth & Matilda Boyer.

[81] Ibid., Accounting Docket GME-1, ff. 206-207, ahp.

[82] Ibid., GME-15, ff. 185-186, ahp.

[83] Hitselberger. Because she was married in 1808, her age given as 50 in 1850 is surely erroneous.

[84] Hurley, ...Lewis Families, pp. 25-28; ibid., ...Book Twelve, Browning Families, pp. 88-93. Both works provide the names of these ten Browning children and should be referenced for later generations.

[85] Lewis family Bible, possession of Edgar Lewis, Johnstown, Harrison Co., WV (1982), may have been the Bible of Jonathan Lewis (b. 1793), family records transcribed and provided, courtesy of Noel Kent Dawson, Springfield, VA.

[86] NARA, Revolutionary War Pension of Daniel Lewis (Jr.) states he, Daniel (Jr.), was b. in Frederick Co. in 1755.

[87] Harrison Co., (W)V, PPTB, 1798-1799; Melba Pender Zinn, comp., *Monongalia County, (West) Virginia: Records of the District, Superior and County Courts, Volume 5: 1802-1805* (Bowie, MD, 1992), p. 118.

[88] Ibid.; information, courtesy of Mrs. Jessie (Lewis) Van Hoose, Annandale, VA.

[89] Lewis family Bible, possession of Edgar Lewis.

[90] Millard Millburn Rice, *This Was the Life, Excerpts from the Judgment Records of Frederick County, Maryland, 1748-1765* (Baltimore, 1984), pp. 133-134, 146 indicates a fourth child was b. to John Trundle between the 19 Mar. 1754 Court & Nov. 1754 Court. Joannah seems to be the youngest of four children named in the will of John Trundle (Frederick Co., MD, Will Liber A-1, ff. 399-400). Lewis family Bible, possession of Edgar Lewis has only the year, 1753, as her birth date.

[91] Frederick Co., MD, Will Liber A-1, ff. 399-400, ahp.

[92] Harrison Co., (W)V, Marriage Bond Book 2, p. 167, author has photocopy of original; ibid., Deed Book 7, pp. 328-329, ahp; ibid., NARA, 1810 census, photostats, v. 7, p. 949.

[93] Frederick Co., MD, Will Liber A-1, ff. 399-400, ahp.

[94] Harrison Co., (W)V, Marriage Bond Book 2.

[95] NARA, Revolutionary War Pension.

[96] Lewis family Bible, possession of Edgar Lewis.

his bay horse "...when she goes for herself..." and she was also to have Sarah Green Tree who seems to have been a Negro, "...to have as her Right to the age of Sixtee...."[97]

In 1776 Montgomery Co. was formed from Frederick Co. and in 1777 David Lewis was taxed in Rock Creek Hundred, Montgomery Co., MD with two taxables in his household. That year his older brother, Jeremiah, was also taxed in Rock Creek Hundred.[98] This was during the American Revolution and in the same year, 1777, David Lewis of Montgomery Co. was a private, 2d Co., 29th (Lower) Bn., Maryland Militia, as was his brother, Jeremiah.[99] In 1778 he signed the Oath of Fidelity to the State of Maryland from Montgomery Co.[100] The same year, 1778, he was again taxed in Rock Creek Hundred, Montgomery Co. as was his brother, Jeremiah.[101] David Lewis further supported the war against the British by supplying the following: beef and corn, bill and receipts 23 Dec. 1780;[102] corn and beef, bill and receipts 29 Dec. 1780;[103] corn, bill and receipt 3 Jan. 1781.[104] Later in 1781, on Sep. 4, David Lewis was named in the will of his father, Daniel Lewis. He was to receive one "hiffer."[105]

David Lewis seems to have moved across the line to nearby Frederick Co. by 1 Apr. 1784. On that date he sold one Negro woman named Fan and her daughter, Ally, to Abraham Faw. The bill of sale was as follows:

At the request of Abraham Faw the following Bill of Sale was recorded on the fifteenth Day of April Anno Domini 1784 To wit.

"Maryland ac[k]. Know all Men by these Presents that I David Lewis of Frederick County in the State abovesaid for and in Consideration of five thousand eight hundred Pounds of Tobacco to me in Hand paid by Abraham Faw of Frederick Town and County in the State abovesaid at and before the Ensealing and delivery of these Presents, the Receipt whereof I do hereby acknowledge have bargained sold released granted and confirmed, and by these Presents do bargain sell release grant and confirm unto the said Abraham Faw his Heirs and Assigns one Negro Woman named Fan, aged about twenty eight years, and her daughter named Ally, aged about four years, which I bought of W. (blank)   To have and to hold all and singular the said Premises, and every of them by these Presents bargained sold released granted and confirmed unto the only proper use[grant behoof]of the said Abraham Faw his Heirs Extrs Admis or Assigns forever freely quietly peaceably and entirely without any Contradiction, Claims Disturbances or Hindrance of any Person whatsoever, and without any Account to me, or to any other whatsoever to be made answered, or hareafter to be rendered, so that neither I the said David Lewis, nor any one for me, or in my Name any Right Title Interest or demand of in to, or for the said bargained Premises, or any part or Parcel thereof ought to exact challenge claim or demand at any Time or Times hereafter but from all Actions Right Estate Title Claim and demand, Possession and Interest thereof shall be wholly barred and excluded by Force and Virtue of these Presents. And I the said David Lewis for myself my Executors and Administrators all and singular the said bargained Premises unto the said Abraham Faw his Executors Administrators and Assigns against me the said David Lewis my Heirs Extrs Adminrs and Assigns, and against all and every Person and Persons whatsoever shall and will warrant and forever defend: Provided always and it is hereby agreed between the said Parties to these Presents, that if I the said David Lewis do and shall well and truly pay or cause to be paid unto the said

[97] Frederick Co., MD, Will Liber A-1, ff. 399-400, ahp. The age "sixtee" must refer to the age of Sarah Green Tree, as Joannah would likely have already reached age sixteen.
[98] Eleanor M.V. Cook, "1777 Tax List of Montgomery County," pp. 15-16.
[99] S. Eugene Clements, p. 198.
[100] *Montgomery Co., Md. Oath of Fidelity & Tax Lists - 1778*, p. 6.
[101] Ibid., pp. 60-61.
[102] Papenfuse, p. 343.
[103] Ibid., p. 344.
[104] Ibid., p. 351.
[105] Montgomery Co., MD, Will Liber 1, ff. 220-221, author has photocopy of original.

Abraham Faw his Heirs or Assigns two thousand Pounds of Crop Tobacco at George Town clear of Cask on at or upon the twentieth day of August next, and three thousand eight hundred Pounds of like Tobacco, at said Ware House on at or upon the twentieth day of August in the year 1785. with legal Interest for the same for Redemption of the said bargained Premises then these Presents, and every Clause Article Condition and Thing herein contained shall erase and be void; otherwise to be and remain in full Force and Virtue in Law In witness whereof I have hereunto set my Hand and affixed my Seal this first day of April 1784.

Signed sealed and ⌐ John Mantz   David Lewis (Seal)
delivered in Presence of⌐ Sneervoot Tillmkiss (?)

On which Bill of Sale was endorsed the following Acknowledgment viz "Frederick County fs[t]. April 1st 1784. Then came the above said David Lewis before me the Subscriber one of the Justices of Peace for the County above said and acknowledged the within mentioned Property to be the Right[Title]and Estate of the said Abraham Faw his Heirs and Assigns forever, according to the within Instrument of writing

          Acknowledged before   Jn° Harrison[106]

The 1784 bill of sale may have been for a good reason. On 1 Aug. 1782 David Lewis entered into a business arrangement with one Ignatius Wathom. One John Mummert and his heir, William Mummert, were owners of two tracts of land known as *Roberts Choice* and *Mummerts Choice* when they became indebted to Ignatius Wathom. Apparently David Lewis was not paid for several years. This debt was eventually settled 8 Aug. 1789 when the two tracts of land were sold at public sale to the highest bidder by the sheriff of Montgomery Co., Benjamin White Jones. The land was purchased by John Trundle, half brother-in-law of David Lewis.[107] The deed was as follows:

At the Request of John Trundle the following deed Was recorded this 5th day of November 1790 To wit This Indenture made the Twelfth day of august in the year of Our Lord one Thousand seven hundred and Ninety. Between Benjamin White Jones Sheriff of montgomery County in the state of maryland of the one Part and John Trundel of the County and State aforesaid of the Other Part Whereas a certain Ignatius Wathom for the use of David Lewis did at the November Court holdin for the County aforesaid The second Tuesday of November seventeen hundred and eighty five before the Justices thereof Obtain a Judgement against a Certain John Mummert of said County as well for the quantity of Two Thousand Two hundred pounds of Crop Tobacco a certain debt with Interest from the first day of August seventeen hundred and eighty Two as the further quantity of Three hundred and eighty One Pounds of Tobacco adjudged unto the said Ignatius Wathom for the use of said David Lewis for his Costs in that am't Expended, and Whereas the said Ignatius Wathom for the use of David Lewis Obtained a writ of Fieri facias against the Lands and Tenements of William Mummert as heir at Law of the aforesaid John Mummert directed to the said Benjamin White Jones sheriff of the County afs'd redeemable to the Court to be holden for said County the second Tuesday of August seventeen hundred and Eighty Nine, directing him the said Sheriff to Levy of the Lands and Tenements of him the said William Mummert as heir at Law of John Mummert, sufficient to Pay and satisfy unto him the said Ignatius Wathom for the use of David Lewis as well the Quantity of Two Thousand Two hundred pounds of Crop Tobacco with Interest from the first Day of august seventeen hundred and Eighty Two the debt aforesaid as the further Quantity of six hundred and fifty Pounds of Tobacco Costs and Thirty six Pounds of Tobacco additional Costs in said Suit Expended In Insurance of which Fieri facias he the said Benjamin White Jones as Sheriff of the County afs'd seized and Took Two Tracts or Parcels of Land lying and Being in the County aforesaid formerly the Right and Property of the aforesaid John Mummert deceased and Then as it was seized the Property of William Mummert heir at Law to the aforesaid John Mummert the One of the aforesaid Two Tracts of land containing fifty nine Acres more or Less, called by the Name of

---

[106] Frederick Co., MD, Deed Liber W R-4, ff. 411-413, ahp.
[107] Ibid., Will Liber A-1, ff. 399-400, ahp.

Roberts Choice, the Other called by the Name of Mummerts Choice, Containing Eleven acres more or Less, which Two Tracts be as afs'd seized and Taken for the uses aforesaid were appraised to the quantity of four Thousand Pounds of Crop Tobacco, and afterwards To wit On the eighth Day of august seventeen hundred and eighty Nine, set up and sold by the Sheriff afs'd at Public Sale to the highest Bidder and he the aforesaid John Trundel, become the Purchaser, the amount of the sale Thereof being Three Thousand five hundred and fifty Pounds Crop Tobacco and seven pounds fifteen shill'gs and seven Pence Specie, all which appears of Record in Now This Indenture Witnesseth that the said Benjamin White Jones as Sheriff of the County for and in Consideration as well of the Premises afs'd as the sums of Quantity of Three Thousand five hundred and fifty pounds of Crop Tobacco and seven Pounds, fifteen shillings and seven Pence specie to him in hand paid by the aforesaid John Trundel at or before the Ensealing and Delivery of These Presents the receipt whereof is hereby acknowledged, he the said Benjamin White Jones as Sheriff of the County afs'd, hath granted Bargained and sold and by these Presents, doth grant Bargain and sell unto him the said John Trundel his heirs and assigns forever all his the aforesaid John and William Mummerts right, Title and Interest of in and unto the aforesaid Two Tracts or Parcels of land called Roberts Choice and Mummerts Choice containing as afs'd, and lying and Being in the County and State afs'd To have and To hold unto him the said John Trundel his heirs and assigns forever Together with all and Singular the rights members and appurtenances of said Lands - and the said Benjamin White Jones for himself his heirs Executors and administrators doth Covenant, Promise, grant and agree to and with the said John Trundel his heirs and assigns that he the said Benjamin White Jones shall Warrant and forever defend unto him the aforesaid John Trundel his heirs and assigns the aforesaid Tracts or Parcels of land against him the said Benjamin White Jones his heirs Executors and administrators In Witness Whereof the said Benjamin White Jones hath hereunto set his hand and affixed his seal the Day and year first within written

Signed, Sealed and delivered in Presence of   Benjamin W Jones sheriff   (seal)
Richard Thompson   J Holmes

On which deed was the following Endorsements To Wit. Rec'd the 12th day of August 1790 of the within Named John Trundel three Thousand five hundred and fifty pounds Crop Tobacco and Seven pounds fifteen shillings and Seven Pence Specie in full for the Consideration within mentioned

Witness   C.P^r. me Benjn. W Jones   Sheriff
Richard Thompson   J Holmes

Montgomery County Ist. Be it Remembered that On the 12th day of august 1790 the within Named Benjamin White Jones came before us Two of the Justices of the Peace for the County afs'd & acknowledged the within Instrument of writing to be his act and deed and the Lands and Premises therein mentioned to be the right and Estate of the within Named John Trundel his heirs and assigns forever awarding To the True Intent and meaning Thereof and the act of assembly in such cases made and Provided

Taken and acknowledged before us Richard Thompson   J Holmes[108]

In 1790 David Lewis was living in Frederick Co. In his household were: two white males 16 years and upward, one white male under 16, four white females, and four slaves.[109]

Perhaps it was late 1796 or early 1797 when David Lewis moved his family to Harrison Co., (W)V. By 1798 he was living there where he was taxed on one horse.[110] He seems to have lived at a place now called Romine's Mill, Harrison Co. On 18 Sep. 1798 he was witness to an agreement as follows in part:

'On demand I promise to deliver unto Thomas LEWIS 2 forge hammers at ROWEN's Forge or works in Harrison County for value received this 18 September 1798,' signed by John WICKWARE in the presence of Robert B. JAMES and David LEWIS.[111]

[108] Montgomery Co., MD, Deed Liber D, ff. 443-444, ahp.
[109] *Heads of Families*, p. 70.
[110] Harrison Co., (W)V, PPTB, 1798. Assessments were usually in the early part of the year, by May.
[111] Zinn.

David Lewis is said to have died at Romine's Mill. His death must have occurred between 18 Sep. 1798 and early 1799 when his widow whose name appeared as Hannah Lewis, was assessed on two horses in Harrison Co., (W)V.[112] Family tradition says David Lewis was killed by a falling tree.[113]

David Lewis was 25 when the American Revolution began and soon became a private in the Maryland Militia. Though a specific occupation for David Lewis was not found, he seems to have been involved in agriculture by 23 Dec. 1780 when he furnished corn and beef to further support the American Revolution. From 1782 to 1789 he apparently managed two parcels of land for Ignatius Wathom. The land was known as *Roberts Choice* and *Mummerts Choice*, a total of 70 acres in Montgomery Co. The land must have been near Frederick Co. as David Lewis was living there by 1784. Probably in late 1796 or early 1797 he moved his family to Romine's Mill, Harrison Co., (W)V. He was certainly in Harrison Co. in 1798 and was probably 48 when his untimely death occurred there. It seems likely his death was the result of an accident during the construction of a cabin. It is possible David Lewis lived for a few years in some other county of Virginia just prior to his arrival in Harrison Co. Apparently he always signed his name in full. Many descendants of David and Joannah (Trundle) Lewis still live in the Romine's Mill and Johnstown area of Harrison Co., WV, as well as in the nearby counties of Lewis and Upshur.[114]

Joannah (Trundle) Lewis seems to have lived at least about ten years after her husband's death. From 1799 through 1804 she was taxed in Harrison Co. By 1799 with one tithable in her family she was taxed on two horses. In those records her given name appears as Hannah, Johannah, and Johanna.[115] The following was recorded 21 June 1802 in Harrison Co.:

> Ordered
> That that the road from the widow Lewis[s] to Samuel Davis[s] be Restablished and that the survey of the present which said road leads through work the said road[116]

When she was summoned to testify 30 June 1806 on behalf of her daughter, Margery Lewis, her name appeared as Joanna Lewis and Johannah T. Lewis.[117]

According to a marriage bond of 18 Aug. 1806, Joannah (Trundle) Lewis married Patrick Burnside. The bond was as follows:

> Know all men by these presents that we Patrick Burnsides and Michal Roby _ Both of the county of Harrison and State of Virginia are held & firmly bound to William L Cabell Chief Magistrate of the Comm[th] & his Sucessors in the just & full Sum of Fifty pounds Lawful Money, To which payment Well & truly To be made we bind our Selves our Heirs Ex[rs] & Adm[rs] firmly by these presents Witness our hands and Seals this 18th Day of Aug[t] 1806

---

[112] Harrison Co., (W)V, PPTB, 1799.
[113] Information, courtesy of Mrs. Van Hoose.
[114] Author, personal knowledge.
[115] Harrison Co., (W)V, PPTB, 1799-1804.
[116] Ibid., Minute Book, 1801-1803, ahp.
[117] Melba Pender Zinn, comp., *Monongalia County, (West) Virginia: Records of the District, Superior and County Courts, Volume 3: 1804-1810* (Bowie, MD, 1991), pp. 110-111.

The Condition of the above Obligation is Such that Should there be no Lawfull cause to Obstruct said Patrick Burnsides Marriage With Joannah Lewis (a widow) Then the above obligation to be Void otherwise to Stand in full force & Virtue

Signed Sealed & Acknowledged   Patrick Burnside   [Seal]
in presence of   his
        Benjamin Wilson   Michal ( ) Roby   [Seal]
                                                              mark[118]

Earlier, 2 Sep. 1801, one Patrick Burnsides acquired 300 acres on Freemans Creek, Harrison Co. (W)V from George Arnold and his wife, Elizabeth, for $500.[119] Later, 16 Dec. 1806, one Patrick Burnsides reported a stray horse at his place in Harrison Co.[120] It is uncertain whether either of these Patrick Burnsides was one and the same as the Patrick Burnside who married Joannah (Trundle) Lewis but one deed found was clearly for this couple. On 16 Apr. 1808 Patrick Burnsides and his wife, Joannah, sold 80 acres on Plummers Run, Harrison Co. to Francis Owen for $400. The deed was as follows:

This Indenture made this E? Sixteenth day of April in the year of our Lord one thousand eight hundred and eight between Patrick Burnsides and Joanna his wife of the county of Harrison and state of Virginia of the one part and Francis Owen of the of the county and state aforesaid of the other part, Witnesseth that the said Patrick Burnsides and Joanna_his wife for and in consideration of the sum of four hundred dollars lawful money of Virginia the receipt whereof is hereby acknowledged have granted bargained sold aliened enfeoffed released and confirmed and by these presents do grant bargain sell alien enfeoff release and confirm to the said Francis Owen his heirs and assigns forever all that tract of land which he the said Francis Owen purchased of Patrick Burnsides lying and being in the County of Harrison and State aforesaid situate on a drain of Plummers run being part of a survey of four hundred acres granted to John Wickwire by patent and bounded as followeth, towit, begining and runing thence North 37D West 20 poles to a poplar thence North 31 D West 36 poles to a hickory thence North 47 degrees East 90 poles to a popular thence South 48 D West 140 poles to a White Oak and Gum thence North 85 1/2 D West 70 poles to the begining containing eighty acres together with all profits_commodities thereunto belonging or in any wise appertaining with all its appertenances To have and To Hold the above described tract of land with the appertenances to the said Francis Owen his heirs and assigns to the only proper use and behoof of the said Francis Owen his heirs and assigns forever and the said Patrick Burnsides and Joanna_his wife for themselves_their heirs do hereby covenant to and with the said Francis Owen and his heirs and assigns they the said Patrick Burnsides & Joanna_his wife the above described tract of land with the appertenances to the said Francis Owen his heirs and assigns shall and will warrant and forever defend against all persons and claims whatsoever. In Testimony whereof the aforesaid Patrick Burnsides and Joanna_ his wife have hereunto set their hands and seal_ the day and year first above written.

                                                    Patrick Burnsides [Seal]
Signed sealed and delivered in the   Joannah Burnsides   [Seal]
presents of
J.A. Sommerville
Virginia SS.
        At a court held for Harrison County April Term 1808
        This deed from Patrick Burnsides and Joannah his wife to Francis Owen was produced in court acknowledged by the said Patrick and Joannah and ordered to be recorded, she having been first privilly examined as the law requires.   Teste   Ben Wilson, C.H.C.[121]

---

[118] Harrison Co., (W)V, Marriage Bond Book 2, p. 167, transcribed by David R. Houchin, 21 Apr. 1993, ahp.
[119] Ibid., Deed Book 4, p. 443, transcribed by David R. Houchin, 7 Apr. 1993.
[120] Ibid., Estray Book, p. 68, ahp.
[121] Ibid., Deed Book 7, pp. 328-329, ahp.

This deed was further noted when the names of Patrick Burnsides and Joanna, his wife, were entered into April 1808 court records when they came into court, she having been first privily examined, and consenting, acknowledged a deed to Francis Owen which was ordered recorded.[122]

In 1810 one Patrick Burnside was head of a family in Harrison Co., (W)V. There was only one female in the family, and she was under ten years of age. There were two males in the family who could have been Patrick Burnside, head of family: one at least 16 but under 26, the other 45 or older. It seems more likely the older male was Patrick Burnside. In addition there were four boys under 16.[123] On 6 Dec. 1816 one Patrick Burnsides of Harrison Co., (W)V, for a sum of $400, sold 100 acres on Freemans Creek, a branch of the West Fork River, Harrison Co., (W)V to Nicholas Stillwell of Reding Twp., Hunterdon Co., NJ. Patrick Burnsides signed by mark. The deed was certified by Samuel Z. Jones and Wm. Powers, Magistrates of Harrison Co.[124] Nothing was found to indicate whether this Patrick Burnsides was one and the same as the Patrick Burnside who married Joannah (Trundle) Lewis. It is possible Patrick Burnside and his wife, Joannah, left the area after they sold the land in 1808 but it seems more probable Joannah had died by 1810, leaving Patrick Burnside a widower.[125]

Children of David and Joannah (Trundle) Lewis:

    i.   Ann[4], b. 17 Nov. 1772[126] Frederick Co., MD;[127] d. 18 Jan. 1790[128] Frederick Co., MD.[129] Ann Lewis was probably named for her maternal grandmother, Ann (---) Trundle, and died at the young age of 17.

10.   ii.   John Trundle, b. 1 Sep. 1774 Frederick Co., MD.

    iii.   Ruth, b. Jul. 1776[130] Frederick Co., MD;[131] d. Sep. 1857 Harrison Co., (W)V[132] prob. Rooting Creek near Johnstown; m. 27 Jan. 1801 Harrison Co., (W)V by Rev. Isaac Morris, **SAMUEL DAVIS**, b. prob. 1762 Loudoun Co., VA; d. 10 Sep. 1847 Harrison Co., (W)V[133] prob. Rooting Creek near Johnstown; poss. s/o John Davis.[134] Samuel Davis m. (1) 13 Apr. 1786 Frederick Co., VA, Phebe Cornell.[135] Ruth Lewis grew up in the homes of her parents, David and Joannah (Trundle) Lewis, which were in Montgomery and Frederick Co., MD, and would have been an adult by the time they moved to Harrison Co., (W)V.[136] On 27 Jan. 1801 in Harrison Co. she married Samuel Davis, a veteran of the American Revolution.[137] He had come to Harrison Co. in 1796

---

[122] Ibid., Minute Book, pp. 124-125, ahp.

[123] Ibid., NARA, 1810 census, photostats, v. 7, p. 949.

[124] Ibid., Deed Book 13, pp. 184-185, ahp.

[125] It can be noted within this work that most of her close relatives died before the age of 60.

[126] Lewis family Bible, possession of Edgar Lewis.

[127] Eleanor M.V. Cook, "1777 Tax List of Montgomery County," pp. 15-16.

[128] Lewis family Bible, possession of Edgar Lewis.

[129] *Heads of Families*, p. 70.

[130] Lewis family Bible, possession of Edgar Lewis.

[131] Eleanor M.V. Cook, "1777 Tax List of Montgomery County," pp. 15-16.

[132] NARA, Revolutionary War Pension, roll 764.

[133] MRHC, p. 14; NARA, Revolutionary War Pension, roll 764.

[134] DRHC, p. 42 has Catherine Romine, b. *ca.* 1776 Loudoun Co., VA, d/o John Davis. She may have been a sister of Samuel. Samuel Davis seems to have named his first son, John.

[135] Eliza Timberlake Davis, comp., *Frederick County, Virginia, Marriages 1771-1825* (Baltimore, 1973), p. 29.

[136] Eleanor M.V. Cook, "1777 Tax List of Montgomery County," pp. 15-16; Frederick Co., MD, Deed Liber W R-4, ff. 411-413, ahp; *Heads of Families*, p. 70; Harrison Co., (W)V, PPTB, 1798.

[137] NARA, Revolutionary War Pension, roll 764.

from Fauquier Co., VA[138] with his first wife, Phebe (Cornell) Davis.[139] From 1796 to 1810 this Samuel Davis seems to have lived on Rooting Creek, Harrison Co., (W)V where he was assessed annually on as many as three horses. By 1799 there was a second, somewhat younger, Samuel Davis in Harrison Co. who lived at Tenmile.[140] No connection between the two was found. On 30 June 1806 Samuel Davis and Ruth (Lewis) Davis were summoned to testify on behalf of Margery Lewis, sister of Ruth.[141] Samuel Davis of Rooting Creek seems to have been the Samuel Davis who in 1810 was head of a family in Harrison Co. In his household were: three white males under ten, one white male at least ten but under 16, two white males at least 16 but under 26, one white male 45 or over, two white females under ten, one white female at least ten but under 16, one white female at least 26 but under 45, and one white female 45 or over. Some of the children would have been from his first marriage.[142] Samuel and Ruth (Lewis) Davis continued to live in or near what became Johnstown, Harrison Co., (W)V where he was assessed annually from 1811 to 1820 on as many as four horses.[143] In 1820 he was enumerated there, but of the two Samuel Davises it is difficult to determine which was he.[144] From 1821 to 1847, the year of his death, he was assessed regularly in Harrison Co. and taxed on as many as three horses.[145] In 1830 he was enumerated in the Eastern part of Harrison Co. In his household were: one white male at least ten but under 15, two white males at least 15 but under 20, one white male at least 20 but under 30, one white male at least 60 but under 70, one white female at least ten but under 15, one white female at least 15 but under 20, one white female at least 20 but under 30, and one white female at least 50 but under 60.[146] On 23 Aug. 1832 Samuel Davis of Harrison Co., (W)V, age 71, in his pension application said in Apr. 1781 he entered service as a substitute for Thomas Sheppards under Capt. Francis Berry of Frederick Co., VA. He was then a resident of Loudoun Co., VA. He served for three months and after his term in service returned to Loudoun Co. Then after a few days he was again in US service by draft as a militiaman under command by Capt. Cannon to join the American Army under Gen. LaFayette. Having done this, while encamped at mills near Williamsburg, he was taken ill and when troops marched to Yorktown he was too sick to accompany them. He was then discharged by Col. Merriweather and as soon as able, returned to his home

[138] Ibid.; Harrison Co., (W)V, PPTB, 1796-1801.

[139] MRUC, p. 51 gives the parents of John Davis as Samuel & Phebe Davis.

[140] Harrison Co., (W)V, PPTB, 1796-1810.

[141] Zinn, v. 3, pp. 110-111.

[142] Harrison Co., (W)V, NARA, 1810 census, photostats, v. 7, p. 156. Known children of Samuel & Phebe (Cornell) Davis: John, b. 26 Feb. 1788 Loudoun Co., VA; James, b. poss. ca. 1790; William, b. 17 Dec. 1795 prob. Fauquier Co., VA ; prob. Sarah, b. 12 Mar. 1798 prob. Harrison Co., (W)V; Israel, b. ca. 1800 prob. Harrison Co., (W)V (information, courtesy of Mrs. Naomi [Davis] Giffin, Columbus, OH; NARA, Revolutionary War Pension, roll 764; HCWV 1850, pp. 87, 89, 91; Lewis family Bible, printed 1870, prob. Bible of Elmore Dow Lewis, owned by Robert Roy Post, Salem, WV [2000]).

[143] Harrison Co., (W)V, PPTB, 1811-1820.

[144] Ibid., NARA, 1820 census, roll 138, p. 88 or 783 or 784 (page numbering system unclear).

[145] Ibid., PPTB, 1821-1847.

[146] Ibid., NARA, 1830 census, roll 190, p. 303.

in Loudoun Co. He states John Welch, John Middleton and John Romine who were then likewise residents of Loudoun Co. and might testify were in service with him. He further states they now live in Harrison Co. His application was signed Sam[l] Davis, his mark. John Middleton served on first tour of duty with him. John Romine served on second tour of duty with him. Their sworn statements signed by mark. He was awarded $20 annually.[147] In 1840 Samuel Davis was enumerated in Harrison Co. In his household were: one white male under five, one white male at least 20 but under 30, one white male at least 70 but under 80, three white females at least 20 but under 30, and one white female at least 60 but under 70.[148] Samuel Davis died 10 Sep. 1847 probably at age 85. On 15 Aug. 1850 Ruth (Lewis) Davis, as a widow of Samuel Davis, first entered a claim for pension. She stated that her maiden name was Ruth Lewis. She died Sep. 1857 at age 81.[149] Children of Samuel and Ruth (Lewis) Davis, all born in Harrison Co., (W)V, in or near now Johnstown: Matilda[5], b. 13 Mar. 1803; Humphrey, b. 1 June 1809; Joseph, b. *ca.* 1811; Gary L., d. Mar. 1853.[150]

iv. Prob. son, b. *ca.* 1779;[151] prob. d. young.

v. Margaret, b. 6 Oct. 1783[152] Montgomery or Frederick Co., MD;[153] d. 5 Aug. 1784[154] Frederick Co., MD.[155]

vi. Margery, b. 20 Aug. 1785[156] Frederick Co., MD;[157] d. prob. aft. 1840 Jefferson Co., IN;[158] m. 3 Oct. 1814 Harrison Co., (W)V by Rev. Joseph Morris, **WILLIAM MILLHOUSE**,[159] b. poss. *ca.* 1785; d. prob. aft. 1840 Jefferson Co., IN.[160] Margery Lewis grew up in the homes of her parents, David and Joannah (Trundle) Lewis, in Frederick Co., MD and Harrison Co., (W)V. When she was about 11 years old David Lewis moved his family to Harrison Co. and he died about a year later. In Oct. 1804 when she was 19, Margery Lewis had a child and she said the father was **JONATHAN RADCLIFFE**.

District Court, Harrison County. Jonathan RADCLIFFE summoned to answer Margery LEWIS in a plea of covenant broken and $2000 damage, 22 March 1805.[161]

---

[147] NARA, Revolutionary War Pension, roll 764, application of Samuel Davis abstracted 28 Mar. 1983.

[148] Harrison Co., (W)V, NARA, 1840 census, roll 562, p. 78.

[149] NARA, Revolutionary War Pension, roll 764.

[150] Ibid., claim for pension in arrears has names of their children; information, courtesy of Mrs. Giffin; Barbara Prince-Tharp, comp., *Where They Lie - Cemeteries of Southern Harrison County* (Lost Creek, WV, 1984), p. 226; DRHC, p. 1 has age of Gary L. Davis as 25 in 1853 (apparently in error), parents as Samuel & Ruth. HCWV 1850, pp. 87, 90, 100, some ages for persons with these names in this census seem questionable.

[151] *Heads of Families*, p. 70 allows for a son b. in this gap between Ruth & Margaret.

[152] Lewis family Bible, possession of Edgar Lewis.

[153] *Montgomery Co., MD Oath of Fidelity & Tax Lists - 1778*, p. 6; Frederick Co., MD, Deed Liber W R-4, ff. 411-413, ahp.

[154] Lewis family Bible, possession of Edgar Lewis.

[155] Frederick Co., MD, Deed Liber W R-4, ff. 411-413, ahp.

[156] Lewis family Bible, possession of Edgar Lewis.

[157] Frederick Co., MD, Deed Liber W R-4, ff. 411-413, ahp.

[158] Jefferson Co., IN, NARA, 1840 census, roll 83, p. 296.

[159] MRHC, p. 34 has her name as Margaret Lewis & his as William Millhome; list of marriages celebrated & signed by Joseph Morris has her name as Margary Lewis & his as William Millhouse, author has photocopy of original (difficult to read), courtesy of Miss Gwen L. Spry, Albuquerque, NM.

[160] Jefferson Co., IN.

[161] Zinn, v. 3, pp. 42, 110-111.

Several people gave depositions and the names of several family members including her mother, Johannah T. Lewis, appear in that record. The index card identifying the file states that the verdict and judgment awarded Margery $25 in damages. There may have been an appeal. The record further states Jonathan Radcliffe married Sarah Caster before the birth of the child, though it may have been after that birth.[162] Jonathan Radcliff is known to have had a son named Louis Radcliff or perhaps Lewis Radcliff, likely for the surname of Margery Lewis. Louis/Lewis seems to have been the right age to have been that child born in 1804 to Margery Lewis and he was the older of two sons of Jonathan Radcliff.[163] The child was not found to be living with Margery Lewis or with other Lewis families so he may have grown up in the home of Jonathan and Sarah (Caster) Radcliff. On 3 Oct. 1814 Margery Lewis married William Millhouse in Harrison Co. In 1820 William Millhouse was head of a family in Harrison Co. In his household were: two white males under ten, one white male at least 26 but under 45, and one white female at least 26 but under 45.[164] They seem to have lived there for the next ten years where in 1830 William Millhouse was enumerated in the Eastern part of Harrison Co. In his household were: one white male under five, one white male at least five but under ten, two white males at least ten but under 15, one white male at least 15 but under 20, one white male at least 40 but under 50, one white female under five, one white female at least five but under ten, and one white female at least 40 but under 50.[165] By 1840 William Millhouse had moved his family to Jefferson Co., IN where he was enumerated in that year. In his household were: four white males at least 20 but under 30, one white male at least 50 but under 60, one white female at least five but under ten, one white female at least ten but under 15, one white female at least 15 but under 20, and one white female at least 50 but under 60. At that time five members of the household were engaged in agriculture.[166] It is not known where William and Margery (Lewis) Millhouse died or how many children they had but some members of the family seem to have been in Iowa at a later time. Child of Margery Lewis and Jonathan Radcliff, born in Harrison Co., (W)V: Louis/Lewis Radcliff, b. Oct. 1804.[167] Known sons of William and Margery (Lewis) Millhouse, both born in Harrison Co., (W)V: Eli[5], b. 1816; William Henry Harrison, b. 13 Feb. 1821.[168]

[162] Ibid.; MRHC, p. 16 gives the date of that marriage as 29 Nov. 1804 Harrison Co., (W)V.
[163] Dennis B. Rodgers, "The Radcliffs of Hacker's Creek," *Hacker's Creek Journal*, v. 6, p. 47.
[164] Harrison Co., (W)V, NARA, 1820 census, roll 138. p. 736. It should be noted, this record does not allow for Louis Radcliff, b. in 1804.
[165] Ibid., 1830 census, roll 190, p. 7.
[166] Jefferson Co., IN, NARA, 1840 census, roll 83, p. 296. Census records seem to indicate William & Margery may have had up to eight children. More research is needed for this family.
[167] Zinn, v. 3, pp. 42, 110-111; Rodgers has Louis, s/o Jonathan Radcliff, died without marrying, though this could be further researched to determine what happened to him.
[168] Information, courtesy of Miss Spry who also has Eli Millhouse m. 11 Feb. 1847 Jefferson Co., IN, Susan Tuttle; William Henry Harrison Millhouse m. 16 Nov. 1842 Jefferson Co., IN, Emeline Minor.

vii.   Delila, b. 1 Oct. 1787[169] Frederick Co., MD;[170] prob. d. young. No other information was found for this daughter.

11. viii.   Jonathan, b. 25 Mar. 1793.

ix.   Rachel, b. 4 Feb. 1797[171] prob. Harrison Co., (W)V;[172] d. aft. 1859 Harrison Co., (W)V;[173] m. 20 Nov. 1815 Harrison Co., (W)V, **SAMUEL DAWSON**,[174] b. *ca.* 1793 prob. Harrison Co., (W)V; d. aft. 1849 Harrison Co., (W)V.[175] Rachel Lewis seems to have been born about the time her parents, David and Joannah (Trundle) Lewis, moved to Harrison Co., (W)V. She would have been no more than two when her father, David, died and would have had no memory of him as she grew up in Harrison Co. Rachel likely lived with her mother, Joannah (Trundle) Lewis, until Joannah died. By 1810 Rachel Lewis was likely living in Harrison Co., (W)V with her older brother, John Trundle Lewis. She was probably the white female in that household who was at least ten but under 16 at that time.[176] She probably lived there until her marriage to Samuel Dawson 20 Nov. 1815. Samuel Dawson was enumerated in Harrison Co., in 1830 and 1840. By 1840 they may have had as many as ten children and four members of the household were engaged in agriculture.[177] In 1850 Samuel Dawson and his wife, Rachel, were living in Harrison Co. with apparently seven of their children still at home. At age 56 Samuel was a farmer. He must have died before 1860 when Rachel (Lewis) Dawson, age 62, apparently a widow and head of family, was living in Harrison Co. with some other family members.[178] Children of Samuel and Rachel (Lewis) Dawson, all born in Harrison Co., (W)V: Russel[5], b. prob. *ca.* 1818;[179] Elizabeth, b. *ca.* 1820;[180] Ervin, b. *ca.* 1823;[181] Massey, b. *ca.* 1825;[182] Bassel, b. *ca.* 1826;[183] Wilson, b. *ca.* 1828;[184] George, b. *ca.* 1831;[185] Samuel (Jr.), b. *ca.* 1834;[186] David L., b. *ca.* 1836.[187]

---

[169] Lewis family Bible, possession of Edgar Lewis.

[170] *Heads of Families*, p. 70.

[171] Lewis family Bible, possession of Edgar Lewis.

[172] HCWV 1850, p. 102.

[173] HCWV 1860, p.132.

[174] MRHC, p. 36 has John & Sarah as her parents, but John was her brother. She was likely living with John & his wife, Sarah, at the time of her marriage, as her mother, Joannah, was likely dead by then.

[175] HCWV 1850, p. 102.

[176] Harrison Co., (W)V, NARA, 1810 census, photostats, v. 7, p. 157.

[177] Ibid., 1830 census, roll 190, p. 303; ibid., 1840 census, roll 562, p. 89.

[178] HCWV 1860, p. 132.

[179] DRHC, p. 23.

[180] DRHC, p. 170. On 9 June 1859 Harrison Co., (W)V, apparently after the death of her younger sister, Massey, Elizabeth Dawson m. Luther L. Cottrill, her former brother-in-law (MRHC, p. 150). In 1860 Luther L. Cottrill & wife, Elizabeth, were living in Harrison Co. with six children, apparently five from his marriage to Massey & one from his marriage to Elizabeth (HCWV 1860, p. 91).

[181] HCWV 1850, p. 102.

[182] DRHC, p. 23; MRHC, p. 109, Massey Dawson m. 28 Jan. 1847 Harrison Co., (W)V, Luther L. Cottrill.

[183] HCWV 1850, p. 102.

[184] Ibid.

[185] Ibid.

[186] Ibid.

[187] Ibid.; DRHC, p. 41 has his name as David L. Dawson.

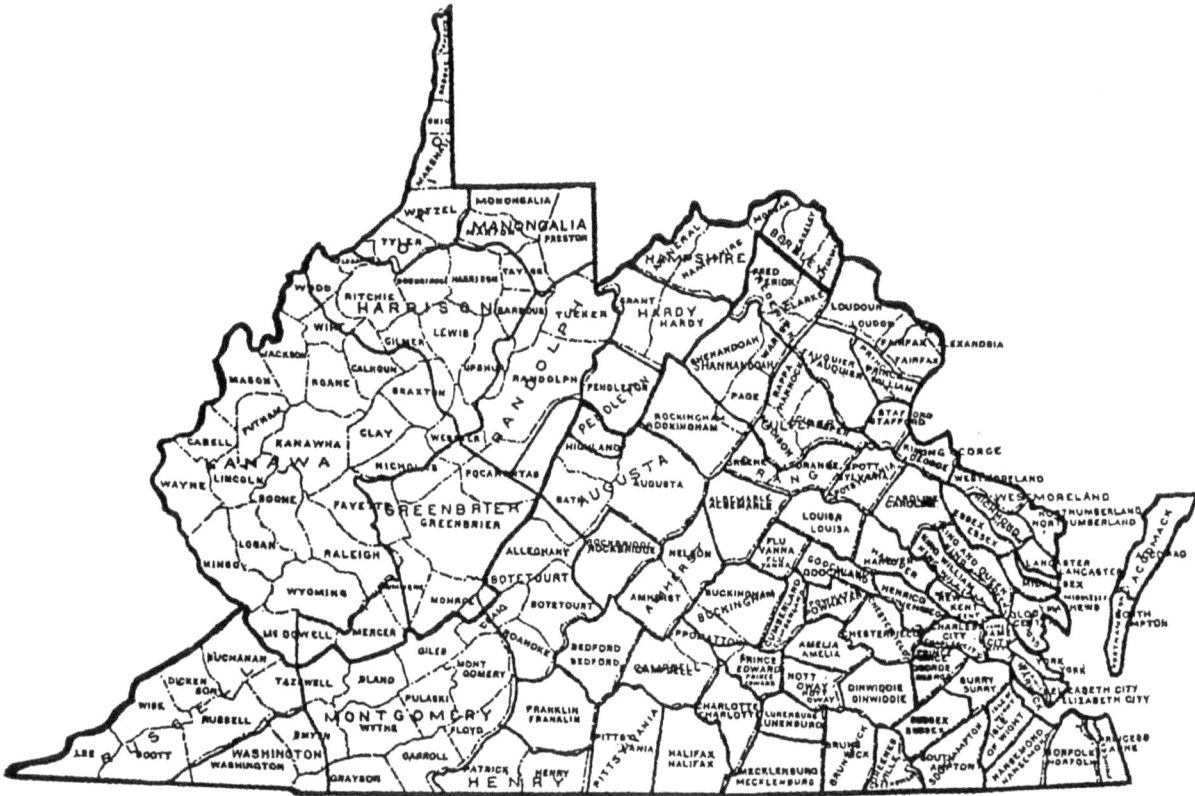

Ill. 7 - Virginia and West Virginia 1790 and 1900. Reproduced from *A Century of Population Growth* (Government Printing Office, Washington, 1909).

6. DANIEL³ LEWIS JR. (Daniel², Jonathan¹) (see 2), b. 1755 Frederick Co., MD;[188] d. 1836 Iredell Co., NC, bur. Lewis Graveyard, near Fifth Creek, Iredell Co., NC;[189] m. (1) 10 May 1778 Montgomery Co., MD by Rev. Alexander Williamson, **MARGERY WATERS**,[190] b. *ca.* 1759[191] prob. Frederick Co., MD; d. 1789 Iredell Co., NC, bur. near husb.;[192] m. (2) *ca.* 1791[193] prob. Iredell Co., NC, **ELIZABETH BELT**, b. *ca.* 1759[194] prob. Frederick Co., MD; d. 1838 Iredell Co., NC, bur. near husb;[195] d/o Thomas Belt.[196]

Daniel Lewis Jr. probably grew up in the homes of his parents, Daniel and Margaret (?Beall) Lewis, in Frederick Co., MD. It is possible his mother was an earlier wife of Daniel Lewis. Though he was not named in the 1781 will of Daniel Lewis (Sr.), he was surely his son. By the time that will was written, Daniel Jr. had been living in Rowan Co., NC for about three years.[197]

By 7 Aug. 1776 his name appeared as Daniel Lewis when, probably at age 21, he was enrolled by Capt. Edward Burgess under Col. Griffith and Gen. R. Beall for service of the Flying Camp, Lower District, Frederick Co., MD.[198] Later in that same year, 1776, the Lower District of Frederick Co., MD became part of the new county of Montgomery. The Militia Act of 1777 resulted in partial reorganization of the battalions[199] and Danl. Lewis of Montgomery Co. was by then a private, 1st Co., 29th (Lower) Bn., Maryland Militia. His likely half brothers, Jere. Lewis and David Lewis, were in the 2d Co.[200]

On 26 Feb. 1778 the name of Daniel Lewis Jr. appears in a list of all "Free Male Persons Names in Lower Newfoundland Hundred above eighteen years old," taken in by George Small, Constable. Also in the list was the name of Daniel Lewis Sr.[201] In the same year, perhaps March 1778, both signed the Oath of Fidelity to the State of Maryland from Montgomery Co. Their names appear with their marks, as Daniel Lewis Junr. with his mark "X" and Daniel Lewis with his mark "DL" in the list delivered to the Court by Edward Burgess.[202]

On 10 May 1778 his name was recorded as Daniel Lewis when he married Margery Waters in Montgomery Co., MD.[203] Later that year, 1778, they moved to Rowan Co., NC[204] where, in future records his name would appear only as Daniel Lewis. Other

[188] NARA, Revolutionary War Pension, roll 1555.
[189] Gravestone, Lewis Graveyard, near Fifth Creek, Iredell Co., NC, cited in Mary Elinor Lazenby, *Lazenby, Some Account of Families in the United States Which Bear the Name* (Washington, 1942, 2d ed.), pp. 38, 41, 43. This work should be referenced by anyone researching this family and other Maryland families who came to Iredell Co., NC.
[190] Gaius Marcus Brumbaugh, *Maryland Records, Colonial, Revolutionary, County, and Church from Original Sources* (Baltimore, 1985 repr. 1928 ed.), v. 2, pp. 521-522.
[191] Gravestone, Lewis Graveyard, cited in Lazenby, p. 43.
[192] Ibid.
[193] Lazenby, pp. 40-42, dau., Margery Lewis, b. 20 Aug. 1792.
[194] Gravestone, Lewis Graveyard, cited in Lazenby, p. 43 .
[195] Ibid.
[196] Iredell Co., NC, Will Book 1, No. 88 , p. 123, cited in Mrs. George H. Malcom, Fourth Creek Chapter DAR, Statesville, NC, *Iredell County, North Carolina Will Abstracts* (1973), p. 88.
[197] NARA, Revolutionary War Pension, roll 1555.
[198] Ibid.; *Archives of Maryland, Muster Rolls and Other Records of Service of Maryland Troops in the American Revolution, 1775-1783* (Baltimore, 1900), v. 18, pp. 42-43.
[199] S. Eugene Clements, p. 10.
[200] Ibid., p. 198.
[201] *Montgomery Co., Md. Oath of Fidelity & Tax Lists - 1778*, pp. 67-68.
[202] Ibid., pp. 3-4.
[203] Brumbaugh.
[204] NARA, Revolutionary War Pension, roll 1555.

families from Montgomery Co. moved there around the same time.[205] In 1781 he joined the army as a volunteer, apparently in Rowan Co., NC, in services of Capt. Abel Armstrong, Col. Davie(?), and Gen. R. Beall.[206] On 28 Feb. 1786 Daniel Lewis, for the sum of £100, acquired 170 acres on Fourth Creek, Rowan Co., NC from Prior Smallwood Roby. One acre was exempted for a burying ground.[207] Upon the formation of Iredell Co., NC in 1788, the area where Daniel Lewis lived and owned land became a part of the new county.[208] In 1789 Margery (Waters) Lewis died at the young age of 30. She was the first buried in the Lewis Graveyard, near Fifth Creek on family land. It became a burying ground for surrounding families who had come from Maryland.[209]

Circa 1791 Daniel Lewis married Elizabeth Belt and in 1810 she was named in the will of her father, Thomas Belt, of Iredell Co., NC.[210] In 1800 Daniel Lewis was taxed in Iredell Co., NC with a house valued at over $100 which, when included with two outbuildings and two acres, had a total value of $115. There was also a barn 26 X 16 valued at $20 and 168 acres valued at $200.[211] When David Beall Sr. wrote his will 15 May 1806, Burges Gaither and Daniel Lewis were named executors.[212] Daniel Lewis was to acquire other lands. According to a deed registered 1 Apr. 1807, for the sum of £150, he acquired from James Taylor, 100 acres lying on both sides of Fifth Creek, Iredell Co., NC, joining Ninian Steel. Witnesses were David Beal and Henry Baggerly jurat.[213] One week later, 8 Apr. 1807, for the sum of $125, he acquired from John Lovelace, 50 acres lying on both sides of Fifth Creek, Iredell Co., NC. Witnesses were B. Gaither and Thomas Galloway jurat.[214] On 29 Apr. 1813, for the sum of $31, Daniel Lewis acquired from William Archibald, nine acres lying in the forks of Fifth Creek, Iredell Co., NC, joining his other land. Witnesses were Samuel Archibald and A. Campbell.[215]

Daniel Lewis continued to live in Iredell Co., NC and in 1820 he was head of a family there. In his household were: one white male at least 16 but under 26, one white male 45 or over, and one white female 45 or over.[216] On 25 Aug. 1832 Daniel Lewis at age 77 applied for his Revolutionary War Pension, signing with his mark "X"[217] as in earlier records. He died in 1836 at age 80[218] and estate papers were filed that year.[219] Elizabeth (Belt) Lewis survived her husband and died in 1838 at age 79.[220]

---

[205] Michael L. Cook, *Pioneer Lewis Families* (Evansville, IN, 1984), v. 4, p.1039; Lazenby, pp. 37-43.

[206] NARA, Revolutionary War Pension, roll 1555.

[207] Rowan Co., NC, Deed Book 10, p. 561, cited in Mrs. Stahle Linn Jr., *Abstracts of the Deeds of Rowan County, North Carolina, 1753-1785, Vols. 1-10* (Salisbury, NC, 1983), p. 220.

[208] Shirley Coulter et al., comp., *Minutes of the Court of Pleas and Quarter Sessions Iredell County, North Carolina, 1789 to 1800* (Statesville, NC), Preface.

[209] Lazenby, pp. 41, 43.

[210] Iredell Co., NC, Will Book 1, No. 88, p. 123, cited in Malcom, p. 88.

[211] Mrs. Lois M.P. Schneider, *Iredell County, N.C. Land Valuations for Direct Tax -1800 -* (Statesville, NC, 1983), p. 41.

[212] Iredell Co., NC, Will Book 1, p. 230, cited in Sharon J. Doliante, *Maryland and Virginia Colonials: Genealogies of Some Colonial Families* (Baltimore, 1991), p. 623.

[213] Iredell Co., NC, Deed Book F, p. 426, cited in Russell C. Black Jr., *Iredell County, N.C. Deed Abstracts Books E & F, 1803-1808* (Statesville, NC), p. 68.

[214] Ibid., p. 437, cited in Black, p. 69.

[215] Ibid., Deed Book H, p. 449, cited in Black, *Iredell County, N.C. Deed Abstracts Books G & H, 1809-1817* (Statesville, NC), p. 69.

[216] Dorothy Williams Potter, *1820 Census of North Carolina, Volume XXVIII, Iredell County* (1973), p. 57.

[217] NARA, Revolutionary War Pension, roll 1555.

[218] Gravestone, Lewis Graveyard, cited in Lazenby, p. 43.

[219] Iredell Co., NC, Will Book 2, p. 159, cited in Schneider, *Inventory of the Estate Papers of Iredell County, North Carolina, 1788-1915* (Troutman, NC, 1987), p. 59.

[220] Gravestone, Lewis Graveyard, cited in Lazenby, p. 43.

Daniel Lewis Jr. was probably 21 when the American Revolution began and within two months became a private in the Maryland Militia. Though he is not mentioned in the will of Daniel Lewis (Sr.), it seems almost certain he was his son. In 1778, in Montgomery Co., MD he married Margery Waters and they left for Rowan Co., NC that same year. Margery (Waters) Lewis was to die in 1789, leaving no known children. In 1781, apparently in Rowan Co., he joined the army as a volunteer. For North Carolina, all records found have his name as Daniel Lewis. His second wife was Elizabeth Belt whom he married *ca.* 1791. By then the area where he lived and owned land was in the new county of Iredell, near other families who had come there from Maryland. He acquired more land and by 1813 he owned 329 acres around Fifth Creek, Iredell Co., NC, suggesting he must have been engaged in agriculture. Late in life as Daniel Lewis he received a pension for his service in the Revolutionary War. Though he probably never learned to read or write, he seems to have been a successful business man and influential in his community. Both he and his second wife, Elizabeth (Belt) Lewis, lived to an advanced age and had children, so it seems likely there are living descendants.

Children of Daniel Jr. and Elizabeth (Belt) Lewis, all born in Iredell Co., NC:

    i.   Margery,[4] b. 20 Aug. 1792;[221] d. 12 Feb. 1881 Iredell Co., NC, bur. New Hope Church, Iredell Co., NC;[222] m. 15 Feb. 1816 Iredell Co., NC, **ROBERT LAZENBY**,[223] b. 24 June 1786 White Oak Branch farm, Iredell Co., NC; d. 20 Aug. 1828 Iredell Co., NC,[224] bur. Lewis Graveyard near Fifth Creek, Iredell Co., NC;[225] s/o Joshua & Keziah (---) Lazenby.[226] Margery Lewis was an heir of Daniel Lewis Jr.[227] and grew up in the home of her parents, Daniel Jr. and Elizabeth (Belt) Lewis, near Fifth Creek, Iredell Co., NC. She was the oldest daughter[228] and it is possible she was named for her father's first wife, Margery (Waters) Lewis, who had died at the young age of 30. On 15 Feb. 1816 Margery Lewis married Robert Lazenby whose parents had also come from Montgomery Co., MD.[229] By the time they married, in addition to farming and school teaching, Robert Lazenby had received a commission as captain in the War of 1812. According to a deed, recorded 29 July 1814, he also had title to a farm on the south side of South Yadkin River, below the mouth of Rocky Creek, Iredell Co., NC, and continued to vary farming with school teaching. Robert and Margery (Lewis) Lazenby continued to live on that farm.[230] In 1820 Robert Lazenby, school master, was head of a family in Iredell Co. NC. In his household were: one white male under ten, one white male at least 26 but under 45, one white female under ten, and one white female at least 16 but under 26.[231] Robert Lazenby died 20 Aug. 1828 at the

---

[221] Lazenby , p. 42.
[222] Ibid., p. 41.
[223] Ibid., p. 40.
[224] Ibid., p. 39.
[225] Gravestone, Lewis Graveyard, cited in Lazenby, p. 41.
[226] Lazenby, p. 39.
[227] Iredell Co., NC, Will Book 2, p. 159, cited in Schneider, *Inventory of the Estate Papers*, p. 59, name is given as Margary E. Lewis.
[228] Lazenby, p. 40.
[229] Ibid., p. 37.
[230] Ibid., p. 39-42.
[231] Potter, p. 56. It seems as if Margery (Lewis) Lazenby should have been recorded as being over 26.

young age of 42,[232] leaving his wife, Margery (Lewis) Lazenby, with six young children.[233] With the help of her oldest son, Daniel Orlando, she managed the family farm until her old age, when she went to live with her youngest daughter, Kesiah Elizabeth. Margery (Lewis) Lazenby died 12 Feb. 1881 at the advanced age of 88.[234] Children of Robert and Margery (Lewis) Lazenby, all born in Iredell Co., NC: Venelia[5], b. 27 Nov. 1816; Daniel Orlando, b. 27 June 1819; Joshua Leroy, b. 30 Jan. 1821; John Milford, b. 3 Feb. 1823; Robert Lewis, b. 6 Mar. 1824; Kesiah Elizabeth, b. 19 Aug. 1827.[235]

ii.   Margaret, b. *ca.* 1794;[236] d. poss. 1838, bur. unmarked grave, Lewis Graveyard near Fifth Creek, Iredell Co., NC;[237] m. poss. 1813[238] prob. Iredell Co., NC, **HENRY FITZGERALD**, d. 1841 Iredell Co., NC, bur. near wife.[239] Margaret Lewis was an heir of Daniel Lewis Jr.[240] and grew up in the home of her parents, Daniel Jr. and Elizabeth (Belt) Lewis, near Fifth Creek, Iredell Co., NC. She was probably named for her probable paternal grandmother, Margaret (?Beall) Lewis, and married Henry Fitzgerald possibly by 1813. In 1820 Henry Fitzgerald was head of a family in Iredell Co., NC. In his household were: one white male under ten, one white male at least ten but under 16, one white male at least 26 but under 45, one white female under ten, one white female at least ten but under 16, and one white female at least 26 but under 45.[241] Known child of Henry and Margaret (Lewis) Fitzgerald, born in Iredell Co., NC: Elizabeth[5].[242]

iii.   Elizabeth, m. bef. 1820[243] Iredell Co., NC, **ELAM LOVELACE**.[244] Elizabeth Lewis was an heir of Daniel Lewis Jr.[245] and grew up in the home of her parents, Daniel Jr. and Elizabeth (Belt) Lewis, near Fifth Creek, Iredell Co., NC. She was probably named for her mother, Elizabeth (Belt) Lewis, and married Elam Lovelace, before 1820. He is probably the same person as Elam Loveless, who in 1820 was head of a family in Iredell Co., NC. In his household were: one white male under ten, one white male at least 16 but under 26, and probably one white female at least 16 but under 26.[246] Probable child of Elam and Elizabeth (Lewis) Lovelace, born in Iredell Co., NC: prob. son[5], b. by 1820.[247]

---

[232] Lazenby, p. 39.

[233] Ibid., p. 42.

[234] Ibid., p. 41. The name of Kesiah Elizabeth given as Mrs. Charles W. Kesler.

[235] Ibid., p. 42.

[236] Potter, p. 56.

[237] Lazenby, p. 43.

[238] Potter, pp. 56-57.

[239] Gravestone, Lewis Graveyard, cited in Lazenby, p. 43.

[240] Iredell Co., NC, Will Book 2, p. 159, cited in Schneider, *Inventory of the Estate Papers*, p. 59.

[241] Potter, p. 56.

[242] Lazenby, p. 43.

[243] Potter, pp. 56-57.

[244] Lazenby, p. 41.

[245] Iredell Co., NC, Will Book 2, p. 159, cited in Schneider, *Inventory of the Estate Papers*, p. 59.

[246] Potter, p. 56 is unclear whether there is a female under 26.

[247] Ibid.

iv.   Ephraim, b. prob. bet. 1795 & 1804;[248] d. aft. 1835.[249] Ephraim Lewis was an heir of Daniel Lewis Jr.[250] and grew up in the home of his parents, Daniel Jr. and Elizabeth (Belt) Lewis, near Fifth Creek, Iredell Co., NC. He was apparently the younger male who, in 1820, was living in the household of Daniel Lewis in Iredell Co., NC.[251] On 27 Mar. 1827 he was enrolled as a scholar with school master, Robert Lazenby, his brother-in-law.[252] Because teachers were often rare or unavailable, many did not learn to read and write until they were adults. No other information was found for Ephraim Lewis.

---

[248] Potter, p. 57.
[249] Iredell Co., NC, Will Book 2, p. 159, cited in Schneider, *Inventory of the Estate Papers*, p. 59
[250] Ibid.
[251] Potter, p. 57.
[252] Lazenby, p. 41.

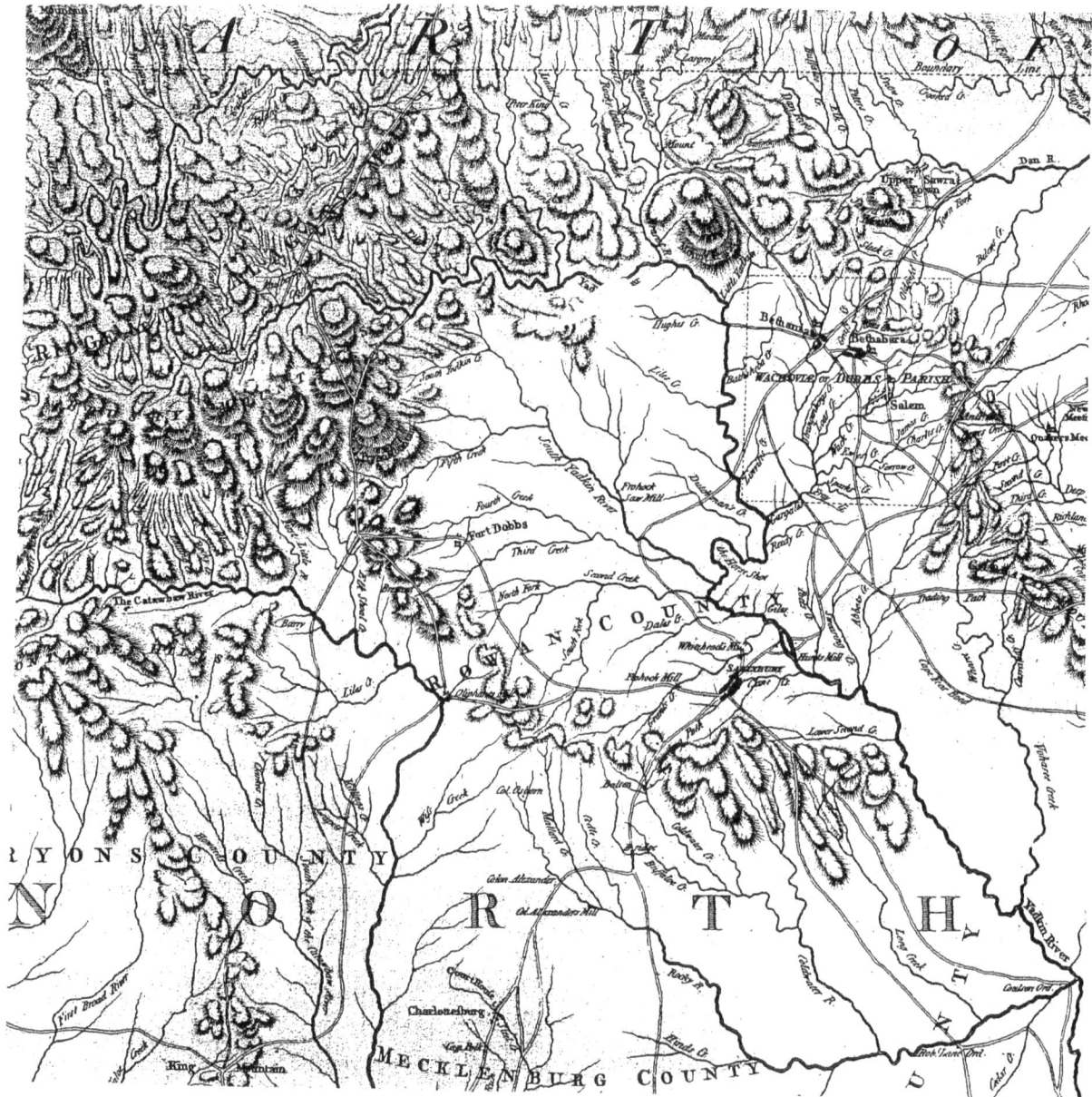

Ill. 8 - Part of North Carolina showing Rowan County, from a 1775 map of North and South Carolina in Raleigh, State Department of Archives (1966). Reproduced from collections of the Library of Congress, Geography and Map Division.

CHAPTER FOUR

LEWIS, FOURTH GENERATION

7. LEVI[4] **LEWIS** (Jeremiah[3], Daniel[2], Jonathan[1]) (see 4), b. *ca.* 1771 Frederick Co., MD;[1] d. bet. 31 Mar. 1812 & 11 Aug. 1812 Montgomery Co., MD;[2] m. 18 Dec. 1798 Montgomery Co., MD, **REBECCA WINDSOR**,[3] b. *ca.* 1778 Montgomery Co., MD;[4] d/o Thomas & Catherine (Ward) Windsor.[5] Rebecca (Windsor) Lewis prob. m. (2) 7 Nov. 1812 Frederick Co., MD, **ARCHIBALD BROWNING JR.**[6]

Levi Lewis grew up in the homes of his parents, Jeremiah and Jane (Fitzgerald) Lewis, which were first in Frederick Co., MD but upon formation of Montgomery Co. in 1776 were in the new county. By 1781 their home was probably on *Trouble Enough* or *Close Tract*, two tracts of land acquired in 1779 by his grandfather, Daniel Lewis.[7] Of eight children mentioned in the 1815 will of Jeremiah Lewis, Levy was named fourth in the list of names given which may mean he was one of the older children.[8] On 18 Dec. 1798 he married Rebecca Windsor in Montgomery Co., MD and in 1800 he was head of a family there. In his household were: one white male at least 26 but under 45, and one white female at least 16 but under 26.[9]

On 21 Dec. 1809 Rebecca (Windsor) Lewis was named in the will of her father whose name appeared as Thomas Winsor.[10] Levi Lewis was still living in Montgomery Co., MD in 1810 when the name, Levi Lewis, appears in the census of that year twice, which may mean he was enumerated a second time, possibly due to a move. One household appears with: three white males under ten, one white male at least ten but under 16, one white male at least 26 but under 45, two white females under ten, one white female at least 26 but under 45, three free persons of color, and 11 slaves.[11] The other household appears with: one white male under ten, two white males at least ten but under 16, one white male at least 26 but under 45, three white females under ten, one white female at least 26 but under 45, three free persons of color, and 11 slaves.[12] Levi Lewis was probably seriously ill by early 1812. On 31 Mar. 1812 as Levin Lewis, planter, of Montgomery Co., MD, he made his will, naming his wife, Rebeckah. According to his will he had six children though he did not give their names.[13] When his father, Jeremiah Lewis, made his will about three years later, 23 Apr. 1815, he mentioned the children of

[1] Montgomery Co., MD, Will Liber 3, ff. 198-200, ahp.; ibid., NARA, 1800 census, roll 11, p. 44 or 224.

[2] Ibid., Will Liber H, f. 24 & Will Liber 2, p. 328, cited in Mary Gordon Malloy et al., comp., *Abstracts of Wills Montgomery County, Maryland, 1776-1825* , p. 85.

[3] Janet Thompson Manuel, comp., *Marriage Licenses Montgomery County, Maryland 1798-1898* (Silver Spring, MD, 1987), p. 194.

[4] Montgomery Co., MD, NARA; ibid., Will Liber G, f. 143 & Will Liber 2, p. 230, cited in Malloy, p. 154; William Neal Hurley Jr., *Our Maryland Heritage, Book Fourteen, Lewis Families* (Bowie, MD, 1999), p. 73. This work should be referenced by those researching Lewis families in Montgomery & Frederick Co., MD.

[5] Montgomery Co., MD, Will Liber G, f. 143 & Will Liber 2, p. 230, cited in Malloy, p. 154; Hurley.

[6] Margaret E. Myers, *Marriage Licenses of Frederick County 1811-1840* (Silver Spring, MD, 1987), p. 146.

[7] Montgomery Co., MD, Deed Liber A, ff. 394-396, ahp; ibid., Deed Liber C, f. 539, ahp.

[8] Ibid., Will Liber 3, ff. 198-200, ahp.

[9] Ibid., NARA.

[10] Ibid., Will Liber G, f. 143, cited in Malloy, p. 154.

[11] Ibid., NARA, 1810 census, roll 14, p. 319 or 932.

[12] Ibid., p. 323 or 936.

[13] Montgomery Co., MD, Will Liber H, f. 24, cited in Malloy, p. 85.

his son, Levy, though not by name, "to Heir the same part as he might do if living ."[14] Levi Lewis had died by 11 Aug. 1812. In records his given name appears as Levi, Levy, and Levin.

Rebecca (Windsor) Lewis was not found to be living in Montgomery or Frederick Co., MD in 1820.[15] She may have been the Rebecca Lewis who on 7 Nov. 1812 married Archibald Browning Jr. in Frederick Co., MD.[16] Three of her children were to marry in Frederick Co., suggesting she may have been living there at the times of those marriages.

Children of Levi and Rebecca (Windsor) Lewis, all born in Montgomery Co., MD:

    i.   Harriet Ann[5], b. *ca.* 1805; d. 26 Aug. 1881 Montgomery Co., MD;[17] m. 28 Nov. 1826 Frederick Co., MD, **ALPHA WATKINS**.[18]

    ii.   Catharine, b. *ca.* 1806; d. 1861 Montgomery Co., MD;[19] m. 1 May 1827 Montgomery Co., MD, **VINCENT BREWER**.[20]

    iii.   John Thomas, b 22 Apr. 1809; d. 29 Oct. 1885 prob. New Market Dist., Frederick Co., MD, bur. Kemptown Methodist Church Cem., Frederick Co., MD;[21] m. 1 Dec. 1834 Frederick Co., MD, **EMELINE MOXLEY**.[22]

    iv.   Jeremiah, b. poss. 22 Apr. 1809, poss. twin of John Thomas;[23] d. 23 Mar. 1891 prob. New Market Dist., Frederick Co., MD, bur. Kemptown Methodist Church Cem., Frederick Co., MD;[24] m. 25 Apr. 1845 Frederick Co., MD, **SARAH JANE CLAGGETT**.[25]

    v.   Thomas Howard, b. 26 Aug. 1810; d. 11 Apr. 1882, bur. Howard Chapel Cem., Long Corner, Howard Co., MD;[26] m. 9 Dec. 1834 Montgomery Co., MD, **LYDIA ELEANOR PURDUM**.[27]

    8.   **JONATHAN**[4] **LEWIS** (Jeremiah[3], Daniel[2], Jonathan[1]) (see 4), b. *ca.* 1778 Montgomery Co., MD;[28] d. aft. 1859 prob. Montgomery Co., MD;[29] m. 20 Dec. 1807 Montgomery Co., MD, **ELIZABETH WATKINS**,[30] b. 9 Mar. 1780 Montgomery Co.,

---

[14] Ibid., Will Liber 3, ff. 198-200, ahp.

[15] Gary W. Parks, comp., *Index to the 1820 Census of Maryland and Washington, D.C.* (Baltimore, 1986).

[16] Myers. More research is needed on Rebecca (Windsor) Lewis ?Browning.

[17] Hurley, p. 93.

[18] Myers; Hurley, p. 93.

[19] Ibid., p. 74.

[20] Manuel, p. 193 has his name as Vinson Brewer. William Neal Hurley Jr., *Montgomery County, Maryland 1850 Census* (Bowie, MD, 1998), p. 284 has Vincent Brewer.

[21] Hurley, *...Lewis Families*, p. 149.

[22] Myers; Mary Fitzhugh Hitselberger & John Philip Dern, *Bridge in Time, the Complete 1850 Census of Frederick County, Maryland* (Redwood City, CA, 1978), p. 245 has her name as Eveline Lewis.

[23] Ibid., gives age of both John T. Lewis & Jeremiah Lewis as 41 in 1850.

[24] Hurley, *...Lewis Families*, p. 73.

[25] Ibid. One Jeremiah Lewis m. Sarah E. Norwood or Sarah J. Norwood in Frederick Co., MD, year not provided (John Stanwood Martin, *Genealogical Index to Frederick County, Maryland, the First Hundred Years* [Malvern, PA, 1992], v. 3, pp. 43-44). Perhaps Sarah Jane Claggett had an earlier marriage to a Mr. Norwood.

[26] Hurley, *...Lewis Families*, p. 88.

[27] Manuel, p. 195 has her name as Lydia E. Purdom; Hurley, *...Lewis Families*, p. 88 gives her name as Lydia Eleanor Purdum.

[28] Hurley, *Montgomery County, Maryland 1850 Census*, p. 54; William Neal Hurley Jr., *Montgomery County, Maryland 1860 Census* (Bowie, MD, 1998), p. 104.

[29] Ibid.

[30] Manuel, p. 194.

MD;[31] d. aft. 1859 prob. Montgomery Co., MD;[32] d/o Jeremiah & Elizabeth (Waugh) Watkins.[33]

Jonathan Lewis grew up in the homes of his parents, Jeremiah and Jane (Fitzgerald) Lewis, in Montgomery Co., MD. By 1781 their home was probably on *Trouble Enough* or *Close Tract*, two tracts of land acquired in 1779 by his grandfather, Daniel Lewis.[34] Of eight children mentioned in the 1815 will of Jeremiah Lewis, Jonathan was named sixth in the list of names given, which may mean he was one of the younger children.[35] It is likely he was named for his great-grandfather, Jonathan Lewis.

On 20 Dec. 1807 Jonathan Lewis married Elizabeth Watkins in Montgomery Co., MD. Apparently Elizabeth Watkins was a sister of Nicholas Watkins who had married his sister, Rachel Lewis. In 1810 one Jonathan Lewis was head of a family in Montgomery Co., MD. In his household were: one white male under ten, one white male at least 26 but under 45, one white female under ten, one white female at least ten but under 16, one white female at least 26 but under 45, and five slaves.[36] Jonathan Lewis and his wife, Elizabeth, probably lived their entire lives in Montgomery Co., MD where he was a farmer. In 1850 they were living in Clarksburg Dist., Montgomery Co. MD where as a farmer he had real estate valued at $1,000.[37] They were still living there in 1860 when the age for each was recorded as 82. They then had real estate valued at $950 and a personal estate valued at $300.[38]

Child of Jonathan and Elizabeth (Watkins) Lewis, born in Montgomery Co., MD:

    i.   Joseph H.[5], b. 10 Nov. 1821;[39] d. 23 Jan. 1906 Montgomery Co., MD, bur. Salem United Methodist Church Cem., Cedar Grove, Montgomery Co., MD;[40] m. 26 Jan. 1849 Montgomery Co., MD, **ALMEDA MILES**.[41]

9. JEREMIAH[4] LEWIS (Jeremiah[3], Daniel[2], Jonathan[1]) (see 4), b. 8 May 1781 Montgomery Co., MD; d. 5 Apr. 1868 Montgomery Co., MD;[42] m. 13 Dec. 1805 Montgomery Co., MD, **MARY WINDSOR**,[43] b. 30 Jan. 1787 Montgomery Co., MD; d. 12 July 1852 Montgomery Co., MD;[44] d/o Thomas & Catherine (Ward) Windsor.[45]

Jeremiah Lewis (Jr.) grew up in the home of his parents, Jeremiah and Jane (Fitzgerald) Lewis, in Montgomery Co., MD and must have been named for his father. By the time Jeremiah (Jr.) was born in 1781, the home of his parents was probably on *Trouble Enough* or *Close Tract*, two tracts of land acquired in 1779 by his grandfather,

[31] Hurley, *...Lewis Families*, p. 15. Other records indicate she was born *ca.* 1778 (Hurley, *Montgomery County, Maryland, 1850 Census*, p. 54; Hurley, *Montgomery County, Maryland, 1860 Census*).

[32] Ibid.

[33] Hurley, *...Lewis Families*, p. 15.

[34] Montgomery Co., MD, Deed Liber A, ff. 394-396, ahp; ibid., Deed Liber C, f. 539, ahp.

[35] Ibid., Will Liber 3, ff. 198-200, ahp.

[36] Ibid., NARA, 1810 census, roll 14, p. 320 or 933.

[37] Hurley, *Montgomery County, Maryland 1850 Census*, p. 54.

[38] Hurley, *Montgomery County, Maryland 1860 Census*.

[39] Hurley, *...Lewis Families*, p. 16; Hurley, *Montgomery County, Maryland 1850 Census*, p. 54.

[40] Hurley, *...Lewis Families*, p. 16.

[41] Manuel, p. 194. There were probably children other than Joseph H.

[42] MSS, Lewis folder, MCHS, "Family Record" compiled, partly from a Lewis family Bible, and signed by Mrs. Myrtle E. (Lewis) Riggs.

[43] Manuel, p. 194; MSS, Lewis folder has 17 Dec. 1805.

[44] Ibid.

[45] Montgomery Co., MD, Will Liber G, f. 143, cited in Malloy, p. 154; Hurley, *...Lewis Families*, p. 29.

Daniel Lewis.[46] Of eight children mentioned in the 1815 will of Jeremiah Lewis (Sr.), his son, Jeremiah, was named seventh in the order of names given, which may mean he was one of the younger children.[47] On 13 Dec. 1805 he married Mary Windsor in Montgomery Co., MD. She was a sister of Rebecca Windsor who had married his brother, Levi Lewis, as well as a sister of Zadock Windsor who had married his sister, Jane Lewis.

On 21 Dec. 1809 Mary (Windsor) Lewis was named in the will of her father whose name appeared as Thomas Winsor.[48] It appears likely in 1810 Jeremiah and Mary (Windsor) Lewis, as well as three of their children, were living with his parents, Jeremiah and Jane (Fitzgerald) Lewis.[49] Jeremiah Lewis (Jr.) is probably the same person whose name appeared as Jerem. Leewis in 1820 when he was head of a family in Montgomery Co., MD.[50] In 1850 Jeremiah Lewis (Jr.) and his wife, Mary, were living in Clarksburg Dist., Montgomery Co., MD where he was a farmer with real estate valued at $1,000.[51] On 12 July 1852 Mary (Windsor) Lewis died at age 65. Jeremiah Lewis (Jr.) survived his wife, Mary, and in 1860 he continued to live in Clarksburg Dist., Montgomery Co., MD. He then had real estate valued at $2,050 and a personal estate valued at $1,150. Apparently living with him in 1860 was a son, Alexander Hanson/Henson Lewis and his family, as well as one farm laborer, Thomas Hilton.[52] Jeremiah Lewis (Jr.) made his will 21 July 1863, naming six sons and six daughters, including two deceased daughters. His son, Edward Lewis, was named executor and witnesses were: W. Viers Bouic, John W. Hurley, and C.T. Anderson.[53] Jeremiah Lewis (Jr.) was nearly 87 when he died, 5 Apr. 1868.

Children of Jeremiah (Jr.) and Mary (Windsor) Lewis, all born in Montgomery Co., MD:

    i.   Alethea Ann[5], b. *ca.* 1807; m. 12 Dec. 1823 Montgomery Co., MD, **ELISHA BEALL**.[54]

    ii.   Edward, b. 19 Nov. 1808; d. 30 Aug. 1884 Boyds, Montgomery Co., MD, prob. bur. Boyds Presbyterian Church Cem., Boyds, Montgomery Co., MD;[55] m. 24 Mar. 1831 Montgomery Co., MD, **MARY ANN T. KING**.[56]

    iii.   Catherine, b. *ca.* 1810;[57] d. by 21 July 1863;[58] m. 24 Jan. 1831 Frederick Co., MD, **SAMUEL WILLIAMS**.[59]

    iv.   Arnold Thomas, b. 14 Mar. 1813; d. 31 Jan. 1884 Montgomery Co., MD, bur. Boyds Presbyterian Church Cem., Boyds, Montgomery Co., MD;[60] m. (1) 12

---

[46] Montgomery Co., MD, Deed Liber A, ff. 394-396, ahp; ibid., Deed Liber C, f. 539, ahp.

[47] Ibid., Will Liber 3, ff. 198-200, ahp.

[48] Ibid., Will Liber G, f. 143, cited in Malloy, p. 154.

[49] Ibid., NARA, 1810 census, roll 14, p. 318 or 931.

[50] Parks, p. 146.

[51] Hurley, *Montgomery County, Maryland 1850 Census*, p. 79.

[52] Hurley, *Montgomery County, Maryland 1860 Census*, p. 96.

[53] Montgomery Co., MD, Will Liber JWS-1, f. 255, cited in Mary Gordon Malloy et al., comp., *Abstracts of Wills Montgomery County, Maryland, 1826-1875*, pp. 93-94.

[54] Ibid. has her name as Letha A., wife of Elisha Beall; Manuel, p. 194 has her name as Lethe Ann Lewis.

[55] MSS, Lewis folder; Hurley, *...Lewis Families*, pp. 40-41.

[56] Manuel, p. 193.

[57] Hurley, *...Lewis Families*, p. 29.

[58] Montgomery Co., MD, Will Liber JWS-1, f. 255, cited in Malloy, *Abstracts of Wills... 1826-1875*, pp. 93-94.

[59] Myers, p. 146.

[60] Hurley, *...Lewis Families*, p. 187.

Dec. 1834 Montgomery Co., MD, **SARAH R. WATKINS**;[61] m. (2) **MARY A. BURDETTE.**[62]

v.   William B., b. *ca.* 1814;[63] m. 18 June 1851 Frederick Co., MD, **MINERVA ANN (BROWNING) GIBBONS.**[64]

vi.   Jeremiah.[65]

vii.   John Robert, b. *ca.* 1816;[66] d. 25 Mar. 1879 prob. Montgomery Co., MD, bur. Hyattstown Methodist Church Cem., Hyattstown, Montgomery Co., MD; m. 29 Aug. 1843, **MARY ELLEN BROWNING.**[67]

viii.   Jane Rebecca, b. prob. *ca.* 1818; d. by 23 Mar. 1844;[68] m. 9 Jan. 1834 Montgomery Co., MD, **SINGLETON KING.**[69]

ix.   Mary Ann, b. 9 Sep. 1820; d. 16 Nov. 1880 prob. Frederick Co., MD, bur. Urbana Methodist Cem., Urbana, Frederick Co., MD; m. 23 Mar. 1844 Frederick Co., MD, **SINGLETON KING.**[70]

x.   Caroline, b. *ca.* 1826; d. 20 Nov. 1902, bur. Hyattstown Methodist Church Cem., Hyattstown, Montgomery Co., MD;[71] m. (1) 5 Feb. 1848 Frederick Co., MD, **GARRISON WARFIELD**;[72] m. (2) 14 May 1885 Frederick Co., MD, **SINGLETON KING.**[73]

xi.   Angeline, b. 11 Sep. 1828; d. 14 Mar. 1898 prob. Frederick Co., MD, bur. Mt. Olivet Cem., Frederick, MD; m. (1) 11 Nov. 1848 Frederick Co., MD, **ASBURY WARFIELD**; m. (2) 6 Oct. 1870, **EDMUND L. WINDSOR.**[74]

xii.   Alexander Hanson, b. *ca.* 1831;[75] d. 22 Aug. 1892 Montgomery Co., MD, bur. Monocacy Cem., Beallsville, Montgomery Co., MD; m. 11 Mar. 1854, **EMALINE BURDETTE.**[76]

10.   JOHN TRUNDLE[4] **LEWIS** (David[3], Daniel[2], Jonathan[1]) (see 5), b. 1 Sep. 1774[77] Frederick Co., MD;[78] d. 1 Jan. 1861 Johnstown, Harrison Co., (W)V, bur. Old Johnstown Church Cem., Johnstown, Harrison Co., WV;[79] m. 1 Apr. 1811 Harrison Co.,

---

[61] Manuel, p. 193.

[62] Hurley, *...Lewis Families*, p. 187.

[63] Hurley, *Montgomery County, Maryland 1850 Census*, p. 79.

[64] Hurley, *...Lewis Families*, p. 31.

[65] Montgomery Co., MD, Will Liber JWS-1, f. 255, cited in Malloy, *Abstracts of Wills... 1826-1875*, pp. 93-94.

[66] Hurley, *Montgomery County, Maryland 1850 Census*, p. 79.

[67] Hurley, *...Lewis Families*, p. 32. John Robert Lewis may have m. (2) Caroline (---).

[68] Ibid., p. 33.

[69] Manuel, p. 194.

[70] Hurley, *...Lewis Families*, p. 33. Singleton King m. (1) Jane Rebecca Lewis, sister of Mary Ann Lewis.

[71] Ibid., p. 37.

[72] Myers, p. 146.

[73] Hurley, *...Lewis Families*, pp. 37, 203. Singleton King m. (1) Jane Rebecca Lewis, m. (2) Mary Ann Lewis, both sisters of Caroline Lewis.

[74] Ibid., p. 33.

[75] Hurley, *Montgomery County, Maryland 1850 Census*, p. 79; Hurley, *Montgomery County, Maryland 1860 Census*, p. 96.

[76] Hurley, *...Lewis Families*, pp. 33-34; Hurley, *Montgomery County, Maryland 1860 Census*, p. 96 has her name as Eveline Lewis.

[77] Lewis family Bible, possession of Edgar Lewis, Johnstown, Harrison Co., WV (1982), may have been the Bible of Jonathan Lewis (b. 1793), family records transcribed and provided, courtesy of Noel Kent Dawson, Springfield, VA.

[78] Eleanor M.V. Cook, "1777 Tax List of Montgomery County," *Maryland Genealogical Society Bulletin* (1990), v. 31, pp. 15-16. Montgomery Co. formed from Frederick Co. 1776.

[79] Gravestone, Old Johnstown Church Cem., Johnstown, Harrison Co., WV.

(W)V, **SARAH WHITE**,[80] b. *ca.* 1788 MD;[81] d. 15 Mar. 1870 Johnstown, Harrison Co., WV, bur. beside husb.;[82] prob. d/o William White.[83]

John Trundle Lewis, probably named for his maternal grandfather, grew up in the homes of his parents, David and Joannah (Trundle) Lewis, which were in Montgomery and Frederick Co., MD. He would have been an adult by the time they moved to Harrison Co., (W)V.[84] He was likely the other white male, 16 years and upward, who in 1790 was living in the household of David Lewis in Frederick Co., MD.[85]

In 1798 he must have been the other tithable with David Lewis in Harrison Co., (W)V.[86] When David Lewis died in late 1798 or early 1799, John Trundle Lewis was about 24 years of age. In 1799 through 1804 he must have been the tithable in Harrison Co., (W)V, living with Johannah/Hannah Lewis, his mother.[87] On 30 June 1806 he was summoned to testify on behalf of his sister, Margery Lewis.[88] John Trundle Lewis was witness to a deed dated 16 Jan. 1808 when James M. and Ann Camp sold land on both sides of Rooting Creek, Harrison Co., (W)V to Job Ward. Another witness was one William White.[89] As John Lewis he was assessed regularly on his personal property in 1805 through 1811 in Harrison Co., (W)V and by 1807 he had four horses.[90] In 1810 John T. Lewis was head of a family in Harrison Co., (W)V. In his household were: one white male under ten, one white male at least 16 but under 26, one white male at least 26 but under 45, one white female under ten, and one white female at least ten but under 16.[91] The two children under ten are unknown but it seems likely the older male under 26 was his brother, Jonathan Lewis, and the older female under 16 was his sister, Rachel Lewis.

On 1 Apr. 1811, as John Lewis, he married Sarah White in Harrison Co., (W)V. According to a Harrison Co., (W)V deed recorded Sep. 1812, John Lewis for a sum of $157.50 acquired 105 acres of land from James McPherson and his wife, Elizabeth. The land was described as

> A ceartain tract or parsel of Land Being part of a tract of Eight hundred and forty acres that Was formly Taken up by James Arnold On Ruting creek and bounded as followeth to witt Begining on the West Side of said creek at a Beech Corner to Land said McPherson sold to John Davis jun[r] and on a line of the Original tract and running thence South twenty Degrees East Eighty one Poles to a Beech annothrn Corner of s[d]. Davisses thence South Seventy two Degrees West two hundred and four poles to a Beech On another of s[d] McPhersons original lines thence with the Same North seven Degrees East one hundred and Eleven poles to Two Suger trees Corner to the s[d] original tract thence

[80] Earle H. Morris Company, ed., *Marriage Records Harrison County Virginia - (West Virginia) 1784-1850* (Clarksburg, 1950), p. 71.

[81] Harrison Co., (W)V, NARA, 1850 census, roll 950, Dist. 22, p. 398, family 405-405; ibid., 1860 census, roll 1351, Clarksburg PO, p. 986, family 1730-1730.

[82] Gravestone, Old Johnstown Church Cem.

[83] Morris. William White signed marriage bond.

[84] Cook; Frederick Co., MD, Deed Liber W R-4, ff. 411-413, ahp; *Heads of Families at the First Census of the United States... 1790 Maryland* (Washington, 1907), p. 70; Harrison Co., (W)V, PPTB, 1798.

[85] *Heads of Families.*

[86] Harrison Co., (W)V, PPTB, 1798.

[87] Ibid., 1799-1804.

[88] Melba Pender Zinn, comp., *Monongalia County (West) Virginia: Records of the District, Superior and County Courts, Volume 3: 1804-1810* (Bowie, MD, 1991), pp. 110-111.

[89] Harrison Co., (W)V, Deed Book 7, p. 226, cited in John David Davis, comp., *Harrison County, (West) Virginia Deed Records 1785-1810* (Bowie, MD, 1993), p. 360, has John Spundle Lewis and Joab Ward.

[90] Ibid., PPTB, 1805-1811.

[91] Ibid., NARA, 1810 census, photostats, v. 7, p. 157.

with another line of the Same North Seventy seven & a 1/2 Degrees East one hundred & fifty five poles to the Begining Containing One hundred and five acres[92]

The creek is now called Rooting Creek and John Trundle and Sarah (White) Lewis were to live there the rest of their lives. In 1820 he was enumerated in Harrison Co., (W)V. In his household were: four white males under ten, one white male over 45, and one white female at least 26 but under 45.[93] Ten years later, in 1830, the area where he lived was identified as Eastern Dist., Harrison Co. and in his household were: one white male at least five but under ten, two white males at least ten but under 15, two white males at least 15 but under 20, one white male at least 40 but under 50, two white females under five, and one white female at least 40 but under 50.[94] By 5 July 1839 he was a trustee of the Methodist Protestant Church in that community where he lived that became known as Johnstown. It is said to have been so named for the many Johns and Jonathans who lived there.[95]

In 1840 as John T. Lewis he was enumerated in Harrison Co., (W)V. In his household were: one white male at least five but under ten, one white male at least 15 but under 20, one white male at least 20 but under 30, one white male at least 60 but under 70, one white female at least ten but under 15, one white female at least 15 but under 20, and one white female at least 50 but under 60.[96] In 1812 through 1860 he was assessed regularly in Harrison Co., (W)V where he had as many as seven horses. His taxable personal property continued to increase. By 1843 he had a gold watch, silver watch, and a brass clock. By 1844 he had a piano, as well as gold and silver plate. His livestock in 1853 included 42 cattle.[97] As a farmer in 1850 his real estate was valued at $6,000.[98] He may have had orchards. Both John and his wife, Sarah, were still living in 1860 when their son, John, and his family were living with them.[99] John Trundle Lewis died 1 Jan. 1861 at the advanced age of 86. His wife, Sarah (White) Lewis, survived him and died 15 Mar. 1870 at about age 82.

Children of John Trundle and Sarah (White) Lewis, all born in an area that became Johnstown, Harrison Co., (W)V:

    i.   Daniel[5], b. 26 Dec. 1811;[100] d. 29 May 1892 Harrison Co., WV,[101] bur. Old Johnstown Church Cem., Johnstown, Harrison Co., WV;[102] m. 11 Jan 1838 Harrison Co., (W)V, **PHEBE DAVIS**.[103]

---

[92] Author has photocopy of original deed, courtesy of and in possession of Noel Kent Dawson, recorded Harrison Co., (W)V, Deed Book 10, p. 332.

[93] Harrison Co., (W)V, NARA, 1820 census, roll 138, p. 779.

[94] Ibid., 1830 census, roll 190, Eastern Dist., p. 317.

[95] *100th Anniversary, 1984, Johnstown United Methodist Church* (Johnstown, WV 1984), n. pag.

[96] Harrison Co., (W)V, NARA, 1840 census, roll 562, p. 77.

[97] Ibid., PPTB, 1812-1860.

[98] Ibid., NARA, 1850 census.

[99] Ibid., NARA, 1860 census.

[100] Information of Mrs. Texie David (Lewis) Dawson, courtesy of Noel Kent Dawson; Patricia B. Hickman, *Harrison County Death Records 1853-1903* (Bowie, MD, 1991), p. 125; gravestone, Old Johnstown Church Cem., cited in Barbara Prince-Tharp, comp., *Where They Lie - Cemeteries of Southern Harrison County* (Lost Creek, WV, 1984), p. 229.

[101] Hickman.

[102] Gravestone, Old Johnstown Church Cem., cited in Barbara Prince-Tharp.

[103] MRHC, p. 90.

   ii.   Allen, b. 8 May 1814; d. 29 May 1896 Harrison Co., WV, bur. New Johnstown Church Cem., Johnstown, Harrison Co., WV;[104] m. 1837 Harrison Co., (W)V, **MATILDA DAVIS**.[105]

   iii.   David, b. 29 June 1816; d. 22 May 1874 Harrison Co., WV, bur. Old Johnstown Church Cem., Johnstown, Harrison Co., WV;[106] m. 30 Nov. 1837 Harrison Co., (W)V, **MARY JENKINS**.[107]

   iv.   Jonathan, b. 16 Apr. 1818 Harrison Co., (W)V; d. 27 Apr. 1899 Lewis Co., WV, bur. Crawford, Lewis Co., WV;[108] m. (1) 10 Nov. 1840 Harrison Co., (W)V, **ELIZABETH ROMINE**;[109] m. (2) 8 Feb. 1877 Lewis Co., WV, **E. JEMIMA HEFNER**.[110]

   v.   Nelson, b. *ca.* 1821;[111] m. 16 Nov. 1848 Harrison Co., (W)V, **ELENOR CONNELLY**.[112]

   vi.   Cassey, b. 1823; d. 1915 Harrison Co., WV, bur. New Johnstown Church Cem., Johnstown, Harrison Co., WV;[113] m. 14 Dec. 1848 Harrison Co., (W)V, **SAMUEL L. DAVIS**.[114]

   vii.   Mary "Polly," b. 13 Aug. 1826;[115] m. 14 Aug. 1856 Harrison Co., (W)V, **RICHARD PERINE**.[116]

   viii.   John, b. 1830; d. 1914 Harrison Co., WV, bur. Old Johnstown Church Cem., Johnstown, Harrison Co., WV;[117] m. prob. 1854 Harrison Co., (W)V, **MARY McPHERSON**.[118]

11. JONATHAN[4] **LEWIS** (David[3], Daniel[2], Jonathan[1]) (see 5), b. 25 Mar. 1793[119] prob. Frederick Co., MD;[120] d. 30 Apr. 1848[121] near Post Mill, Lewis Co., (W)V,[122] bur. Old Johnstown Church Cem., Johnstown, Harrison Co., WV;[123] m. 14 Oct. 1817 Harrison Co.,

---

[104] Information of Mrs. Dawson; gravestone, New Johnstown Church Cem., cited in Barbara Prince-Tharp, p. 253.

[105] MRHC, p. 89.

[106] Information of Mrs. Dawson; gravestone, Old Johnstown Church Cem., cited in Barbara Prince-Tharp, p. 231.

[107] MRHC, p. 90.

[108] Research information, courtesy of Hartzel Guy Strader, Miamisburg, OH. Though others have not placed this Jonathan Lewis in this family, records of 1820, 1830 , & 1840 clearly allow for him in the household of John T. Lewis (Harrison Co., [W]V, NARA, 1820 census, roll 138, p. 779; ibid., 1830 census, roll 190, Eastern Dist., p. 317; ibid., 1840 census, roll 562, p. 77). Record of 1880 has his father b. in MD, mother in VA (WV 1880, v. 1, p. 121). Jonathan & Elizabeth (Romine) Lewis appear to have named a son, John T., & a dau., Sarah (LCWV 1850, p. 26), prob. for his parents, John Trundle & Sarah (White) Lewis.

[109] MRHC, p. 96.

[110] MRLC, p. 92.

[111] Information of Mrs. Dawson; HCWV 1850, p. 91; LCWV 1860, p. 39; LCWV 1870, p. 16.

[112] MRHC, p. 113.

[113] Information of Mrs. Dawson; gravestone, New Johnstown Church Cem., cited in Barbara Prince-Tharp, p. 248.

[114] MRHC, p. 113.

[115] Information of Mrs. Dawson; DAR, ed., *Marriage Records Harrison County Virginia*, v. 1, p. 59; MRHC, p. 137 gives her parents as John T. & Sarah Lewis.

[116] Ibid.

[117] Information of Mrs. Dawson; gravestone, Old Johnstown Church Cem., cited in Barbara Prince-Tharp, p. 230; MRHC, p. 126 gives his parents as John T. & Sarah Lewis.

[118] Ibid.

[119] Lewis family Bible, possession of Mr. Lewis; Lewis family Bible (1870), prob. Bible of Elmore Dow Lewis, possession of Robert Roy Post, Salem, WV (2000); gravestone, Old Johnstown Church Cem.

[120] *Heads of Families*; WV 1880, v. 1, p. 380, Davis Lewis gives father b. in MD; ibid., v. 3, p. 153, Ruth (Lewis) Jenkins gives father b. in MD. Other children living in 1880 give father b. in VA (WV 1880, v. 3). By 1880 Jonathan Lewis had been dead over 30 years and information may have been confused.

[121] Lewis family Bible, possession of Mr. Post; gravestone Old Johnstown Church Cem.

[122] Information, courtesy of Mrs. Mary "Mollie" (Lewis) Reger, Buckhannon, WV; information, courtesy of Mrs. Jessie (Lewis) Van Hoose, Annandale, VA.

[123] Lewis family Bible, possession of Mr. Post; gravestone, Old Johnstown Church Cem.

(W)V, **SARAH DAVIS**,[124] b. 12 Mar. 1798 prob. Harrison Co., (W)V; d. 30 Jan. 1875 Johnstown, Harrison Co., WV, bur. beside husb.;[125] prob. d/o Samuel & Phebe (Cornell) Davis.[126]

Jonathan Lewis was probably born in Frederick Co., MD and would have been a mere lad when his parents, David and Joannah (Trundle) Lewis, moved to Harrison Co., (W)V where he was to grow to manhood. When David Lewis died, Jonathan Lewis was about six years of age and probably continued to live with his mother, Joannah (Trundle) Lewis. In 1806 his mother married Patrick Burnside and he probably lived in their home, perhaps until she died. By 1810 Jonathan Lewis was likely living in Harrison Co., (W)V with his brother, John Trundle Lewis. He was probably the white male in that household who was at least 16 but under 26 at that time.[127] He was a volunteer in the War of 1812,[128] probably late, and may not have participated in military activity.

In 1815 through 1817 Jonathan Lewis was assessed in Harrison Co., (W)V where he had one horse.[129] On 14 Oct. 1817 he married Sarah Davis in Harrison Co., (W)V. She was probably a daughter of Samuel Davis and his first wife, Phebe Cornell. Samuel Davis was a soldier in the Revolutionary War. As his second wife, Samuel Davis married Ruth Lewis, sister of Jonathan Lewis.[130] In 1818 through 1820 Jonathan Lewis was assessed on two horses in Harrison Co., (W)V[131] and in 1820 he was head of a family there. In his household were: two white males at least 16 but under 26, one white male at least 26 but under 45, one white male at least 45 or older, one white female at least ten but under 16, and one white female at least 26 but under 45. Some of the age breaks in this record appear to be in error, but perhaps it does suggest there was another family living with Jonathan Lewis in 1820.[132]

A truer picture of this family shows up in 1830 when Jonathan Lewis was enumerated in Eastern Dist., Harrison Co., (W)V. In his household were: one white male at least five but under ten, one white male at least 30 but under 40, three white females under five, one white female at least 20 but under 30, and one white female at least 30 but under 40.[133] By 5 July 1839 he was a trustee of the Methodist Protestant Church in that community where he lived that became known as Johnstown. It is said to have been so named for the many Johns and Jonathans who lived there.[134] When he was enumerated in 1840, in his household were: one white male under five, one white male at least 15 but under 20, one white male at least 40 but under 50, one white female under five, one white female at least five but under ten, two white females at least ten but under 15, one white female at least 15 but under 20, and one white female at least

[124] Morris, p. 104.

[125] Lewis family Bible, possession of Mr. Post; gravestone, Old Johnstown Church Cem.

[126] Morris, p. 104. Samuel Davis signed marriage bond. Harrison Co., (W)V, NARA, 1810 census, photostats, v. 7, p. 156 allows for a girl of her age in the household of Samuel Davis.

[127] Harrison Co., (W)V, NARA, 1810 census, photostats, v. 7, p. 157.

[128] Bernard L. Butcher, ed., *Genealogical and Personal History of the Upper Monongahela Valley* (New York, 1912), v. 2, p. 437-438.

[129] Harrison Co., (W)V, PPTB, 1815-1817.

[130] NARA, Revolutionary War Pension, roll 764. More information on Samuel Davis and his family appears elsewhere in this work.

[131] Ibid., PPTB, 1818-1820.

[132] Ibid., NARA, 1820 census, roll 138, p. 779.

[133] Ibid., 1830 census, roll 190, Eastern Dist., p. 317.

[134] *100th Anniversary.*

40 but under 50.[135] Assessment records in 1821 through 1848 indicate he was in Harrison Co., (W)V. By 1847 he was taxed on five horses and one clock.[136]

Jonathan Lewis was employed in agriculture in 1840.[137] Apparently he had fruit orchards where he lived in Johnstown, Harrison Co., (W)V.[138] In Apr. 1848 when he was on a trip selling fruit trees near Post Mill in then Lewis Co., (W)V he became ill and died there rather suddenly on 30 Apr. 1848.[139] Family tradition says his body was brought back to Johnstown in a wagon.[140] His widow, Sarah (Davis) Lewis, survived him and as Sarah Lewis, she was assessed on one horse and one clock in Harrison Co. in 1849, the year following the death of her husband.[141] In 1850 she was living in Dist. 22, Harrison Co., (W)V with four of her children.[142] From 1851 through 1860 she was assessed regularly on personal property in Harrison Co., (W)V. In 1855 she had one horse and 14 cattle.[143] In 1860 she was living with her son, Elmore D. Lewis, in Harrison Co., (W)V with a post office address of Clarksburg.[144] By 1870 she was living in Elk Twp., Harrison Co., WV with a post office address of Clarksburg. She then had real estate valued at $600 and a personal estate valued at $180 and was unable to read or write.[145] As a widow, Sarah (Davis) Lewis, was responsible for her younger children and lived to see them all marry. She died 30 Jan. 1875 at age 76.

Children of Jonathan and Sarah (Davis) Lewis, all born in an area that became Johnstown, Harrison Co., (W)V:

    i.   Delila[5], b. 10 Sep. 1819; d. bef. 13 Dec. 1826 Harrison Co., (W)V.[146]

    ii.   Wilson, b. 20 Sep. 1821;[147] d. 17 June 1915 Harrison Co., WV, bur. New Johnstown Church Cem., Johnstown, Harrison Co., WV;[148] m. 29 Aug. 1844 Harrison Co., (W)V, **RACHEL BLAIR**.[149]

    iii.   Nancy, b. 25 Feb. 1824;[150] d. 5 Feb. 1915 prob. Clarksburg, WV, bur. IOOF Cem., West Milford, WV;[151] m. 12 Mar. 1846 Harrison Co., (W)V, **ISAAC PERINE**.[152]

    iv.   Delila, b. 13 Dec. 1826;[153] m. 3 Sep. 1846 Harrison Co., (W)V, **LEMUEL DAWSON**.[154]

    v.   Roanna, b. 16 June 1829;[155] d. 1918 prob. Harrison Co., WV, bur. Old Johnstown Church Cem., Johnstown, Harrison Co., WV;[156] m. (1) 16 Apr.

---

[135] Harrison Co., (W)V, NARA, 1840 census, roll 562, p. 77.

[136] Ibid., PPTB, 1821-1848.

[137] Harrison Co., (W)V, NARA, 1840 census, roll 652, p. 77.

[138] Butcher, v. 2, p. 437.

[139] Information, courtesy of Mrs. Reger. Since 1851 Post Mill has been in Upshur Co., WV.

[140] Information, courtesy of Mrs. Van Hoose.

[141] Harrison Co., (W)V, PPTB, 1849.

[142] Ibid., NARA, 1850 census, roll 950, Dist. 22, p. 398, family 402-402.

[143] Ibid., PPTB, 1851-1860.

[144] Ibid., NARA, 1860 census, roll 1351, Clarksburg PO, p. 1032, family 2061-2061.

[145] Ibid., 1870 census, original, Elk Twp., Clarksburg PO, p. 177, family 144-146.

[146] Lewis family Bible, possession of Mr. Lewis.

[147] Ibid.; gravestone, New Johnstown Church Cem., cited in Barbara Prince-Tharp, p. 251.

[148] Ibid.

[149] Morris, p. 239.

[150] Lewis family Bible, possession of Mr. Lewis.

[151] Gravestone, IOOF Cem., West Milford, WV, cited in Barbara Prince-Tharp, p. 27, read her name as Mandy Perine; Butcher, v. 2, pp. 811-812.

[152] Morris, p. 245 has his name as Isaac Prine.

[153] Lewis family Bible, possession of Mr. Lewis.

[154] Morris, p. 246.

1846 Harrison Co., (W)V, **WILLIAM DAWSON**;[157] m. (2) 13 Nov. 1883 Harrison Co., WV, **JAMES B. LAMBERT**.[158]

vi. Maria, b. 9 Oct. 1831;[159] d. 13 June 1908 prob. Harrison Co., WV, bur. Old Batton Cem., Batton Hollow, Hastings Run Rd., Harrison Co., WV;[160] m. 5 Sep. 1850 Harrison Co., (W)V, **GEORGE W. CONLEY**.[161]

vii. Davis, b. 8 Mar. 1835;[162] d. 1916 poss. Harrison Co., WV, bur. Old Johnstown Church Cem., Johnstown, Harrison Co., WV;[163] m. (1) **MARGARET E. WALKER**;[164] m. (2) 30 Apr. 1872 Lewis Co., WV, **CAROLINE Y. (BONNETT) RINEHART**.[165]

viii. Ruth, b. 28 Oct. 1837;[166] d. 12 Dec. 1929 prob. Harrison Co., WV, bur. Old Johnstown Church Cem., Johnstown, Harrison Co., WV;[167] m. 17 May 1855 Harrison Co., (W)V, **JAMES P. JENKINS**.[168]

ix. Elmore Dow, b. 28 Dec. 1841;[169] d. 3 May 1889[170] prob. Spencer, WV;[171] m. (1) 8 Feb. 1866 Upshur Co., WV by Rev. Oliver Lowther, **SARAH POST**;[172] m. (2) 20 Dec. 1881 Lewis Co., WV, **PARTHENIA F. LINGER**.[173]

---

[155] Lewis family Bible, possession of Mr. Lewis.

[156] Gravestone, Old Johnstown Church Cem., cited in Barbara Prince-Tharp, p. 231.

[157] Morris, p. 245.

[158] MRHC, p. 303.

[159] Lewis family Bible, possession of Mr. Lewis.

[160] Gravestone, Old Batton Cem., cited in Barbara Prince-Tharp, p. 171.

[161] Morris, p. 261.

[162] Lewis family Bible, possession of Mr. Lewis.

[163] Gravestone, Old Johnstown Church Cem., cited in Barbara Prince-Tharp, p. 230.

[164] Paul C. Hawkins & Judith Hawkins, *Upshur County Death Records. An Alphabetical Listing of Deaths Recorded in the Upshur County Courthouse, Buckhannon, West Virginia, 1853-1928* (Bowie, MD, 1993), p. 81.

[165] MRLC, pp. 62, 82.

[166] Lewis family Bible, possession of Mr. Lewis; gravestone, Old Johnstown Church Cem., cited in Barbara Prince-Tharp, p. 228 has her b. 22 Oct. 1837.

[167] Ibid.

[168] MRHC, p. 132.

[169] Lewis family Bible, possession of Mr. Lewis; Lewis family Bible, possession, Mr. Post.

[170] Ibid.

[171] Lewis family research, courtesy of Robert Howard Reger, Buckhannon, WV; Fred J. Linger & Hartzel G. Strader, *The Linger Family History* (Baltimore, 1989), pp. 133-134 has Roane Co., WV hospital.

[172] Upshur Co., (W)V, MR, Book 1853, p. 16. For more information on this family, see Doris Jean Post Poinsett, *Valentin Pfost/Post 1740-1800 of Hardy County (West) Virginia and Some of His Descendants* (Baltimore, 1989), pp. 108-110.

[173] Lewis family Bible, possession of Mr. Post; Linger.

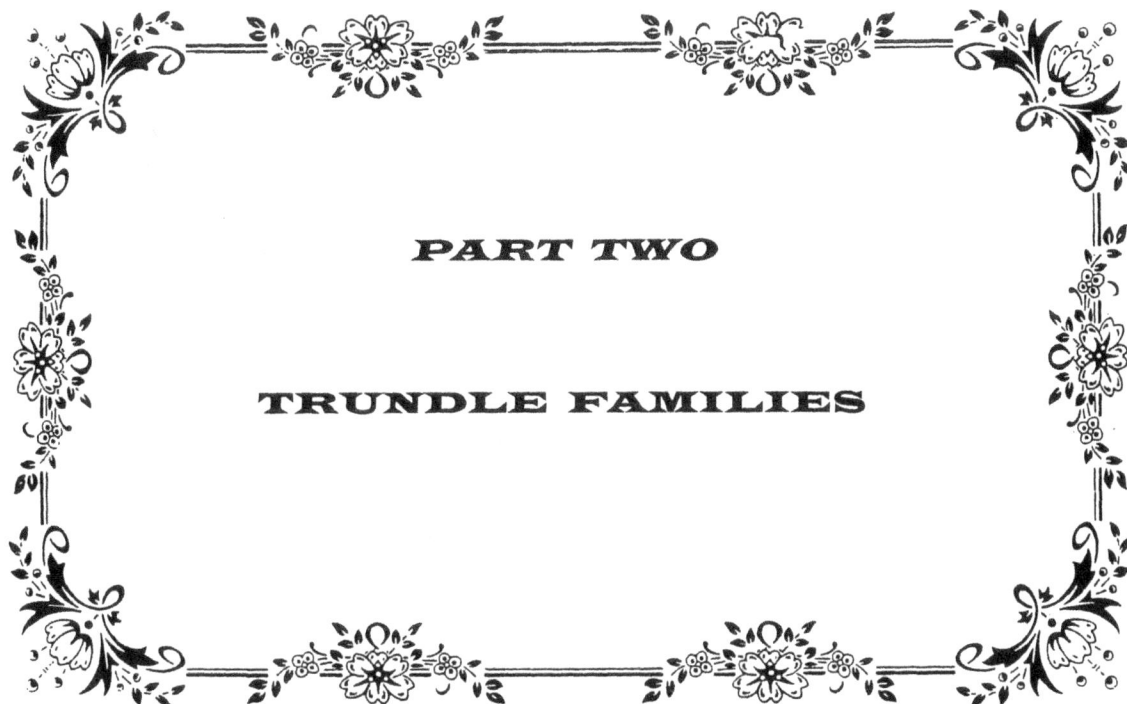

PART TWO

TRUNDLE FAMILIES

Ill. 9 - Map of Anne Arundel Co., MD showing Herring Creek. Reproduced from Rosemary B. Dodd & Patricia M. Bausell, ed., *Abstracts of Land Records Anne Arundel County, Maryland, Volume 1* (Pasadena, MD), p. vii, by permission of Mrs. Rosemary B. Dodd via Betty deKeyser, Librarian, The Anne Arundel Genealogical Society.

CHAPTER FIVE

JOHN TRUNDLE, THE PROGENITOR

1. JOHN[1] TRUNDLE and his wife, **MARY**, had a son named John Trundle who was born 26 Dec. 1687. The son, John, was baptized 4 June 1699 at St. James Parish (Anglican), Anne Arundel Co., MD.[1] St. James Parish, earlier called Herring Creek Parish, was established in 1692. In 1699 the rector was Henry Hall.[2] Earlier in that year, 20 Jan. 1698/99, John Trundle, planter, of Herring Creek, Anne Arundel Co., MD, had made his will naming an only son, John Trundle. The will was as follows:

In the name of God Amen This Twentieth day of January ano one Thousand Six hundred ninety Eight Nine I John Trundle of Herring Creek in Ann Arundell County planter being Sick of body yet thanks be to God of Sound and perfect Memory do make and ordain This to be my Last Will and Testament in Maner and form following Imprimis I Comitt my Soule into the hand of my blessed Saviour and Redeemer who purchased it with his most precious blood in hopes of a Joyfull resurrection att the Last day my body I comitt to the Earth to be buried in Such Decent Manner as to my Executrix hereafter named Shall Seem right most and to that Earthly Good God hath been pleased to bestow on me I bequeath in maner and form following

It I give and bequeath unto my dear and only Son John Trundle and unto the heires of his body forever all that my plantation whereon I now dwell containing two hundred and fifty acres of Land to which the appurtenances thereunto belonging or in any wise appurteining for him to enjoy the Same & when he Shall arrive att the age of one and Twenty Years provided that his Mother my Loving wife Mary Trundle be then departed out of this life.

Item. I give and bequeath unto my Said Loving Son John Trundle one feather bed and furniture & Too Iron potts and hooks & Chests and the one halfe of the pewter the Gun bought of Mr. John Chapple the halfe dozen of Chaires one paire of (?), one frying pann halfe a dozen of Spoons what Carpenter and Cooper tools, I have one halfe of the Sider Casques, a pair of Large Stilliards, one paire of Small Stilliards one grind stone, one Iron pestle one feather dutch(?) Case with the bottles One large brass Kettle one halfe dozen of (?) Three Negro Slaves viz: Color the Negro Boy and the Negro Girle Hager and one other Negro boy named Will four Cows and Calfs one young Mare with her increase Except the first mare fold she brings and four Sows with Pigs when he shall arrive to his full age and my Intent and meaning of giving my Son the above mentioned Goods is in Case my Loving wife and Son should differ when my Said Son John Trundle doth arrive att his full age.

Item I give unto my Son in Law Benj. Thorly the great Gun which was his fathers and Seaven pounds Ster P money when he shall arrive to the full age of one and Twenty Years

It[m] I give and bequeath unto John Christian Son to John Christian the full mare fold of either my Too mares the increase of the said mare fold to run on for the use of the said John Christian and Seaven pounds Ster P money when he shall arrive to the full age of one and Twenty Years but if in Case the above said Benj. Thorly and John Christian or either of them shall happen to dye then my will is that my said Dear Son John Trundle have the part allotted of him that dyes before age

It[m] I give and bequeath unto my Sons in Law, Edward, John, and Samuel Thorly one Ster P (?) apice and no more I having done my honest part to them and brought them up to gett their Livings. And if in Case it should happen my Loving wife and my Dear Son Jo[n]. Trundle should happen to dye that is before my Said Son arrive at his full age and my Said Son have no issue then my will and desire is that my Loving friend John Chapple my Trustee Hereafter named have the plantation before bequeathed with the appurtenances thereunto belonging to his the Said Chapples use and to be wholy att his disposal his heires or assigns.

[1] F. Edward Wright, *Anne Arundel County Church Records of the 17th and 18th Centuries* (Westminster, MD, 1989), p. 152.
[2] Ibid., pp. viii-ix.

Item my will and desire is that in Convenient time after my decease and my body buried by my Executor my personall estate be brought to an appraisment and Still remain in the hands of my (?) and Loving wife Mary Trundle The dischargeing my Just debts and funerall Charges, And also my Reall Estate in her possession and by her to be managed for the benefit of my dear Son John Trundle during her widdowhood but if in Case my Dear and Loving wife Mary Trundle (after my decease) betake her Love to another husband & Harbour and Entertain the Said Thorlys viz. Edward John and Samuel my will & desire is that my Trustees hereafter named sought out and prosecute the Said Thorlys, and if in Case my Wife Intermary as afs[d] my will is that the third of my personall Estate be to sole use benefitt of my Said Son Jo[n]. Trundle And the wife if in Case my Said Son John Trundle should happen to be oppresive burthensome abusive and Troublesome to my dear wife after my Said Son Shall arrive to his full age my will and desire is that my Said Son betake himselfe Lately to the Lower plantation and that he have the halfe of the home Orchard.

Item my will and desire is that no part of the Land above the Road going along the uper Cornfield of my Said Land and plantaion be Cleared or the Timber fallen or wasted till my Said son John Trundle arrive att his full age

Item I Constitute and appoint my Loving wife Mary Trundle my Sole Executrix of this my Last Will and Testament not doubting her Love and Care to my Dear Son John.

Item I Constitute and appoint my Loving friends M[r]. John Chapple and M[r]. Anthony Smith both of Ann Arundell County Trustees to See this my Last Will and Testament fulfilled and performed if my Said wife should happen to depart this life before my said Son John Trundle do arrive to his full age that then and in that Case they my Trustees do take upon theme the full Execution of this my Last Will and Testament and take under their Care and Managem[t]: my Said son and his Estate In Witness whereof I have hereunto Sett my hand and Seale the day and year first above written

John Trundell   (Seale)

Signed Sealed published, delivered
and declared to be the Last Will
and Testam[t]: of John Trundell
in the presence of us   John Chappell
                               The mark of John Morlemore
                               The mark of John Attwood
                               Ch[r]: Vernon

Under oath wth. Will was thus written viz. August the 3[d] Ano Dmi 1699

By Virtue of a Com[o]: to me directed out of the Comissarys office Came before me John Chappell, John Attwood and Chr: Vernon and made oath upon the holy Evangelist that they Saw the within mentioned John Trundle Sign Seale & publish the written to be his Last Will and Testament

Jural Coramme

Jn[o]: Thomson[3]

It can be noted from his will that John Trundle named: Edward, John, Samuel, and Benjamin Thorly/Thorley as his "sons in law," who are more clearly understood to be his step-sons. When Edward Thorley (Sr.) made his will 11 Dec. 1678, he named his wife, Mary, as executrix and sons: Edward, John, and Samuel, though not Benjamin. His will was as follows:

In the Name of God Amen I Edward Thorley of y[e] County of Anne Arundell in y[e] Province of Maryland Planter being very sick & weake in body but of sound and perfect memory the Lord be praysed for it doe make and ordaine this my last will & testam[t] in writing as followeth and first I bequeath my soule to Almighty God my Creator trusting that by y[e] merrite of my Saviour Jesus christ my reedeemer to be made Part as for of Everlasting happinesse my Body I Committ to y[e] ground from whence it was originally taken to be decently buried by my Executrix hereafter named and for my worldly estate which god of his gracious mercy hath sent me I dispose of as followeth.

---

[3] Anne Arundel Co., MD, Will Liber 6, ff. 297- 299, ahp.

Ill. 10 - Will of John Trundle, Anne Arundel Co., MD, Liber 6, f. 297, on file, Maryland State Archives, Annapolis, MD.

Ill. 11 - Will of John Trundle continued, f. 298.

Ill. 12 - Will of John Trundle continued, f. 299.

Imprimis I doe give devise & bequeath unto my three sonnes Edward John & Samuell my plantacon or seate of Land called by yᵉ name of pascalls chance Lying in Talbott County in a Creeke called Coursegoe Chreeke to be equally devided between them to them & theire heires for ever when they shall attaine to yᵉ age of Eighteene yeares a peice and if in case either of my Sonnes should depart this Life without heires or before such by mee as they shall attaine to yᵉ age of Eighteene yeares then my will is that his share or divident of yᵉ Plantacon being in all two hundred fifty acres of Land shall fall to yᵉ survivʳ or survivʳˢ of them and theire heires and in case they all should dye before they attaine to yᵉ age of Eighteene having noe heirs of theire bodyes lawfully begotten then my will is that it be devided betweene yᵉ rest of my Children then Lyveing males or females and to theire heires for ever & for want of such issue to yᵉ next relacon either male or female and theire heires forever and I give each of my Sonnes a yearelying heiffer with theire Increase both male & female

Item I doe give unto my two daughters each of them a yeareling heiffer with theire Increase both male & female. Item I doe give unto my Cozen Thomas Keene a Cow Calfe with yᵉ female increase when he is ffree to be delivered to him And as for yᵉ rest of my goods Chattells Cattell & household stuffe unbequeathed my debts being first paid I doe give & bequeath unto my Loving wife Mary Thorley whome I doe make whole & sole Executrix of this my last will & testamᵗ In testimony whereof I have hereunto set my seale & subscribed my hand this eleaventh day of december In yᵉ yeare of o. Lord one thousand six hundred seaventy & eight

Signed sealed and   his
published in the   Edward ET Thorley   Sealed
presence of viz   marke
Tho: Knighton
Thos: Sheppard
Thomas Williams
And on yᵉ back side of this will was thus written
Feb: yᵉ 10 1678/79
Mary Thorley Executrix of yᵉ within Written will & Thomas Sheppard & Thomas Williams Witnesses of yᵉ same came before me and made affidavit (?) yᵉ within written Will was signed sealed & published by yᵉ testator Edward Thorley to be his last will & testament

Samuell Lane[4]

On 16 May 1679 Mary (---) Thorley acted as executrix of the will of Edward Thorley and the inventory was as follows:

A True and Perfect Inventory of all and Singular the goods ᶜʳᵉᵗᵗⁱˢ Chattells of Edward Thorly Late of Anne Arundell county in the Province of Maryland decd taken this 16ᵗʰ day of May Anno Domini 1679 By mary Thorly relict and Executrix of the Last Will and Testament of the Said Edward Thorley.

Imprimis - Fourteene Pewter dishes and ffifteene Pewter Porringers and Six Pewter Basons Two
    Pewter Tankards and a three pint Pewter fflaggon and a Pewter Salt seller and two pewter
    Chamber Potts
Item - Three Iron Potts and an Iron Kettle Three Brass Skilletts an Iron Ladle and a brass Ladle
    and a small Brass Kettle an Iron Spitt
Item - Two Pailes and two Piggins
Item - two fflock bedds and two Cattaile beds
    Seaven Pillow veers and a boulsten case & two paire of Sheets & paire of curtaines and Valliance
Item - Twelve Napkins and two table Clothes
Item - Three Ells of (?) and fourteene ells of bamborough Linnen
Item - Three Suites of his Wearing clothes
Item - Three Shirts
Item - Three pairs of white Drawers and two White Wast coats and three paire of Stockings
Item - a yard and a halfe of Broad Cloth and two yards of serge and three paire of Mens Shoues and
    three paire of Childrens Shoues

---

[4] Ibid., Will Liber 10, ff. 12-15, ahp.

Item - four Chest

Item - A Lott of Coopers tooles and a Lott of carpinters tooles and two Cross cutt sawes and a
    tennant saw & a lott of Wedges and two Maule rings three axes and five howes and Eight
    thousand nayles

Item - A Brass Candlestick and a paire of Stilliards and two Smoothing Irons and Three bibles and
    A Common Prayer Booke

Item - A Looking glass and a Cupboard and three (?) Lockes

Item - two Gallion dishes and an Earthen basen and a Couch a paire of Spring tongues and a paire
    of snuffers and three gunns

Item - A fire shonece and a paire of tongues and paire of Bellows a gridiron and nine milck trayes

Item - Two Trowelles three reaping hooks and a hatchett and three Drinking glasses and a Childs
    Baskett and a Chaffing dish and two Iron pestells and a Mill

Item - Two ffrying pans and a Lanthorne and three Wooden Bowles

Item - A Boat Sixteene foot by yᵉ Koil and riggin

Item - a Colt nine months old

Item - Thirty two heads of hoggs

Item - Twenty Six head of Cattle young and old

Item - (?) Cropp twenty one tons? of Tobacco (?) and thousands of one hundred and ffifteene pounds

Item - Goods Sold amounting to twelve hundred and Eighty pounds of Tobacco

Item - two Cows sold for Sixteene hundred pounds of Tobacco

Item - more goods sold for two hundred and fifty two pounds of Tobacco

Item - A Servant that hath eight yeares to serve

Item - A Servent that hath till this Middle of next February to serve besides some time for Running
    away and Tobacco paid for his larking up by yᵉ Just time for (?) is at Present time unknowne

Item - a Silver Seale

Item - Six A (?) Spoones

Item - A Brass Skiwer and a (?) a Pr of flesh forkes Iron pan a Bell (?) and (?) Two Leather Jacks a
    powdering Tubb two Tramells two bedsteads a brush and a slick stone and two Chaires

Item - fourteene yards of Woollen cloth

Item - A pewter bed Pan[5]

The name of Edward Thorley appears in Anne Arundel Co., MD land records as
early as 14 Feb. 1670/71 when, for a valuable consideration, he was deeded a grant
containing 40 acres on the south side of South Creek by John Gray. On 14 March
1670/71 he deeded that grant to Christopher Gardiner for a valuable consideration.[6] On
28 Oct. 1673 George Paskall of Anne Arundel Co., MD assigned a patent called *Paskall's
Chance* in Talbot Co., MD to Edward Thorley of Anne Arundel Co., MD. The land was
described as being

> on the south side of Chester River, east side of Corsica Creek - adjoining land laid out for Ezekial
> Croscomb.[7]

Magdelen, wife of George Paskall, consented to the assignment and Rowland Morgan
was a witness.[8] This was the land that Edward Thorley bequeathed to the three sons:
Edward, John, and Samuel, named in his 1678 will. When Queen Anne's Co., MD was
formed in 1707, *Paskall's Chance* became part of the new county and apparently in 1708

[5] Ibid., Inventory Liber 6, ff. 38-41, ahp.
[6] Ibid., Land Record Book WH 4, pp. 311, 333, cited in Rosemary B. Dodd & Patricia M. Bausell, ed., *Abstracts of Land Records,
Anne Arundel County, Maryland, Volume 1* (Pasadena, MD), pp. 148, 150-151.
[7] Talbot Co., MD, Land Record Vol. 1, p. 290, cited in R. Bernice Leonard, comp., *Talbot County, Maryland Land Records, Vols. I
and II* (St. Michaels, MD), p. 61.
[8] Ibid.

the sons: Edward, John, and Samuel Thorley were still in possession of that Queen Anne's Co. land.[9]

Edward Thorley (Sr.) had died by 10 Feb. 1678/79. Benjamin Thorley, named in the will of John Trundle, was likely born after Edward Thorley made his will and must have been his youngest child. By 17 Aug. 1705 Benjamin Thorley, age about 25, was living in Calvert Co., MD.[10] At the time of Edward Thorley's death, he and his wife, Mary, held a lease on land in Anne Arundel Co., MD, formerly owned by William Paggett whose wife was Amy Pascall. Edward's widow, Mary (---) Thorley, was left in possession of 400 acres.[11] In 1705 Benjamin Thorley stated in a deposition that his mother [had] lived as the owner of *Pascall's Purchase*. Further, in another deposition, Susannah, age about 36, wife of Thomas Tracy, and relict of John Sivick, son of William Sivick, stated that Mary Trundle was the mother of Benjamin Thorley by a former husband.[12] Many descendants of Edward and Mary (---) Thorley spell the surname, Thawley.[13]

Though the name, John Trundle, was found in one *ca.* 1636 Cambridge, MA record, it can be argued that the name found was for John Trumble/Trumbull. The name appears in a list of 49 persons called "The Confessions of diverse p'pounded to be received and were entertained as members." Their names are in the autograph of Rev. Thomas Shepard, who succeeded Messers. Hooker and Stone, as minister of that town.[14] The name, John Trundle, was not found in other records of the Cambridge, MA area. Rev. Thomas Shepard was installed as minister of the church in New Towne, now Cambridge, by June 1636, and remained there until his death 25 Aug. 1649.[15] From June 1638 to 7 Dec. 1647 John Trumble and his wife, Elizabeth, had five children whose names and birth dates appear in records of the church in Cambridge.[16] The name of John Trumble also appears in "The Proprietors' Records" for New Towne and Cambridge around this time.[17] In records of the town his name was spelled John Thrumble.[18] This John Trumble, a mariner of Cambridge, MA, moved to Charlestown, MA in 1655. Later the surname was spelled Trumbull.[19]

It seems likely that, either because the name John Trumble sounded similar to John Trundle, or because of a poorly transcribed Massachusetts record, the name of John Trumble became John Trundle in one record. It has naturally caused some Trundle

---

[9] "Kith and Kin - from Queen Anne's County Land Records, Volume E.T. A 1707-1713," *Chesapeake Cousins*, (Easton, MD), v. 22, p. 28.

[10] Chancery Court Liber PC, p. 538, cited in Debbie Hooper, *Abstracts of Chancery Court Records of Maryland, 1669-1782*, p. 15.

[11] Chancery Court Vol. LI, pp. 234, 263, cited in Hooper, p. 5.

[12] Chancery Court Liber PC, p. 538, cited in Hooper, p. 15.

[13] William E. Thawley, *Thorley - Thawley Families* (Cape May, NJ, 1989), p. i, copy on file, Talbot County Free Library, Easton, MD.

[14] Thomas Shepard, of Cambridge, *Manuscript Volume*, under "Book Notices," *The New England Historical & Genealogical Register...* (Boston, 1869), v. 23, p. 369.

[15] Hollis R. Bailey, *The Beginning of the First Church in Cambridge*, from v. 10, Publications of the Cambridge Historical Society, printed separately by permission of the Society (Cambridge, 1917), pp. 101-105. The name of the church in Cambridge was the Church of Christ at Cambridge (ibid. p. 105).

[16] Thomas W. Baldwin, comp., *Vital Records of Cambridge Massachusetts, to the Year 1850, Volume 1, Births* (Boston 1914), p. 710.

[17] *The Register Book of the Lands and Houses in the "New Towne" and the Town of Cambridge...* (Cambridge, 1896), pp. 61-64, 106-116, 335-339.

[18] *The Records of the Town of Cambridge (Formerly Newtowne) Massachusetts 1630-1703...* (Cambridge, 1901), pp. 54-56, 77, 95-96.

[19] "Trumbull" or "Contributions to a Trumbull Genealogy," pp. 3-5, repr. from *The New England Historical & Genealogical Register* (1895).

researchers to try and connect that John in the *ca.* 1636 Massachusetts record, to John Trundle of Anne Arundel Co., MD who made his will in 1698/99.[20]

One work without sources and known to have inaccurate information for early Trundle families in Maryland,[21] states that John Trundle who settled at Herring Creek, Anne Arundel Co., MD, was born in 1624 in Suffolk, Eng. and came to America in 1649. That work further states John Trundle was the son of one David Trundle of Suffolk, Eng., who was born in 1574 and died in 1671.[22] The given name of David was not found in the first four Trundle generations living in Maryland. Research notes give the place of death for this David Trundle as Rotherhite (Rogherhite), Eng.[23] There is some family tradition that John Trundle came with Lord Baltimore's colonists to Maryland but nothing has been found to substantiate this.[24] The surname of Trundle may have been somewhat common in England. It seems reasonable to think that the roots of John Trundle are in England and that he was likely the immigrant. Nevertheless, more research is needed to determine the names of his ancestors and where they lived.

According to a 1707 rent roll of Anne Arundel Co., MD, two hundred and fifty acres surveyed 18 Nov. 1659 for William Paget/Paggett was later granted to John Trundle.

> This Land was escheated for want of ye heirs of Paget & order'd by his Ldp to be granted to John Trundle ffather of yᵉ possor John Trundle.[25]

By 3 May 1679 William Paggett had died,[26] so it was likely near that date that John Trundle received the grant. The land called *Paggetts Land*[27] was on the west side of a branch running north out of Herring Creek Bay called Beaver Dam Branch in Anne Arundel Co., MD.[28] In his 1698/99 will, John Trundle referred to the 250 acres as "my plantation whereon I now dwell."

John Trundle married **MARY (---) THORLEY** after 1678, perhaps nearer 1685. It seems likely he could have had an earlier marriage. Mary already had several children from her first marriage and may have been 40, or older, when their son, John Trundle, was born. One published work offers the possibility that her maiden name was Mary Ross, but that work questions the possibility.[29] An effort to verify that Edward Thorley and John Trundle had a wife whose maiden name was Mary Ross, failed.

John Trundle was almost certainly in Maryland before 1679.[30] He was a planter in Anne Arundel Co. and seems to have prospered in his lifetime. He signed his will with a full signature as John Trundell, indicating he was literate, perhaps even well educated

---

[20] Trundle/Trunnell web page, probably that of Ed Carroll (inactive 2 Mar. 1999), photocopy, courtesy of Mrs. Janice (Beall) Taylor, Urbanna, VA.

[21] George Norbury Mackenzie, ed., *Colonial Families of the United States of America...* (Baltimore, 1966), v. 2, pp. 718-720. This author attempts herein to provide information with cited sources.

[22] Mackenzie, p. 718.

[23] MSS, Trundle folder, MCHS, notes of Mrs. Janice (Beall) Taylor.

[24] Ibid.

[25] *Maryland Rent Rolls: Baltimore and Anne Arundel Counties, 1700-1707, 1705-1724 - A Consolidation of Articles from the Maryland Historical Magazine* (Baltimore, 1976), p. 114.

[26] Chancery Court Vol. LI, p. 234, cited in Hooper, p. 5.

[27] Anne Arundel Co., MD, Deed Liber PK, ff. 278-280, ahp.

[28] *Maryland Rent Rolls.*

[29] Mackenzie, p. 718.

[30] *Maryland Rent Rolls*; Chancery Court Vol. LI, p. 234, cited in Hooper, p. 5.

for his time. He had died by 3 Aug. 1699.[31] A record of the inventory and appraisal of the estate of John Trundle was found and is as follows:

A true & perfect Inventory of all the Goods Chattells & Creditts of John Trundle late of Ann Arundell County in the province of Maryland dec[d]: taken & appraised by us whose names are hereunto subscribed (having first taken our oaths to make a true appraisem[t]: of the same) this 3[d]: day of August Anno Dmi (1699) --

Imp[rs] To a Negro Man	30=00=00
To a Negro Woman	25=00=00
To a Negro Boy	26=00=00
To a Negro Girl	10=00=00
To a Negro Boy of a year old	05=00=00
To 2 Cows & Calves	05=10=00
To a Cow without a Calf	02=10=00
To a 4 year old Bull	01=10=00
To a Steer of 4 years old	02=00=00
To a 2 year old hiefer & 2 two years old & a yearling	04=10=00
To 20 head of hoggs	10=00=00
To a Mare and foale & a Mare without a fole	06=00=00
To a feather bed and furniture	05=00=00
To another old Bed Bedstead & furniture	03=00=00
To a par cell of old Bedding	01=05=00
To a Couch & Couch Bed	01=15=00
To 78 [lb] of pewter	01=19=00
To 2 gunns at 25[d]: = & 2 p[r]: of Stily[ds]: at 25[d]:	01=10=00
To a brass Kettle and skellet at 20[d]: to 3 old Iron Potts and old Iron Kettle & 2 old frying pans 20[d]	02=00=00
To a warming pan Box Iron & Beaters	00=07=00
To 6 Wooden Chairs 10[d]: To a Small Trunck	01=05=00
To 5 Chests 30[d]: (?) Dutch (?) & Bottle 30[d]:	02=10=00
To a Hand mill 20[d]:To a par cell of Coopers & Carpenters Tools	01=15=00
To 3 p[r] = of (?) a spade wier Lifter an Iron (?) and a p[r] of Pot hocks - 12 Iron Skewers & (?)	00=15=00
To a par cell of old Irons & a par cell of Earthen ware	00=13=00
To a doz[n] = of Quart Bottles at 13[d]: to 5 Books 5[d]:	00=08=00
To 2 Hammocks 1 p[r]: of Sheets with a little old Linnen	01=10=00
To a par cell of old Sider Cask	01=00=00
To par cell of nailes	00=15=00
To ? 5[d]: to his wearing apparrell 44[d] =	02=10=00
To ? Goods as per Envoice	07=12=00
To 4 Ells of Holland & 12 Ells of Dutch Linnen	01=07=00
To 46 Ells of Ozen briggs at 10[d] per Ell	01=13=00
To 8 1/2 y[ds] of (?)	00=10=00
To 1 p[r] of Boys Shoes 2 p[r] of mens plains 1 p[r] of Woosled Stockings & a par cell of Thread	00=15=00
To a par cell of pailes 3 Baggs with some old Tubbs	01=00=00
To a grind stone & a foyer pot & a small brass Ladle	00=08=00
To 2 old saddles and bridles & a huir Bagg	00=10=00
To a p[r] of Leather Breeches 20[d] = a (?) 2[d] = 6[d] 2 Lancets 4[s] = 6[d] - to 8 y[ds] of blew & 4 ells of Ozen brigg p[r] of woosled Hose a p[r] of shoes 20[d] a p[r] of spring 14[s] = 6[d] =	02=16=10
Sum Total	172=00=02

[31] Anne Arundel Co., MD, Will Liber 6, ff. 297-299, ahp.

Debts due to yᵉ Estate in money
To Job Evans accs _   10=00=00
To Benj. Chews (?) Accts _   05=00=00
To Gerrard Hopkins Accᵗs _   08=00=00
To James Ffords (?) Accᵗ: _   <u>00=04=02</u>
                                                                         23=04=02

                            023= 4=2
                            <u>175=10=2</u>
                Sum total   198=14=4

    Debts due in Tobb =   Tob:
To John Turners Accᵗ: _   1053
To Alexander Chappells Accᵗ. _ _ _ _ _ _ _ _ _ _ _ _ _   0260
To William Smiths Accts _ _ _ _ _ _ _ _ _ _ _ _ _ _ _ _   0435
To to b: upon yᵉ plantation at my husbands Death _ _   <u>5402</u>
                                                       7150

The whole appraisemt: amounts to one hundred ninety & Eight pounds fourteen Shillings and four
pence in money Sterling. And Seaven thousand one hundred & fifty pounds of Tob: appraised by us

        his mark
    John W Atwood (Sigill)
        his mark
    John G Gale (Sigill)[32]

Though Mary (---) Thorley Trundle did not appraise the estate of her husband, John
Trundle, she made a statement as to the amount of tobacco "upon yᵉ plantation at my
husbands Death." This clearly indicates she was living 3 Aug. 1699, the date of the
appraisal. By 15 June 1700 Mary had died and on that day there was an inventory and
appraisal of her estate which was as follows:

A true and perfect Inventory of all the goods Chattles and Creditts of Mary Trundle late of Ann
Arundell County widd Decd Taken and appraised this ffifteenth day of June Anno Dm: 1700=
By us whose names are hereunto Subscribed having first taken our Oaths to make a true
appraismᵗ. of yᵉ Same in money Sterpˢ:
(vizˡ)

	£ S d
To 4 Cows and Calves _	11=10=00
To 2 heifers one 3 yeares Old yᵉ other 2 yeares Old _ _ _ _ _ _ _ _	04=10=00
To 2 Yearlings _	01=00=00
To 10 head of hoggs _	05=00=00
To 13 Shoats _	02=00=00
To 2 Mares and one colt _	07=10=00
To a Negro Man _	30=00=00
To a Negro Woman _	25=00=00
To a Negro Boy _	26=00=00
To a Negro Girle 5 yeares Old _ _ _ _ _ _ _ _ _ _ _ _ _ _ _ _ _	10=00=00
To a Negro Boy of 2 yeares Old _ _ _ _ _ _ _ _ _ _ _ _ _ _ _	05=00=00
To 79ᴸ of Pewter _	01=19=06
To a ffeather Bed and furniture _ _ _ _ _ _ _ _ _ _ _ _ _ _ _	04=00=00
To another ffeather Bed & furniture _ _ _ _ _ _ _ _ _ _ _ _	03=00=00
To a pʳ cell of old Bedding & fflock Bed _ _ _ _ _ _ _ _ _ _	01=00=00
To Couch & Couch Bed and furniture _ _ _ _ _ _ _ _ _ _ _	01=15=00

---

[32] Ibid., Inventory & Accounts Vol. 19 1/2 A, ff. 75-77, ahp. Some amounts in this account are barely decipherable due to ink
smudging on the court copy. This may explain why amounts as interpreted do not add up to the first sum total of 172.00.02.

To " p^r of mens Pollonia Shoues _ 01=05=04
To " p^r of Irish hose _ 00=09=00
To 44 yards of Narrow Blew _ 01=00=02
To a (?) of Carseg _ 01=14=00
To 5 yards of Coulourd Linnen _ 00=02=06
To 3 Ells of osinbridg white _ 00=01=09
To 3 Ells of holland _ 00=04=08
To 21 1/2 Ells of hammells _ 00=10=06
To 3 Ells of Course w^t Linnen _ 00=03=00
To 9 1/2 yards of Dimaty _ 00=07=00
To 2 yards of hairs Cloth _ 00=03=00
To Thread and Buttons _ 00=03=00
To her wearing apparrell _ 00=04=00
To 3 p^r of womens yarn Stockings _ _ _ _ _ _ _ _ _ _ _ _ _ _ _ _ _ _ _ 00=02=00
To a p^r cell of Old wearing linnen _ _ _ _ _ _ _ _ _ _ _ _ _ _ _ _ _ _ _ 00=12=00
To 55^L of Brazen ware _ 01=12=00
To a parcell of Iron ware as p^r Invoyce _ _ _ _ _ _ _ _ _ _ _ _ _ _ _ _ 04=19=03
To 3 Iron Potts 1 Iron ketle & p^r pott hocks
   2 p^r of Tongs & ffrying panns a grid iron
   ludls and fflesh fork _ 01=10=00
To a box iron a warming pan a pestell
   & morter a ginger grater & a Tin lanthorne _ _ _ _ _ _ _ _ _ _ _ 00=07=00
To a Case and Bottles and a Trunck _ _ _ _ _ _ _ _ _ _ _ _ _ _ _ _ _ 01=05=00
To 5 wooden Chaires & a Small red Trunck _ _ _ _ _ _ _ _ _ _ _ _ 01=00=00
To a gun a Sword & 2 p^r of Stilliards _ _ _ _ _ _ _ _ _ _ _ _ _ _ _ _ 01=00=00
To a Chafing dish & 2 Setts of Skewers _ _ _ _ _ _ _ _ _ _ _ _ _ _ 00=07=00
To 5 Chests 30^s a dozen of q^{rt} Bottles 3^s _ _ _ _ _ _ _ _ _ _ _ _ _ 01=13=00
To a p^r cell of Old carpenters & Coopers Tooles
   4 Cross cut Saws 4 ffalling axes 4 Grubbing axes
   3 Hilling Hows a Spade & an Iron pestell _ _ _ _ _ _ _ _ _ _ _ _ 02=00=00
To a p^r cell of Tin ware _ 00=13=00
To a p^r cell of Old Bookes 72^d Sisers & a Drain line 4^d _ _ _ _ _ _ <u>00=11=00</u>
                                                                 163=05=02

             John W Atwood (Seale)
             Augusustin
             Hawkins (Seale)

To a Pad C: to Some Earthen ware _ _ _ _ _ _ _ _ _ _ _ _ _ _ _ _ 00=08=00
To a hand mill 20^d to a p^r cell of Old
   Casque tubs and Payles 25^d _ _ _ _ _ _ _ _ _ _ _ _ _ _ _ _ _ _ 02=05=00
To 5 Bushells of Salt _ 00=12=06
To a Barrell of Indian Corn _ 00=10=00
To 55^L of Bacon _ <u>01=07=06</u>
                                      in all   168=08=02

Soe the whole appraism^t amounts to one hundred Sixty and Eight pounds Eight Shilling and Two pence Ster P: as appraises by us-   his marke
             John W Atwood   (Seale)

             Augustin Hawkins   (Seale)[33]

Though some amounts in the inventory and account of 15 June 1700 do not balance, the "in all" amount is accurate. It agrees with the final account of 6 Apr. 1709 nearly nine

---

[33] Ibid., Vol. 11 B, ff. 4-7, ahp. A few amounts were difficult to read and may not have been transcribed accurately which likely explains why amounts do not add up to totals.

years later when the estate of Mary (---) Thorley Trundle was finally settled. The final account was as follows:

> The ffinall account of John Chappell & Anthony Smith ad^ts
> of Mary Trundle Dec^d The s^d account^ts Charge themselves with
> the Invty_ 168 8 2
> And humbly Craves allowance for their
> former accounts past made up amt^s _ _ _ _ _ _ _ _ _ _ 97 09 4
> and for Countys fees paid as by}
>   acc^s & rec^ts from Robert Wood} _   396
> be paid Rich^d- Dallain a fee in}
>   behalf of the Orphan} _   200
>   596
> To a legacy paid John Christian left}
> him by John Trundle as per ac^t proct} _ _ _ _ _ _ _ _   7 _ _
> 596^lb Tob^o- at 1^d _ _ _ _ _ _ _ _ _ _ _ _ _ _ _ _ _ _ _   2 9 8
> com^th- of 9:13:8 _   19 4
>   107 18 4
> Countys fees for this account etc
> tob^o- & sallary for D^o- at 10^P}
> is 7 inall 79 at 1^d- etc to be p^d} _ _ _ _ _ _ _ _ _ _ _   6 7
>   108 04 11
> Ball due to John Trundle ye Orphan _ _ _ _ _ _ _ _ _ _ 60 03 03
>   proof _ _ _ _ _ 168 08 02
>   Aprill the 6th 1709
> The above account^ts- John Chappell & Anth^o Smith make oath
> that the above is a just & true account of their asm^t of the s^d
> Mary Trundles Estate _ _
>   Before me W Bladen County Gent[34]

John Trundle, son of John and Mary (---) Thorley Trundle, seems to have been 12 years of age when his mother died. In a June 1706 list of orphans his name appeared as John Trondle when he was living with Jeremiah Larkins in Herring Creek Hundred, Anne Arundel Co., MD.[35] Because the name, John Trundle, occurs in all generations that follow in this work, the name hereinafter will be referred to as John Trundle I, John Trundle II, and so forth in order by generation.

In summary, **JOHN TRUNDLE I**, b. prob. by 1640 poss. Eng.; d. bet. 20 Jan. 1698/99 & 3 Aug. 1699 Herring Creek, Anne Arundel Co., MD; m. prob. *ca.* 1685 Anne Arundel Co., MD, **MARY (---) THORLEY**, b. prob. *ca.* 1647; d. bet. 3 Aug. 1699 & 15 June 1700 Herring Creek, Anne Arundel Co., MD. **MARY** --- m. (1) prob. by 1665, **EDWARD THORLEY**, d. bet. 11 Dec. 1678 & 10 Feb. 1678/79 Anne Arundel Co., MD.

Child of John I and Mary (---) Thorley Trundle, born at Herring Creek, Anne Arundel Co., MD:
2.   i.   John II², b. 26 Dec. 1687.

---

[34] Ibid., Account Liber, ff. 137-138, ahp.
[35] Dorothy H. Smith, "Orphans in Anne Arundel County, Maryland, 1704-1709," *Maryland Magazine of Genealogy*, v. 3, pp. 36-37.

CHAPTER SIX

TRUNDLE, SECOND GENERATION

2. JOHN² **TRUNDLE II** (John I¹) (see 1), b. 26 Dec. 1687¹ Herring Creek, Anne Arundel Co., MD;² d. prob. aft. 1724³ Prince George's Co., MD;⁴ m. prob. *ca.* 1710 Anne Arundel or Prince George's Co., MD, **HANNAH** ---,⁵ d. prob. aft. 1724 Prince George's Co., MD.⁶

John Trundle II was 11 years of age when he was baptized 4 June 1699 at St. James Parish (Anglican), Anne Arundel Co., MD,⁷ apparently by its first rector, Rev. Henry Hall.⁸

> St. James Parish, earlier called Herring Creek Parish was established in 1692 under the act of Assembly and consisted of Herring Creek Hundred and a major part of West River Hundred.⁹

John II had grown to the age of 11 in the home of his parents, John I and Mary (---) Thorley Trundle, who lived on Herring Creek, Anne Arundel Co., MD. Also living in their home were his older half brothers: Edward, John, Samuel, and Benjamin Thorley.¹⁰ There were likely two of his older half sisters living there as well.¹¹ By 20 Jan. 1698/99 his father, John I, was seriously ill and was to die by 3 Aug. 1699.¹² His mother, Mary, survived only briefly, leaving John Trundle II an orphan by 15 June 1700.¹³

In a June 1706 list of orphans his name appeared as John Trondle when he was living with Jeremiah Larkins in Herring Creek Hundred, Anne Arundel Co., MD.¹⁴ According to rent rolls, by 1707 he was of age to possess the 250 acre plantation called *Paggetts Land*¹⁵ bequeathed to him by his father, John Trundle I.¹⁶

On 17 Oct. 1707 John Trundle II, who signed his name John Trundell, was witness to a deed from Wᵐ Mitchell, son of Wᵐ Mitchell, late of Anne Arundel Co., MD, to Seth Biggs, merchant of Anne Arundel Co., MD. The deed was for half of a 200 acre tract of land known as *Poplar Neck* on the south side of South River, Anne Arundel Co. In 1684

---

¹ F. Edward Wright, *Anne Arundel County Church Records of the 17th and 18th Centuries* (Westminster, MD, 1989), p. 152.

² Ibid. pp. viii-ix; *Maryland Rent Rolls: Baltimore and Anne Arundel Counties, 1700-1707, 1705-1724 - A Consolidation of Articles from the Maryland Historical Magazine* (Baltimore, 1976), p. 114.

³ Son, John III, b. 1724 (DAR membership papers of Florence Michele Remmele #524815 descendant of John III & Alethia [---] Trundle via John IV & Ruth [Lewis] Trundle; "Old family document passed down through the Trundle/Thomas family," n. pag., copy courtesy of Mrs. Janice [Beall] Taylor, Urbanna, VA).

⁴ Prince George's Co., MD, Deed Liber F, f. 275, ahp.

⁵ Ibid.

⁶ Probable son, John III, b. 1724 (DAR membership papers; Old family document; Prince George's Co., MD, Deed Liber F, f. 275, ahp).

⁷ Wright, p. 114.

⁸ Ibid., p. ix.

⁹ Ibid., p. viii.

¹⁰ Anne Arundel Co., MD, Will Liber 6, ff. 297-299, ahp.

¹¹ Ibid., Will Liber 10, ff. 12-15, ahp.

¹² Ibid., Will Liber 6.

¹³ Ibid., Inventory & Accounts, Vol. 11 B, ff. 4-7, ahp.

¹⁴ Dorothy H. Smith, "Orphans in Anne Arundel County, Maryland, 1704-1709," *Maryland Magazine of Genealogy,* v. 3, pp. 36-37. Jeremiah Larkin m. 6 Oct. 1702 St. James Parish, Anne Arundel Co., MD, Margaret Brown (Wright, p. 153).

¹⁵ *Maryland Rent Rolls*; Anne Arundel Co., MD, Deed Liber PK, ff. 278-280, ahp.

¹⁶ Ibid., Will Liber 6.

the 200 acres had been bequeathed to Wm Mitchell and John Mitchell by their father, Wm Mitchell. Other witnesses to the deed were John Deaver and Musquet Simnas.[17]

John Trundle II kept the 250 acre plantation known as *Paggetts Land* only about three years. Between 1707 and 1710 he moved to Prince George's Co., MD. On 11 May 1710 for the sum of 112 pounds sterling he sold the plantation to William Lock and Anthony Smith who were already tenants on that Anne Arundel Co. land. The deed was as follows:

This Indenture this Eighth Day of May Anno Dm Seventeen hundred and Tenn Between John Trundle of prince Georges County Joyner of the One part and William Lock of Ann Arundel County Chyrurgen and Anthony Smith of the Same County Gent of the other part Witnesseth that the Said John Trundle for & in Consideration of the Sum of One hundred and Twelve pounds Ster & Secured to be paid the said John Trundle the receipt whereof he doth hereby acknowledge and himself therewith to be fully Secured Hath given Granted bargained Sold Enfeoffed and Confirmed and^by these presents doth for himself and his heires fully and absolutely give Grant Enfeoff and Confirm as well as Bargain and Sell unto the Said William Lock and Anthony Smith all that Tract or p^r cell of Land Caleed paggetts Land Situate Lying and being near Herring Creek in the County of Ann Arundell according to the Certificate of the Same Land returned into the Land Office formerly Taken up by one pagett Containing and Laid out for Two hundred & fifty acres to the Same Moore or Less and now in the Tenure or Occupation of the Said ------ William & Anthony -

To have and to hold the Said Tract of p^r cell of Land with all the Deeds Evidences Escripts & Writing to the Same belonging or in any wise appertaining together with all the Edifices or building woods underwoods Timbers Timber Trees Ways Waters Gardens Emoluments Libertys Corners Wasts Wast or Surplus Land or Lands whatsoever to the Same belonging or in anywise appertaining to the Said Wm Lock and Anthony Smith and their heires & assignes for ever to be Equally Divided Between them And To hold and Occupy and Enjoy the Land as tenants in Comon - free and Clear and Freely and Clearly Acquitted Exonerated and Discharged of and from all and all manner of former gifts Grants Bargaines Sales Mortgages Judgments and Incumbrances whatsoever heretofore had made Comitted done or Suffered by the Said John Trundle And the Said John Trundle doth for himself his heires Ex^trs: Ad^mrs. & Assignes Covenant promise Grant and Agree to and with the Said William Lock and Anthony Smith or either of them their or either of their heires Ex^trs: Adm^rs. or assignes that he the Said John Trundle Shall and Will att any time or times hereafter at the request of the Said W^m. and Anthony or either of them or their or either of their heires make doe acknowledge and Suffer or cause to be made done acknowledged and Suffered all Such furth^er & other Deeds Acts things or Matters as Shall by the Said William and Anthony or either of them their or either of their heires or assignes and the Learned councill in the Law of them the Said William and Anthony or either of them be reasonably advised devised or required and further that he the Said John Trundle for him and his heires hereby doth and Shall the afs^d Lands and premises wth the appurtinences to them the said William and Anthony and their heires against him the Said John and his heires and all Claiming or to Clayme by from or under him and also ag^st. all p^r son or p^r sons whatsoever Warrant and for ever Defend.-

In Wittness whereof the Said John Trundle hath herewith Sett his hand and Seale the day and Year first within Mentioned

Sealed and Delivered   John Trundell   (S)
in the presence of
Wornell Huntt
Bay^rd. Rawleigh
Ja: Earle

17 Anne Arundel Co., MD, Land Record Book WT 2, p. 588, cited in Rosemary B. Dodd & Patricia M. Bausell, ed., *Abstracts of Land Records, Anne Arundel County, Maryland, Volume II* (Pasadena, MD), p 179.

May the 11th 1710

Then came John Trundle party to this Indenture and acknowledged the within Land & premises to be the Right of the within named Wm Lock & Anthony Smith their heires and assignes for ever before us the Subscribers two of her Maj^{tys}. Justices of Ann Arundell County.

D: Mariarte

Th°. Larkin[18]

John Trundle II signed the deed in full as John Trundell indicating that he was literate. His occupation in 1710 was that of joiner so he may have had no interest in being a planter. He must have married Hannah --- around the 1710 date. When John Beall of Prince George's Co. died 21 May 1711, John Trundle II was paid one pound for making the coffin.[19] On 25 Sep. 1713 John Trundle II of Prince George's Co., carpenter, deeded certain gift items to his wife, Hannah. That deed was as follows:

To All Christian People to whome these Presents shall Come Greeting Know Yee That I John Trundell of Prince Georges County Carpenter as well for and in Consideration to the Naturall Love and Affection which I have and bear to my well beloved wife Hannah Trundell As allsoe for divers other Good Causes and Considerations me at this Present Especially moveing Have given and granted and by these Presents doe give grant and Confirme unto the said Hannah Trundell all and Singular the following goods (viz:) One New Feather Bedd and furniture One Looking Glass One Iron Pott One Square Table One Frying Pann One grid Iron One Box Iron and Two Trunks One Browne Box and One Ink horne To Have & To hold all and Singular the said Goods unto the said Hannah Trundell dureing her Naturall life without my matter of Challenge Claime or demand of me the said John Trundell or of any person or persons whatsoever And after her decease unto Thomas Trundell Sonn of the said John & Hannah Trundell his heires and Assignes for Ever and to noe other Use intent or Purpose whatsoever and I the said John Trundell all and Singular the afs^d- Goods to the use afs^d- against all persons will warr^t. and for ever defend by these Presents And further that I the said John Trundell have Put the s^d- Hannah in Peaceable and quiet Possession of the afs^d- Goods by delivering unto her an Inkhorne at the Ensealing and delivery hereof In Witness whereof I have hereunto Sett my hand and Seale

this 25th day of September Anno Domini 1713 ·

Signed Sealed & Delivered   John Trundell   {Seale}

In the Presence of

    Rich^d: Rudyard[20]

It should be noted that John Trundle II seems to have been consistent in signing his name as John Trundell which was the same spelling used by John Trundle I on his will. This seems to have been the spelling used by literate family members of those generations.

It seems appropriate to digress briefly at this point. One Queen Anne's Co., MD record of 24 Nov. 1709 indicates a mulatto child was born to Catherine Hawkins *ca.* 1707 as follows:

Presented that Cath. Hawkins of St. Paul's Parish in Queen Anne's Co., servant to John Hawkins on 10 July 1708 committed fornication and begat a bastard child. John Hawkins is to have the service of the said mulatto child (now being 2 years old) until it attains the age of 31 years, he paying the county 500 lbs. of tobacco. Cath. Hawkins to have her time of servitude extended.[21]

---

[18] Anne Arundel Co., MD, Deed Liber PK, ff. 278-280, ahp.

[19] F.M.M. Beall, *The Beall and Bell Families*, p. 48.

[20] Prince George's Co., MD, Deed Liber F, f. 275, ahp.

[21] Queen Anne's Co., MD, Judgment Record Liber E.T. No. B, p. 7, cited in F. Edward Wright, "Queen Anne's County Judgment Records," *Maryland Genealogical Society Bulletin*, v. 36, p. 419.

Perhaps one Elizabeth Trundle cared for this mulatto child for a while or had one of her own. Another Queen Anne's Co., MD record of 29 Mar. 1711 has the name of a woman whose name was transcribed as Elizabeth Trundle. The transcribed record:

> Ordered that Major John Hawkins pay the sum of 500 lbs. of tobacco for Elizabeth Trundle's(?) mulatto child.[22]

Nothing else was found for this Elizabeth Trundle. Because her surname seems to have been questioned in the record as transcribed, it may be that the woman's surname was not Trundle.

John Trundle II of Anne Arundel Co., MD became an orphan by the age of 12. As a young man he was literate and his trade was that of joiner or carpenter. He was living in Prince George's Co., MD by 1710 and may have married Hannah --- that same year. They lived in Prince George's Co. but after 1713 their names seem to disappear from records. They had a son, Thomas, who will be referred to as Thomas Trundle I in this work. He was surely the Thomas Trundle who was in Frederick Co., MD by 3 Nov. 1758,[23] and whose brother, John Trundle III, was in Frederick Co., MD by 1754.[24]

Children of John II and Hannah (---) Trundle, probably born in Prince George's Co., MD:

3.   i.   Thomas I[3], b. *ca.* 1711.
4.   ii.   John III, b. 1724.

---

[22] Queen Anne's Co., MD, Judgment Record Liber E.T., no page provided, cited in F. Edward Wright, "Queen Anne's County Judgment Records," *Maryland Genealogical Society Bulletin*, v. 36, p. 432. It can be noted in two records that a John Hawkins was to pay 500 lbs. of tobacco for a mulatto child but it is not clear whether there were two mulatto children. More research is needed.
[23] Frederick Co., MD, Land Liber F, p. 595, cited in Patricia Abelard Andersen, *Frederick County Maryland Land Records Liber F Abstracts, 1756-1761* (Montgomery Village, MD, 1995), p. 62 has Thomas Trundel & John Trundell, Frederick Co., MD.
[24] Millard Milburn Rice, *This Was the Life, Excerpts from the Judgment Records of Frederick County, Maryland* (Baltimore, 1984), pp. 133-135, 146; Frederick Co., MD, Deed Liber M, f. 221, ahp, has Thomas Trundle Sr. (Thomas I) to nephew, Thomas Trundle Jr. (Thomas III), 1769. In his will John Trundle Sr. (John III), 1771, named children: Thomas Bob (Thomas III), John Basel (John IV), Josiah, and Joanna (later called Hannah), likely named for her paternal grandmother, Hannah (ibid., Will Liber A-1, ff. 399-400, ahp).

CHAPTER SEVEN

TRUNDLE, THIRD GENERATION

3. THOMAS[3] TRUNDLE I (John II[2], John I[1]) (see 2), b. *ca.* 1711[1] prob. Prince George's Co., MD;[2] d. bet. 18 July 1791 & 11 Sep. 1792 Montgomery Co., MD;[3] m. (1) 22 Aug. 1738 Anne Arundel Co., MD, **MARY FARQUSON[4]/FERGUSON**, b. *ca.* 1717 Prince George's Co., MD;[5] d. prob. by 1768 Frederick Co., MD;[6] prob. d/o John & Mary (Williams) Ferguson;[7] m. (2) prob. *ca.* 1769 Frederick Co., MD, **JOHANAH WOOD**,[8] b. *ca.* 1733 prob. Prince George's Co., MD;[9] d. *ca.* 1 June 1805 Montgomery Co., MD;[10] prob. d/o Thomas & Mary (Lashley) Wood.[11]

On 25 Sep. 1713 Thomas Trundle I was living in Prince George's Co., MD with his parents, John II and Hannah (---) Trundel.[12] Nothing was found as to where his parents lived in later years or when they died. By 1733 Thomas Trundel I was living in Mount Calvert Hundred, Prince George's Co., MD where his name appeared as Thomas Trundell in a list of taxables.[13]

On 22 Aug. 1738 he married Mary Ferguson in Anne Arundel Co., MD. In 1748 Frederick Co., MD was formed from Baltimore and Prince George's Co. On 3 Nov. 1758 in Frederick Co., John Beall, son of Robert, settled for 399 lbs. of tobacco and costs recovered against John Trundell, Thos Trundel, and Benjamin Becraft.[14] This John Trundell must have been his brother, John III, who was in Frederick Co. by 1754.[15] Apparently the two brothers, Thomas I and John III, and Ninian Edmonston of Frederick Co. were in debt to the estate of John Johnson 2 Sep. 1759 when 3300 lbs. of tobacco and costs were recovered by Thomas Cramphin, administrator.[16] Thomas Trundle I was a planter and on 17 Apr. 1766 for the sum of £100 he acquired 145 1/2 acres of land in Frederick Co., MD. This tract of land, purchased from Daniel Stephenson of Prince George's Co., was known as *Addition to Easy Purchase.* The deed was as follows:

---

[1] Gaius Marcus Brumbaugh, *Maryland Records, Colonial, Revolutionary, County, and Church from Original Sources* (Baltimore, 1985 repr. 1928 ed.), v. 1, p. 223.

[2] F.M.M. Beall, *The Beall and Bell Families,* p. 48; Prince George's Co., MD, Deed Liber F., f. 275, ahp.

[3] Montgomery Co., MD, Will Liber C, f. 7, author has photocopy of original.

[4] Nicholas Russell Murray, comp., *Anne Arundel County, Maryland 1693-1800 Computer Indexed Marriage Records* (Hammond, LA, 1986), p. 58.

[5] MSA, Inventories Box 10, Folder 4, Prince George's Co., MD, inventory of John Forgoson/Farguson, abstracted by Benjamin Franklin Poinsett, 22 June 1999. Mary Farguson & Ann Farguson, as kin, signed by mark 2 November 1734. John Ferguson m. 29 Nov. 1715 Queen Anne Parish, Prince George's Co., MD, Mary Williams (Helen W. Brown, comp., *Prince George's County, Maryland, Indexes of Church Registers 1686-1885* [1979], v. 1, p. 308.)

[6] Brumbaugh.

[7] Brown.

[8] Brumbaugh; *Maryland Genealogical Society Bulletin,* v. 28, p. 368.

[9] Ibid.; MSA.

[10] Brown, v. 2, part 2, p. 305.

[11] *Maryland Genealogical Society Bulletin.*

[12] Prince George's Co., MD, Deed Liber F, f. 275, ahp.

[13] Publications of the Hall of Records Commission No. 1, *Calendar of Maryland State Papers, No. 1 The Black Books, State of Maryland* (Baltimore, 1967), #163, p. 269.

[14] Frederick Co., MD, Land Liber F, p. 595, cited in Patricia Abelard Andersen, *Frederick County Maryland Land Records, Liber F Abstracts, 1756-1761* (Montgomery Village, MD, 1995), p. 62.

[15] Millard Milburn Rice, *This Was the Life, Excerpts from the Judgment Records of Frederick County, Maryland* (Baltimore, 1984), pp. 133-135, 146.

[16] Frederick Co., MD, Land Liber F, p. 872, cited in Andersen, p. 87.

At the request of Thomas Trundle the following Deed was Recorded the 17th Day of April 1766 to wit - This Indenture made this tenth day of April in the year of our Lord one thousand seven Hundred & sixty six Between Daniel Stephenson of Prince Georges County in the Province of Maryland Merchant of the one part & Thomas Trundle of Frederick County and Province aforesaid planter of the other part Witnesseth that the said Daniel Stephenson for and in Consideration of the sum of One Hundred Pounds Sterling money of Great Britain to him in hand paid by the said Thomas Trundle the Receipt whereof the said Daniel Stephenson doth hereby acknowledge and of every part thereof doth hereby acquit exonerate & fully discharge the said Thomas Trundle Hath granted Bargained and sold as by these Presents the said Daniel Stephenson doth Give grant Bargain & sell unto the said Thomas Trundle his heirs and assigns forever att that tract or parcell of Land called the Addition to Easy Purchase lying Situate & being in Frederick County Begining at abounded white Oak standing on the west side of TS Branch and runing thence south Twenty degrees west Eleven Perches then north forty-nine degrees west forty five and a half Perches then south Twenty One Degrees west One Hundred & thirty one perches then north Eighty two Degrees west fifty two Perches then north Eleven degrees west One Hundred & five Perches north fifty three degrees East fifty four Then north twenty three Degrees west forty five Perches then north fifty six Degrees west ninety four perches then north forty seven Degrees East seventy eight & a half Perches then with a straight line to the Begining Tree containing and now laid out for One Hundred & forty five & a half Acres of Land more or less To have & to hold the said Land & Premises together with all & singular the Improvements Conveniences & advantages to the said One Hundred & forty five & half acres of Land contained within the miles & limits afore expressed belonging or in any manner of way appertaining to the only proper use and behoof of him the said Thomas Trundle his heirs & assigns forever & no other use intent or purpose whatsoever and the said Daniel Stephenson doth for himself his heirs Executors & administrators Convey promise grant and agree to and with the said Thomas Trundle his heirs and assigns the aforesaid one Hundred and forty five & ᵒⁿᵉ half Acres of Land and every part and parcell thereof against all manner of Persons whatsoever forever hereafter to warrant & defend & further the said Daniel Stephenson doth for himself his heirs, Executors & administrators Covenant promise grant and agree to and with the said Thomas Trundle his heirs and assigns that he the said Daniel Stephenson his heirs & assigns shall & will from time to time and at all times hereafter at the reasonable request of and at the proper Costs and Charges in the law of him the said Thomas Trundle his heirs and assigns do make acknowledge Infer Execute any further Deed or Instrument of writing such as the said Thomas Trundle his heirs or assigns his or their Councel Learned in the Law shall reasonably devise advise or require for the further and better assurance surely & sure making the Land & Premises aforesaid unto him the said Thomas Trundle his heirs and assigns forever In witness whereof the said Daniel Stephenson hath hereunto set his hand & Seal the Day & year above Written --Danˡ Stephenson {seal}

Signed sealed and delivered in the Presence of
Josi Beall Andrew Heugh

On the back of which Deed was the following Indorsements Viz. April 10th 1766 Received of Thomas Trundle the sum of One Hundred Pounds Sterling money of great Britain it being in full Satisfaction and Payment for the within Land & Premises witness   Josi Beall Andrew Heugh

& Daniel Stephenson Frederick County Sᵈ April 10th 1766   then came Daniel Stephenson party to the within deed before the subscribers two of his Lordships Justices of the Peace for the County aforesaid and acknowledged the within Deed as his act and Deed and the Land & Premises to be the right of the within mentioned Thomas Trundle his heirs & assigns forever

Josi Beall
Andrew Heugh

Recd April 17th 1766 of Thomas Trundle the sum of five Shillings & ten pence Sterling as an Alienation fine on the within mentioned Land by order of Edward Lloyd Esq. agent to his Lordship the Right Honʳble the Lord Proprietary of Maryland----------------r---------------------o John Darnall[17]

Mary (Ferguson) Trundle probably died by 1768 and she probably had no children.[18] On 16 May 1769 there was a deed of gift by Thomas I whose name appeared as Thomas

---

[17] Ibid., Deed Liber K, ff. 455-456, ahp.

Trundell Sen[r] to his nephew Thomas III whose name appeared as Thomas Trundell Jun[r]. The deed was as follows:

> At the Request of Thomas Trundell Jun[r]. the following Deed of Gift Ordered Recorded May 16th: 1769 To Wit-- To all People to whome these presents shall Come I Thomas Trundell of Frederick County and province of Maryland Planter Send greeting Know ye that I the said Thomas Trundell for and in Consideration of the natural love and affection which I have and bear unto my Beloved nephew Thomas Trundell Junior of the County and province aforesaid planter and for divers other good causes and Considerations me hereunto moving have given and granted and by these Presents do give and grant unto the said Thomas Trundell Junior One negro girl named Sarah and her increase now in the Possession of the said Thomas Trundell Jun[r]: To have and to Hold the said negro girl named Sarah and her Increase unto the said Thomas Trundell Jun[r]: his Executors administrators & assigns for Ever and the said Thomas Trundell the said negro girl named Sarah and her increase to the said Thomas Trundle Junior his Executors administrators and assigns against all Persons whatsoever shall and will for Ever defend by these presents In Witness whereof I have hereunto Set my hand and affixed my seal the Eighteenth Day of April annoque Domini 1769.......   his
> Signed Sealed & Delivered in the Presence of us   Thomas T Trundell Sen[r] (seal)
> Andrew Heugh Martha Heugh   mark
> On the foot of which Deed of Gift was the following acknowledgment To Wit...
> Frederick County ? On the Eighteenth Day of April.. A.D: 1769 came Thomas Trundell before the subscriber one of his Lordships Justices of the peace for the County aforesaid and acknowledged the above Deed of Gift to be his act and Deed and the negro girl therein named Sarah and her Increase to be the Right property and ? ? of the above named Thomas Trundell Jun[r]: his heirs & assigns for Ever   Acknowledged Before   Andrew Heugh.......[19]

As of the 1769 date Thomas Trundle I probably had no children. It may have been for this reason that he decided to make a gift to his nephew and namesake, Thomas Trundle III, son of his brother, John Trundle III. John III seems to have had health problems[20] and was to die in 1771,[21] so Thomas I may also have wanted to help the family of his brother, John III.

Perhaps it was soon after the deed to his nephew, about 1769, that Thomas Trundle I married Johanah "Hannah" Wood, a much younger wife.[22] He negotiated a lease in 1770 or 1771 for 100 or 120 acres in Frederick Co., MD with Charles Carroll Jr. of Prince George's Co., MD. That tract of land was known as the *Girls Portion* and had an orchard on its premises. Terms of the lease called for him to construct a tobacco house on the land.[23] He was probably the person whose name appears as Thomas Trunnel in a Frederick Co. list of those reporting stray livestock between 1765 and 1775.[24] In 1776 he was surely the Thomas Trundle, age 65, who was living in North West Hundred, Frederick Co., MD. In his household were Johanah, age 43; Johannah J., age five; Rachol, age three; Mila, age one. In addition there were 14 Negroes: Darkus Kor, age 14; Negor Dottor, age 50; Janney, age 30; Lib, age 22; Jacob, age 19; Florah, age 14; Tom, age 13;

---

[18] Brumbaugh.

[19] Frederick Co., MD, Deed Liber M, f. 221, ahp.

[20] Rice.

[21] Frederick Co., MD, Will Liber A-1, ff. 399-400, ahp. As John Trundle Sr. he named a son, Thomas Bob, referred to herein as Thomas Trundle III.

[22] Brumbaugh; Montgomery Co., MD, Will Liber C, f. 7, author has photocopy of original.

[23] Frederick Co., MD, Deed Liber P, ff. 143-144, ahp; ibid., ff. 144-145., ahp. Two leases are on file and based on dates in the deeds it is difficult to determine the difference, though it seems to be about 20 acres in the tract of land.

[24] F. Edward Wright, *Early Lists of Frederick Countians*, p. 8.

Dottor, age 14; Jenney, age 11; Will, age nine; Peg, age five; Ester, age six; Nan, age four; and Ann, age two.[25]

In late 1776 the part of Frederick Co. where he lived became part of newly formed Montgomery Co. It was surely Thomas Trundle I who in 1777 was living in North West Hundred, Montgomery Co. where his name appeared as Thomas Trundle in the tax list.[26] He was probably the Thomas Trundle taxed in Northwest Hundred, Montgomery Co. in 1778.[27] He must have been the Thomas Trundle who in 1783 was assessed in a district composed of Lower Newfoundland, Rock Creek, and North West Hundreds.[28] In 1790 Thomas Trundle I was head of a family in Montgomery Co., MD. In his household were: one white male 16 years and upward, one white male under 16, three white females, and 19 slaves.[29] On 18 July 1791 as Thomas Trundle Sr. he made his will. The original will was found and was as follows:

July yᵉ 18: 1791 In the name of God Amen I Thomas Trundle Sener of Montgomery County in the State of Maryland being in Perfect health thanks be to God for it and being willing to Destrebet the Worldly things which it hath Pleased the Almighty to Bless me with I do hereby order and Derrict my Excecatricx hereafter named to fulfeill this my Last will and Testament in Manner and form following first I give my Soul to Almighty God that first gave ᶦᵗ me my body to be Berried with a Christan Berriel at the Dischristion of my Exzectrix -
Item I give to My Daughter Hannah Barnes one Negro fellow named Jacob after her Mothers Desece or Widdowhood to her and her Heirs forever---
Item I give to my Daughter Rachel Trundle the following Negros to wit: Nan & Sall Jib and ᵃⁿᵈ ᵗʰᵉʳᵉ ᴵⁿᶜʳᵉ Born to her ᵃⁿᵈ ʰᵉʳ Heirs Lawfuly Begoten of her Bodey and after her Mothers Decese or Widdowhood I gave her one Negro Felow named Bill
Item I give to My Daughte Ameli Wilson the following Negros to wit ᵗʰᵉʸ ᵃⁿᵈ ᵗʰᵉʳᵉ ᴵⁿᶜʳᵉ Easter pegg noll Margary to her and her Heirs of her Body and after her Mothers Deth I give her one Negro fellow Named James
Item I give to ᵐʸ son Thomas Trundle the following Negros to wit ᵗʰᵉʸ ᵃⁿᵈ ᵗʰᵉʳᵉ ᴵⁿᶜʳᵉ Negro Moll Back and Cato and after his Mothers Desece or Widdow hood I give also to him the following Negros Petter and Pegg allso I give him my Gun and Pair of Pistoles and one Mair Named Pleasshar and my Sadale and Bridle and give to ᵐʸ Son Thomas in of ᵃⁿᵈ all my Lands after his Mothers Desece or Widdowhood but if my Son Thomas Should Marrey before his Mothers Death he is to have one piece of Land which his Mother thinks proper and if anay of my Children Should Dey without Ishsew then there devedand to be Equaly Devided Amungst the Serviveing partes or there Repprenstivs
Item I give to ᵐʸ beloved Wife Hannah Trundle all the Remander of ᵐʸ whole Eastate Both Raile and Persnel during her Life or Widdow hood and after her death all to ᵇᵉ Sold and the money to be devided amongst my Children and I do hereby Constatute her my Whole and Sole Exzectrix of this my Last will and Testament herby Revocking and Disanuling all Wills and Testaments herby formaly by me made and do Make and ordain this to be my Last
Signed Sealed Pronounced and Declared
and Published this my Last will and Testament   his
and at the Same time Revoking and Disalowing   Thomas T Trundle (seal)
all Wills by me formely maide   mark

[25] Brumbaugh.

[26] Eleanor M.V. Cook, "1777 Tax List of Montgomery County," *Maryland Genealogical Society Bulletin*, v. 31, pp. 16-17.

[27] *Montgomery Co., Md. Oath of Fidelity & Tax Lists - 1778*, pp. 54-56, presented by Mrs. Lilly C. Stone through the Janet Montgomery Chapter, DAR (1949).

[28] Eleanor M.V. Cook, *1783 Maryland General Assessment Montgomery County, Maryland and 1782 Maryland General Assessment Upper Potomac Hundred* (1997), p. 9. There is information that his nephew, Thomas Trundle III, was not living in Montgomery Co. at that time (Montgomery Co., MD, Deed Liber B, ff. 15-16, ahp; ibid., Deed Liber C, ff. 530-531, ahp; Helen W. Brown, comp., *Prince George's County, Maryland, Indexes of Church Registers 1686-1885* [1979] , v. 1, p.138).

[29] *Heads of Families at the First Census of the United States... 1790 Maryland* (Washington, 1907), p. 86.

in the Presents of the Subscribing Witnesses   her
Zadoc Harris   Hannah X Trundle seal
James Shaw   mark
Charles Selby[30]

Thomas Trundle I probably grew to manhood in Prince George's Co., MD where he was a taxable in 1733. He married Mary Ferguson as his first wife. and they seem to have had no children. As his second wife he married Johanah Wood and they lived in North West Hundred, Frederick Co., MD. After Montgomery Co., MD was formed in 1776, the area where they lived was in the new county. As a planter he owned and leased land and probably had fruit orchards and grew tobacco. He signed his name by mark and was likely unable to read or write. When he died by 11 Sep. 1792 Thomas Trundle I had reached the age of about 81.[31]

Johanah (Wood) Trundle who signed her husband's will as Hannah Trundle by mark, survived her husband. As Joana Trundle in 1800 she was head of a family in Montgomery Co., MD, apparently living near her son, Thomas Trundle[32] II, who was the youngest of four children. In her household were: one white female at least 16 but under 26, one white female over 45, and three slaves.[33] She died around 1 June 1805 at about 72 years of age.

Children of Thomas I and Johanah (Wood) Trundle, probably all born in Frederick Co., MD or, after 1776, Montgomery Co., MD:

> i. Johannah J.[4], b. *ca.* 1771; m. prob. by 1790 Montgomery Co., MD,[34] **GREENBURY BARNES**.[35] Johannah J. Trundle was the oldest child of Thomas I and Johanah (Wood) Trundle and in 1776 she was living in North West Hundred, Frederick Co., MD with her parents. She may have been named for both her paternal grandmother and her mother. She married Greenbury Barnes and on 18 July 1791 she was named as "Hannah" Barnes in the will of her father, Thomas I. After the death of Johanah (Wood) Trundle, she was to receive one Negro fellow named Jacob. Jacob was with Johannah's parents in 1776 and would have been about age 35 in 1791. In 1800 there was a Greenbury Barnes who was head of a family in Dorchester Co., MD. In his household were: one white male at least 16 but under 26, and one white male 45 or over.[36] By 1810 one Greenbury Barnes was head of a family in Prince George's Co., MD. In his household were: three white males at least ten but under 16, one white male 45 or over, two white females under ten, one white female at least 26 but under 45, one white female 45 or over, and 13 slaves.[37] Nothing more was found for the family of Greenbury and Johannah J. (Trundle) Barnes.

---

[30] Montgomery Co., MD, Will Liber C, f. 7, author has photocopy of original.

[31] Ibid., Will Liber 1, f. 246.

[32] Ibid., NARA, 1800 census, roll 11, p. 66 or 246.

[33] Ibid.

[34] *Heads of Families.*

[35] MSS, Trundle folder, MCHS.

[36] Dorchester Co., MD, NARA, 1800 census, roll 11, p. 668 or 725.

[37] Prince George's Co., MD, NARA, 1810 census, roll 16, New Scotland, Oxen, & Bladensburg Hundreds, p. 53 or 551, more research needed.

ii.   Rachel, b. *ca.* 1773; m. 14 Feb. 1792 Prince George's Co., MD, **LANCELOT WILSON**,[38] b. 10 Apr. 1768 Prince George's Co., MD;[39] s/o Lancelot Wilson Sr.[40] Rachel Trundle was the second child of Thomas I and Johanah (Wood) Trundle and in 1776 she was living in North West Hundred, Frederick Co., MD with her parents. In 1790 she would have been one of three white females in the household of Thomas Trundle I.[41] On 18 July 1791 she was named as Rachel Trundle in the will of her father, Thomas I, and was to receive Negros: Nan and Sall Jib. After the death of Johanah (Wood) Trundle, she was to receive one Negro fellow named Bill. Nan was with Rachel's parents in 1776 and would have been about age 19 in 1791. On 14 Feb. 1792 Rachel Trundle married Lancelot Wilson in Prince George's Co., MD. Her surname appeared as Trunnell in that record. In 1800 Lancelot Wilson was living in Prince George's Co., MD. In his household were two white males at least 26 but under 45, two white females under ten, one white female at least 26 but under 45, and three free people of color.[42] Lancelot Wilson was enumerated in Bladensburg Dist., Prince George's Co., MD in 1820 with two persons engaged in manufactures, four male slaves at least 45 or over, one female slave at least 14 but under 26, and one female slave at least 26 but under 45[43] In 1828 the name of Launcelot Wilson was found in New Scotland, Oxen, and Bladensburg Hundreds, Prince George's Co., MD when he had lands known as *Littleworth.*[44] More research is needed for the family of Lancelot and Rachel (Trundle) Wilson.

iii.   Ameli, b. *ca.* 1775; m. by 18 July 1791 prob. Montgomery Co., MD, --- **WILSON**. Ameli Trundle was the third child of Thomas I and Johanah (Wood) Trundle. In 1776 she was living in North West Hundred, Frederick Co., MD with her parents when her name appeared as "Mila." In 1790 she was probably one of three white females in the household of Thomas Trundle I.[45] On 18 July 1791 she was named as Ameli Wilson in the will of her father, Thomas I, indicating she had married a Mr. Wilson by then. She was to receive Negros: Easter, Pegg, Noll, and Margary. After the death of Johanah (Wood) Trundle, she was to receive one Negro fellow named James. In 1791 Easter/Ester would have been about age 21 and Pegg/Peg would have been about age 20. Ester and Peg were with Ameli's parents in 1776. By 1820 Ameli (Trundle) Wilson was probably a widow. She was probably the Amelia Wilson living in First Election Dist., Prince George's Co., MD where she was head of a family. In her household were: one white male at least 16

---

[38] Nicholas Russell Murray, *Prince George's County, Maryland 1702-1886 Computer Indexed Marriage Records* (Hammond, LA, 1986), p. 175. Her name appears as Rachel Trunnell.

[39] Piscataway or St. John's Parish, Prince George's Co., MD, 1689-1878, reference found, MSS, Wilson folder, MCHS.

[40] MSA, Will Box 11, Folder 38, Prince George's Co., MD, reference found, MSS, Wilson folder. In 1771 Lancelot Wilson Sr. had a wife, Elizabeth, who was the mother of some of his children. Elizabeth in her own will of 1775 did not name Lancelot as a child (MSA, Will Box 12, Folder 21, Prince George's Co., MD, reference found, MSS, Wilson folder).

[41] *Heads of Families.*

[42] Prince George's Co., MD, NARA, 1800 census, roll 11, p. 291.

[43] Ibid., 1820 census, roll 44, p. 197. The enumerator counted no one as white.

[44] Shirley Langdon Wilcox, ed., *1828 Tax List Prince George's County Maryland* (1985), p. 81.

[45] *Heads of Families.*

but under 18, one white female at least ten but under 16, three white females at least 16 but under 26, one white female at least 26 but under 45, and eight foreigners not naturalized. There were three people engaged in manufactures, two male slaves under 14, three male slaves at least 26 but under 45, two male slaves 45 or over, and one female slave under 14.[46] Nothing more was found for this Wilson family.

5.   iv.   Thomas II, b. *ca.* 1777.

4. JOHN³ TRUNDLE III (John II², John I¹) (see 2), b. 1724[47] prob. Prince George's Co., MD;[48] d. bet. 12 Mar. 1771 & 15 Apr. 1771 Frederick Co., MD;[49] m. prob. (1) *ca.* 1744[50] Prince George's Co., MD, **ALETHIA** --- ;[51] d. poss. *ca.* 1749 Frederick Co., MD;[52] m. prob. (2) *ca.* 1751 Frederick Co., MD, **ANN** --- ;[53] d. aft. 21 Oct. 1786 prob. Montgomery Co., MD.[54]

John Trundle III was a brother of Thomas Trundle I making him a son of John Trundle II and probably Hannah (---) Trundle.[55] John III had a daughter whose name was Joannah Trundle,[56] probably named for her paternal grandmother, Hannah (---) Trundle. As Joannah (Trundle) Lewis, his daughter used the name "Hannah" in some later records.[57] The birth year of John III is given as 1724. On 5 Nov. 1748 he was a soldier in the Maryland Militia. He served with Capt. Thomas Sappington's Company, Prince George's Co., MD.[58] In that same year Frederick Co., MD was formed from Baltimore and Prince George's Co.

John Trundle III was living in Frederick Co., MD on 15 Feb. 1754 when he received a grant of 41 acres called *Trundles Folley* which was surveyed on that date.

> John Trundles Cert. 41 acres Trundles Folley
> Pat: 15 February 1754 Rent &C Am^t 1/0 Med
> Ch to the Rent Roll
> Frederick County Js^t. By virtue of a warrant granted out of his Lordships land office of this Province to John Trundle of the County afs^d for forty one acres of land bearing date by Renewment February 8 1754 - Therefore certify as Deputy Surveyor under his Exc^y Horatio Sharpe Esq Governor of Maryland that I have carefully laid out for and in the name of him the said Trundle all that tract of land called Trundles Folley lying and being in Frederick County Afs^d: Beginning at abounded white oak standing in a valley on the eastside of the West Paint Branch and running thence north twenty

---

[46] Prince George's Co., MD, NARA, 1820 census, roll 44, p. 180A.

[47] DAR membership papers of Florence Michele Remmele #524815 descendant of John III & Alethia (---) Trundle via John IV & Ruth (Lewis) Trundle; "Old family document passed down through the Trundle/Thomas family," n. pag., copy, courtesy of Mrs. Janice (Beall) Taylor, Urbanna, VA.

[48] Prince George's Co., MD, Deed Liber F, f. 275, ahp.

[49] Frederick Co., MD, Will Liber A-1, ff. 399-400, ahp.

[50] DAR membership papers of Anita Claire Willison #462691, descendant of Thomas III & Rachel (Lewis) Trundle, has this Thomas Trundle b. 16 Jan. 1746/47. Thomas Trundle III had the name of Thomas Bob in the will of John Trundle Sr. or John III (Frederick Co., MD, Will Liber A-1, ff. 399-400, ahp).

[51] "Old family document...," has her name as Alethea and wife of John III; Pauline Beard Cooney, comp., *History of the Beard - Bedichek - Craven and Allied Families* (1979), p. 159 has her name as Aletha and mother of John IV. The name seems to have been used in later generations sometimes in other forms such as Lethe, to be noted later.

[52] Brumbaugh, p. 226 implies son, John IV b. *ca.* 1749. Perhaps she died at his birth.

[53] Frederick Co., MD, Will Liber A-1, ff. 399-400, ahp.

[54] Montgomery Co., MD, Deed Liber C, ff. 403-404, ahp.

[55] Prince George's Co., MD, Deed Liber F, f. 275, ahp; Frederick Co., MD, Deed Liber M, f. 221, ahp.

[56] Frederick Co., MD, Will Liber A-1, ff. 399-400, ahp.

[57] PPTB, Harrison Co., (W)V, 1799-1801.

[58] Murtie June Clark, *Colonial Soldiers of the South 1732-1774* (Baltimore, 1983), p. 26.

four degrees west sixty four perches north sixty six degrees west fifty six perches south forty east ninty perches then by a straight line to the Beginning tree containing and now laid out for forty one acres of land to be held of Conogocheage Manor

Surveyed February 15. 1754 ---- .. ---- .. ---- ..

       24 June 1756 Examined and Passed

                           Ross Exam(?)

                         Isaac Brooke [59]

Trundles Folley on the east side of West Paint Branch was in Montgomery Co., MD after 1776.[60] At the Frederick Co. March Court of 1754 John Trundle III petitions the Court

'that he has lost the sight of his eyes for a long time past and has been with Dr. Hamilton and sundry others for help and with great fatigue and expense finds no benefit, has a wife and three small children and has no way to support them so prays Your Worships will take his case in consideration in letting him be levy free and making him some allowance from the County as Your Worships shall seem meet.

The Court ordered that Trundle be levy-free for the future and 'that he be allowed one shilling in the next County levy as a pension.'[61]

At the Frederick Co. November Court of 1754 John Trundle III petitions the court that

'he was taken blind of one eye three years since and one year with the other, that he has a wife and four small children and was with Dr. Hamilton and sundry others for help and great fatigue and expense and could get none, that he stayed three months and his wife seven weeks which prevented him from making corn, that he got some help there but not capable of doing his business.' He asks to be levy free and for some additional help.

The court grants his petition and allows him 600 pounds of tobacco till next November Court.[62]

In 1758 and 1759 there were records of debt for him and his brother, Thomas I. On 3 Nov. 1758 in Frederick Co., John Beall, son of Robert, settled for 399 lbs. of tobacco and costs recovered against John Trundell, Thos Trundel, and Benjamin Becraft.[63] Apparently the two brothers, Thomas I and John III, and Ninian Edmonston of Frederick Co. were in debt to the estate of John Johnson 2 Sep. 1759 when 3300 lbs. of tobacco and costs were recovered by Thomas Cramphin, administrator.[64] At the Frederick Co. Court of 1760

Juliana Benninger presents a petition to the Court in which she states that a certain John Trundle, a tenant farmer, 'hath detained Catherine Wolphin, daughter of the said Juliana, illegally although the said Catherine hath demanded of John Trundle [her freedom]. From time to time he has refused to let her depart from him.' She asks the Court to proceed according to their sentiments in such a case.

The Court orders a summons to issue returnable in the June Court for John Trundle.[65]

On 27 Oct. 1766 John Trundle III acquired two tracts of land in Frederick Co., MD from Mary Spires, 100 acres called *Benjamin* and 25 1/4 acres called *Labrinth*. The 100

[59] Frederick Co., MD, Warrant Liber BC & GS #5, f. 157, found and transcribed by Benjamin Franklin Poinsett, MSA, 13 June 1998.
[60] Ibid.
[61] Rice, pp. 133-135.
[62] Ibid., p. 146.
[63] Frederick Co., MD, Land Liber F, p. 595, cited in Andersen, p. 62.
[64] Frederick Co., MD, Land Liber F, p. 872, cited in Andersen, p. 87.
[65] Rice, pp. 202-203.

acres were formerly deeded to Benjamin Thrasher by John Beall Sr. The 25 1/4 acres were formerly deeded to Mary Thrasher by William Beall and James Edmonstone. Apparently Mary Spires was Mary (---) Thrasher Spires and a former wife of Benjamin Thrasher.[66] On 18 July 1767 Thomas Thrasher, farmer, of Frederick Co. deeded these same parcels of land to John Trundle III, planter, of Frederick Co. for the sum of £60 current money. Thomas Thrasher must have been an heir of Benjamin Thrasher and probably an heir of Mary (---) Thrasher Spires as well. The 1767 deed was as follows:

At The request of John Trundle the following Deed was Recorded July the 18th 1767 to wit, This Indenture made this eighteenth day of June in the year of our Lord one thousand seven hundred and sixty seven Between Thomas Thrasher of Frederick County and Province of Maryland Farmer of the one Part and John Trundell of the said County and Province Planter of the other Part Witnesseth that the said Thomas Thrasher for and in Consideration of the sum of Sixty Pounds Current money to him in hand by the said John Trundell the receipt whereof he doth hereby acknowledge and thereof and of every Part and Parcel thereof doth release acquit and for ever Discharge the said John Trondell his Executors and Administrators by these Presents Hath given granted bargained sold aliened Released enfeoffed and confirmed and by these Presents Doth give grant bargain sell Alien release enfeoff and confirm unto the said John Trundell all that Part of a Tract of Land called Benjamin Lying in Frederick County and Province aforesaid and Beginning at a bounded White oak being in the Corner aforesaid and Running thence North Sixty two Degrees East Sixty Perches then North forty six degrees East one hundred Perches then North Eighty degrees East Eighty four perches then North thirty two degrees West Sixty four Perches then South Sixty Degrees West Sixty Degrees West Twenty eight perches then South Eighty Degrees West one hundred perches then South seventy Perches then West Eighty eight Perches then south twenty five Degrees East one hundred Perches then with a straight line to the first Bounded tree Containing and laid out for one hundred acres of Land more or less and also all that Tract of Land hereafter mentioned being part of a Tract of Land called Laybrinth lying in the County and Province aforesaid Beginning at the Northeast Corner of said land at or near the Northwest corner of a Tract of Land Called the Benjamin on the North West side of the Plantation where the widow Thrasher lately lived and running thence South Twenty five degrees East one hundred perches South Nineteen degrees West Thirty two perches West thirty two perches then North eight degrees West one hundred Twenty and one half Perches to a line of said Laybrinth then with a Straight line to the first Boundary Containing Twenty five acres and one Quarter of an acre of Land more or less To have and to hold the said Parcell of Land with all and Singular the Houses buildings and improvements on or to the same belonging or in any wise appertaining as also the revertion and revertions remainder and remainders are to him the said John Trundell his heirs and assigns forever and to the only proper use and behoof of him the said John Trundell his heirs and assigns forever and to no other use intent or Purpose whatsoever and the said Thomas Thrasher doth hereby for himself his heirs Executors and administrators Covenant Promise grant and agree to and with the said John Trundell his heirs and assigns that the said parcells of Land and Premises at the Time of ensealing and delivery of these Presents are freely and clearly acquitted exonerated and discharged of and from all former grants bargains sales mortgages and incumbrances whatsoever (the Rent to become due to the Lord Proprietary only excepted) and that the said Thomas Thrasher hath good right lawfull and absolute Authority to Sell transfer convey and make over the said Parcels of Land and premises to as in manner and form aforesaid And Lastly the said Thomas Thrasher doth hereby for himself his heirs Executors and Administrators covenant Promises and grant that he the said Thomas Thrasher his heirs Exrs. and Admrs. the said Parcels of Land and Premises to the said John Trundell against all manner of Persons claiming any right or Interest therein or thereunto claiming under him the sd. Thomas Thrasher Shall and will Warrant and for ever defend by these Presents In Witness whereof the said Thomas Thrasher hath hereunto set his hand and affixed his Seal the day and year first above written
Signed Sealed & Delivered in the Presence of

---

66 Frederick Co., MD, Deed Liber K, ff. 713-714, ahp; ibid., ff. 1382-1384, ahp.

the words Claiming under him the s^d. Thomas Thrasher between the ^thirty sixth & ^thirty seventh lines being first underlined

John Darnall   Thomas Thrasher   (seal)

On the Back of which Deed was the following Indorsment to wit,

Received the 18th day of June 1767

by John Trundell Sixty Pounds Current money

it being the full Consideration of the within Parcels of Land and Premises

Witness John Darnall   Thomas Thrasher

Frederick County (?) June the 18th 1767 In the day and year within written came Thomas Thrasher party to the within deed and acknowledged the same to be his act and deed and the parcels of Land & Premises within mentioned to be the right property & Estate of the within Jno. Trundell his heirs and assigns for ever also Martha the wife of the said Thomas Thrasher being privately examined acknowledged her right of Dower to the same to be likewise the right and Estate the said Jno. Trundell his heirs & Assigns and Declared that she made the said acknowledgement freely and willingly without any Threats from her said husband or fear of his Displeasure and according to the form of the act of assembly in such cases made & Provided

Acknowledged before   John Darnall

Received the 18th day of July 1767 of John Trundell five shillings and one farthing sterling an alienation fine on the within mentioned one hundred and Twenty five acres and one Quarter of an Acre of Land by order Edward Loyd Esq. agent of his Lordship the right Honourable the Lord Proprietary of Maryland   John Darnall[67]

Earlier, on 9 Apr. 1767, Patrick Connerly, Irish, 22, was reported as a runaway from John Trundle and Walter Beall of Frederick Co.[68] On 10 Oct. 1767 in Frederick Co. regarding Walter Beall against Jacob Wilson, John Trundell, and Caleb Cass, there was a judgment to Walter Beall for £2 current money, recorded 8 Aug. last against Jacob Wilson, for use of Walter Beall, by 10 Feb. next, before Andrew Heugh.[69] It must have been John Trundle III who reported stray livestock 17 Aug. 1768 in Frederick Co. and it must have been John Trundle III whose name was on a list of those with rent due on land in Frederick Co. in 1768 and 1769.[70]

In a deed recorded 25 Sep. 1769, for the sum of 20 pounds, ten shillings, John Trundle III as John Trundle Sr., planter, of Frederick Co., deeded to John Hoskinson *Trundles Folley*, acquired in 1754. As John Trundell he signed the deed by mark. His wife, Anne/Ann (---) Trundle, acknowledged her Right of Dower as follows:

On the 30 day of august 1769 Came the within named John Trundel before us the subscribers being two of his lordships Justices for Frederick County and acknowledged his Right to the within mentioned land and premises to be the Right of the within named John Hoskinson his heirs and assigns for Ever also Anne the wife of the said John Trundell being Privately Examined before us out of the hearing of her said Husband acknowledged her Right of Dower to the said land and Premises to be the Right of the said John Hoskinson his heirs and assigns for Ever and that she made the same freely and voluntarily without any threats or ill usage of her said husband or fear of his Displeasure according to an act of assembly in that Case made and Provided taken and acknowledged before us ... Charles Jones, Andrew Heugh...

Rec^d. Septr. 25th 1769 of John Hoskinson one Shilling & Eight pence sterling an alienation fine on the within land by order of Daniel of s^d. Thomas Jenifer Esqr. his Lordships agent (?)[71]

---

[67] Ibid.

[68] Peter Wilson Coldham, *The King's Passengers of Maryland and Virginia*, p. 272.

[69] Frederick Co., MD, Land Liber K, p. s1, cited in Patricia Abelard Andersen, *Frederick County Maryland Land Records Liber K Abstracts, 1765-1768* (Montgomery Village, MD, 1997), p. 1.

[70] Wright, pp. 8, 13, 18. By 1769 John III had a son, John IV, who was about age 20.

[71] Frederick Co., MD, Deed Liber M, f. 491, ahp.

On 12 Mar. 1771 John III as John Trundle Sr. made his will in Frederick Co., MD. It was as follows:

Fradrick County Mary Land Ts[t] I John Trundle Sen[r] in my perfect Sence & Noledge in March 12th in the year of our Lord God one thousand seven hundred & seventy one I make my Last Will & Testament. I leave my Wife ann Trundle holy Exceatary & Likewise my Land Horses, Cattle Sheep & hoggs and all my houshold Furnitude and all Lets, due to live in as we formely did in durcing her Life or widderhood & if she marry to be cut out of the hole. Likewise the three Olphen Boys to my three Sons To to Thomas Bob. to John Basel to Josiah If tha will assist Thar mother to pay the dets If not then must do as well as she can. Likewise my bay Horse to my Dauter Joanna Trundle when she goes for herself & Likewise my Land to my Son Josiah after my Wife Death or marry to have and to hold forever. And likewise when the Leats is paid to make the two children Equil with the others & what is left to be equil divided at her Death ~~and~~[or] if she marrys among my fore Children and likewise Sarah Green Tree to my Daughter Joannen Trundle to have as her Right to the age of Sixtee & so assi[n]ds my self to God

The fift Line underlined before signed   his
                                                              John X Trundle Sen[r]
                                                                        mark
Signed & Sealed in the presants of these Witnesses
            his   his
Mordice   M   Mitchel   Clem   X   Sellbe   Henry Wilson
            mark   mark

On the 15th Day of April 1771 Came Mordica Mitchel & Colim Sellby two of the subscribing Witness to the aforegoing Will & made oath on the holy Evangelists of Almighty God, that they did see the Testator John Trundle sign and seal the said Will & heard him publish pronounce and declare the same to be his Last Will & Testament and that at the Time of his so doing he was to the best of their apprehension of a sound and disposing mind & memory & that they also saw Henry Willson the other subscribing Witness to the said Will sign his Name as a Witness there to & that they severally subscribed their Names as Witnesses to the said Will in presence of the said Testator & in presence of each other

                    Sworn before   J Bowles Dy Comy
Prerogative office to wit
On the 10th Day of June 1771 Came Henry Wilson the third Subscribing Evidence to the within Will & made oath that he saw the Testator therein named sign and Seal & heard him publish pronounce and declare the same to be his Last Will and Testament and that at the Time of his so doing he was of a sound & disposing mind Memory & understanding & that he together with Mordecai Mitchel & Clement Sellby the other two subscribing Witnesses did Sign their Names as Witnesses to this Will in the presence and at the Request of the Testator & in the presence of each other

                    Sworn before Eli Nalette Reg[r][72]

John Trundle III had died by 15 Apr. 1771. Earlier, on the 15 Sep. 1768, he had granted his son, Josiah, a special warrant to *Resurvey on the Benjamin.* On 24 Aug. 1771 a petition for resurvey was recorded as follows:

John Trundle his Certificate - 152 acres
The resurvey on The Benjamin Patented to Josiah Trundle 27 Aug. 1771 Rent per annum 6 pence charged to the Rent Rolls
Frederick County... by virtue of a warrent of Resurvey granted out of his Lordships Land office... to John Trundell of the County aforesaid bearing date by renewment 5 Sep. 1768 to Resurvey 100 Acres part of a tract of land called The Benjamin originally on 5 Sep. 1729 granted unto a certain John Beall for 239 acres under now rent to Resurvey the aforesaid land to amend all errors and to

---

[72] Ibid., Will Liber A-1, ff. 399-400, ahp.

Ill. 13 - Will of John Trundle Sr. on file in Frederick Co., MD, Liber A-1, f. 399.

Ill. 14 - Will of John Trundle Sr. continued, f. 400.

add the contiguous vacancy... certified ... the old land and find that it contains 102 acres and I have added one parcel of vacancy containing 50 acres... reduced the whole into one tract... (degrees and perches)... to behold of Conococheague Manor... Resurveyed 8 Mar. 1769...

The Petition of Josiah Trundle of Frederick County

Humbly showeth that your Petitioners father John Trundell has on the fifteenth of September 1768 granted him a special warrant to Resurvey 100 acres part of a tract called the Resurvey on the Benjamin... containing... 152 acres... That before the said John Trundell obtained his Lordships grant for the same, he died, and by his last will and Testament duly made and recorded devised the aforesaid land to his wife Ann Trundell during her life and after her decease to your Petitioner - that the said Ann Trundell having renounced her Right and Title to the said land in favor of Your Petitioner (as will appear by her Certificate hereto Annexed) - he prays your Honours will grant him Patent of confirmation the Certificate aforesaid.

This is to Satisfy your Honour that I have agreed to lett my son Josiah Trundell have the hole Right to aforesaid land that I was to have my life in for he has fully satisfied me for it therefore if Patent is grant for he was to have it by his father John Trundell Senior after my death or widderhood by his will no more at Present but from me

27 Aug. 1771   Your Humble Servant
                  Ann Trundle[73]

John Trundle III as John Trundle Sr. in his will, seemed to indicate Josiah and Joannah were his two youngest children. The petition by his son, Josiah, with the renouncement by the widow of John III, Ann (---) Trundle, surely makes it clear that Ann was the mother of Josiah and therefore the mother of the younger Joannah. Ann (---) Trundle was the executrix of the estate of John Trundle III and submitted an account of record 23 Apr. 1772 as follows:

Prerogative Office to wit - The Account of Ann Trundel Executrix of John Trundle late of Frederick County Deceased -

This Accountant chargeth herself with the Inventory
of the Deceased Amounting to _ _ _ _ _ _ _ _ _ _ _ _ _ _ _   £133-18-11

And she Craves Allowance for the following Payments to wit -

Of current Money due from the deceased to Richard
Anderson on Acc^t. of - In Glasford Merch^d. in London
on his Bond and paid by this Accountant as Bond Cred^t.
appl. _   161-11- 7

Of Ditto Money due from the Deceased to the said
Richardson on acc^t. of said In Glasford on Book Account
and paid by this Accountant as per Acc^t. proved & receipt
appears _   53-16- 8 1/2

Of Ditto Money due from the Deceased to Watter on his
Bond and paid by this Accountant as per Bond proved &
receipt appears _   12-10- 6

Of Tobacco fees Secured to be paid for Letters recording
& recording Inventory _ _ _ _ _ _ _ _ _ _ _ _ _ _   345
Of D^o Fees Secured to be paid for recording this
Account & Securing Ballance _ _ _ _ _ _ _ _ _ _   75
                                               420   2-12-6
                               at 12/6
Of Funeral Expences Allowed _ _ _ _ _ _ _ _ _ _ _ _ _ _ _   3 ------
Of 10 per c^t. Com^n. on paying the above Sums   23- 7- 1 3/4
                  Amount _ _ _ _ _ _   £256-18- 5

---

[73] MSA, Drawer 54, Land Patent Vol. BC & GS #42, f. 62-63, 479, Frederick Co., MD, copy of transcription, courtesy of Mrs. Taylor.

Deduct 1/5 to reduce it to Gold Curr^c. _ _ _ _ _ _ _ _ _ _ _ 51- 7- 8 1/2

205-10- 8 1/2

Estate Over Paid _ _ _ _ _ _ _ _ _ _ 71-11- 9 1/2

£133-18-11

Prerogative Office to wit April 23^d 1772 Came Ann Trundle the aforegoing Accountant and made Oath that this Account is Just and True as Stated which thereupon is Passed by -[74]

John Trundle III seems to have grown to manhood in Prince George's Co., MD, where he was in the Colonial Militia in 1748. It is possible that before he married he lived some years with his brother, Thomas Trundle I, who was about 13 years older. No record of when their parents died was found. John III must have married at least twice. Probably as his first wife he married Alethia ---, and they lived in a part of Frederick Co., MD that after 1776 became a part of Montgomery Co., MD. As his probable second wife he married Ann ---. John Trundle III was a planter and land owner who was apparently unable to read or write. Though he seems to have suffered from poor health he managed to prosper. He died by 15 Apr. 1771, not having reached the age of 50. On that date Ann (---) Trundle, widow, was living near Walter Beall's Mill in Frederick Co., MD when she reported stray livestock.[75] This must have been the family home probably located on *Resurvey on the Benjamin*. Perhaps there was a family connection to Walter Beall.

Having survived her husband, Ann (---) Trundle served as executrix of his estate 23 Apr. 1772. She may have lived with her son, Josiah Trundle, in Montgomery Co., MD. He sold property to his mother, Ann, many years later on 10 July 1786.

At the request of ann Trundell the following bill of sale was recorded this 10th day of July 1786 (to wit) Know all men by these presents that I Josiah Trundell of montgomery County and state of maryland for and in consideration of the sum or Quantity of two thousand & one hundred pounds of merchantable Tobacco to him in hand paid by Ann Trundell of the same County and state, the receipt whereof I do hereby acknowledge and myself herewith fully satisfied and paid, have bargained, sold transferred, (?) and delivered and by these presents bargain, sell Transfer (?) and deliver unto the said ann Trundell her heirs and assigns the following goods and Chattels, namely two horses two feather Beds and eight head of hogs; To have and to hold the said horses beds and hogs to the said Ann Trundell, her, heirs, and assigns to the only proper use and whereof of the said Ann Trundell and ^{her} heirs and assigns forever and I the said Josiah Trundell, for myself, my heirs Executors and Administrators the aforesaid bargained Goods and Chattels unto the said Ann Trundell her heirs and assigns against every and all manner of persons whatsoever will warrant and forever define by these presents In Witness whereof I have hereunto set my hand and seal this twenty sixth day of June one thousand seven hundred and Eighty six -

Signed and sealed   his
in the presence of   Josiah I Trundell (seal)
                                        his   mark
John I Speake, his mark Henry H Cambron
                                        mark

---

[74] Frederick Co., MD, Will Liber B-2, ff. 193-194, ahp.
[75] Wright, p. 8.

On the back of which bill of sale was the following Endorsements (to wit)
Received on the day and year within written of the within named Ann Trundell the sum or Quantity of two thousand & one hundred pounds of merchantable Tobacco being the Consideration within mentioned. Witness

his
my hand, Josiah I Trundell
mark

Witness John I Speake, his mark, Henry H Cambron, his mark
State of maryland, Montgomery County to wit On the day and year within written came John Speake and Henry Cambron subscribing witnesses to the within Indorsement of writing and the above receipt, and made oath before the undersigned one of the Justices of said County, that they saw Josiah Trundell sign and seal the same, and declared them to be his act and Deed for the uses and puroses herein mentioned at the same time the said Josiah Trundell acknowledged the within Instrument of writing to be his act and Deed, and the goods and Chattels herein mentioned to be the right and property of the within named Ann Trundell, her heirs and assigns forever - Sworn and acknowledged before Richard Thompson[76]

Later that year, 21 Oct. 1786, Ann (---) Trundle and Josiah Trundle deeded the two parcels of land, *Resurvey on the Benjamin* and *Labrinth*, then in Montgomery Co., MD, to Benjamin Gittings. On that date Josiah was residing on *Resurvey on the Benjamin*. The two parcels of land had, in 1767, been deeded to his father, John III, by Thomas Thrasher. Ann and Josiah whose surnames were spelled Trundell in the deed, each signed the deed by mark. They were to receive the sum of £100 current money of Maryland.[77] Earlier, on 24 Aug. 1771 Ann (---) Trundle appeared to have signed her name in full.[78] No death date was found for Ann (---) Trundle.

Children of John III and probably Alethia (---) Trundle:

6.   i.   Thomas Bob or Thomas III[4], b. 16 Jan. 1746/47 prob. Prince George's Co., MD.

7.   ii.   John Basel or John IV, b. *ca.* 1748 prob. Frederick Co., MD.

      Children of John III and Ann (---) Trundle, born in Frederick Co., MD:

8.   iii.   Josiah, b. *ca.* 1752.

     iv.   Joannah, b. bet. 19 Mar. 1754 & Nov. 1754; d. prob. by 1810 Harrison Co., (W)V;[79] m. (1) *ca.* 1771 prob. Frederick Co., MD, **DAVID LEWIS** (see Lewis Families, Chapter Three, No. 5); m. (2) 18 Aug. 1806 Harrison Co., (W)V, **PATRICK BURNSIDE** .

---

[76] Montgomery Co., MD, Deed Liber C, ff. 360-361, ahp.

[77] Ibid., ff. 403-404, ahp.

[78] MSA, Drawer 54, Land Patent Vol.

[79] Harrison Co., (W)V, Marriage Bond Book 2, p. 167, author has photocopy of original; ibid., Deed Book 7, pp. 328-329, ahp.; ibid., NARA, 1810 census, photostats, v. 7, p. 949.

CHAPTER EIGHT

TRUNDLE, FOURTH GENERATION

5. THOMAS[4] **TRUNDLE II** (Thomas I[3], John II[2], John I[1]) (see 3), b. *ca.* 1777 Montgomery Co., MD;[1] d. prob. bet. 1806 & 1810 Montgomery Co., MD;[2] m. *ca.* 1796 prob. Montgomery Co., MD, **LEAH ?SHAW**;[3] b. poss. *ca.* 1777 Montgomery Co., MD; d. aft. 1809 likely Montgomery Co., MD.[4]

Thomas Trundle II grew up in the home of his parents, Thomas I and Johanah (Wood) Trundle, who lived in Montgomery Co., MD. In 1790 he was surely the white male under 16 living there with Thomas Trundle I.[5] When Thomas Trundle I made his will 18 July 1791, he named his son, Thomas, unmarried, who was to receive Negroes: Moll Back and Cato. After the death of Johanah (Wood) Trundle, Thomas II was to receive Negroes: Petter and Pegg, and all lands. In addition, he was to have his father's gun, a pair of pistols, one mare, saddle, and bridle.[6]

Circa 1796 Thomas Trundle II married Leah ?Shaw and they had children born in 1797 and 1800 whose births were recorded in Prince George's Parish, Montgomery Co., MD.[7] In 1800 Thomas Trundle II, as Thomas Trundle, was living in Montgomery Co., MD. In his household were: two white males under ten, one white male at least 26 but under 45, two white females under ten, one white female at least 26 but under 45, and three slaves.[8] Apparently at that time they would have been living on *Addition to Easy Purchase* which he had inherited from his father, Thomas I. In 1805 Thomas Trundle II began dividing and selling parts of *Addition to Easy Purchase*. On 4 Nov. 1805 he sold 35 3/10 acres for the sum of £105.18 to Patrick Orme. The deed was as follows:

> At the request of Patrick Orme the following Deed was Recorded the 4th day of November 1805 to wit This Indenture made this twentieth day of September Eighteen hundred and five Between Thomas Trundel of Montgomery County and state of Maryland of the one part and Patrick Orme of the County and state aforesaid of the other part Witnesseth that the said Thomas Trundle for and in consideration of the sum of one hundred and five pounds Eighteen shillings current money to him in hand paid by the said Patrick Orme at or before the ensealing and delivery of these presents the receipt whereof he doth hereby acknowledge and himself fully paid and satisfied hath granted bargained sold aliened released enfeoffed and confirmed and by these presents doth grant bargain sell alien release enfeoff and confirm unto the said Patrick Orme his heirs and assigns forever part of a tract of land called "the addition to Easy purchase beginning at a stone standing at the end of twenty two perches on the third line of said tract and runing thence south twenty one degrees west sixty six perches to a stone standing upon the tenth line of Isaac Sansdales part of Easy purchase then with it south eighty six degrees and an half west sixty five perches to the thirteenth line of Easy Purchase then with it north fifteen degrees west fifty two perches to a stone standing at the

[1] Gaius Marcus Brumbaugh, *Maryland Records, Colonial, Revolutionary, County, and Church from Original Sources* (Baltimore, 1985 repr. 1928 ed.), v. 1, p. 223; Montgomery Co., MD, Will Liber C, f. 7, author has photocopy of original.

[2] Ibid., Deed Liber M, ff. 466-467, ahp; ibid., NARA, 1810 census, roll 14, p. 314 or 927.

[3] Helen W. Brown, comp., *Prince George's County, Maryland, Indexes of Church Registers 1686-1885* (1979), v. 2, Part 2, p. 305, named a dau., Sarah Shaw.

[4] Montgomery Co., MD, NARA.

[5] *Heads of Families at the First Census of the United States... 1790 Maryland* (Washington, 1907), p. 86.

[6] Montgomery Co., MD, Will Liber C.

[7] Brown.

[8] Montgomery Co., MD, NARA, 1800 census, roll 11, p. 66 or 246.

end of said line then north fifty three degrees east fifty four perches to a stone then south fifty three and an half degrees east thirty six perches to a stone then to the beginning containing thirty five acres and three tenths of an acre of land To have and To hold unto the said Patrick Orme his heirs and assigns forever the aforesaid piece or parcel of land with all and singular the rights profits benefits and priviledges thereunto belonging and all the estate right title interest property claim and demand whatsoever whether in Law or equity of him the said Thomas Trundel his heirs executors or administrators of in and to the said piece or parcel of land or to any part or parcel therof and the said Thomas Trundel for himself his heirs executors and administrators doth by these presents covenant promise grant and agree to and with the said Patrick Orme his heirs and assigns that the said Thomas Trundel his heirs executors and administrators shall and will warrant and forever defend all and singular the aforesaid and above described Land and premises unto the said Patrick Orme his heirs and assigns against all manner of persons whatsoever In Testimony whereof the said Thomas Trundel hath hereunto set his hand and affixed his seal the day and year first within written Signed sealed and delivered in presence of

Wᵐ Smith Thoˢ Simpson   Thomas Trundel   {Seal}

On the back of the aforegoing Deed are thus endorsed to wit, Montgomery County Let Be it remembered that on the 20th day of September 1805 the within named Thomas Trundel came before us two of the Justices of the peace for the County aforesaid and acknowledged this instrument of writing to be his act and deed and the Land and premises therein mentioned to be the right and estate of the within named Patrick Orme his heirs and assigns forever according to the true intent and meaning thereof and the act of assembly in such cases made and provided At the same time came Leah the wife of the said Thomas before us and she being privately examined apart from and out of the hearing of her husband she renounced all her right and title of dower of in and to the within mentioned land and premises unto the said Patrick Orme his heirs and assigns and declared she did the same freely and voluntarily without being induced therto by fear of threats or of ill usage from her husband or through fear of incurring his displeasure

   Taken and acknowledged before Wᵐ Smith Thoˢ: Simpson[9]

On 14 Jan 1806 he sold 49 4/10 acres for the sum of £148.4 to Robert Jones. The deed was as follows:

At the request of Robert Jones the following Deed was Recorded the 14 January 1806 to wit, This Indenture made the twentieth day of September Eighteen hundred and five Between Thomas Trundle of Montgomery County and State of Maryland of the one part and Robert Jones of Prince Georges County and state aforesaid of the other part Witnesseth, that the said Thomas Trundle for and in consideration of the sum of one hundred and forty eight pounds four shillings current money to him in hand paid by the said Robert Jones at or before the ensealing and delivery of these presents the receipt whereof he doth hereby acknowledge and himself fully paid and Satisfied hath granted bargained sold released enfeoffed and confirmed and by these presents doth grant bargain sell alien release enfeoff and confirm unto the said Robert Jones part of a tract of land called the Addition to Easy purchase lying and being in Montgomery County aforesaid beginning at a stone standing at the end of the fifteenth line of Easy purchase and runing thence north fifty six degrees west nine perches to the Seventh line of the Addition to Easy purchase then north twenty three degrees west thirty three perches to a stone standing at the end of said seventh of the Addition to Easy purchase then north fifty six degrees west eighty perches to a stone north forty seven degrees east Eighty perches to a stone south thirty eight degrees and one quarter of a degree east one hundred and twenty eight perches to a stone then by a straight line to the beginning containing Forty nine acres and four tenths of an acre of land To have and To hold unto the said Robert Jones by his heirs and assigns forever the aforesaid piece or parcel of land with all and singular the rights profits benefits and priviledges thereunto belonging and all the estate right title property interest claim and demand whatsoever whether in law or equity of him the said Thomas Trundle his heirs executors or administrators of in or to the same or to any part or parcel thereof and the said Thomas Trundle for himself his heirs Executors and administrators doth by these presents

⁹ Ibid., Deed Liber M, ff. 346-347, ahp.

covenant promise grant and agree to and with the said Robert Jones his heirs and assigns that he the said Thomas Trundle his heirs Executors or administrators shall and will forever warrant and defend all and Singular the aforesaid and above described land and premises unto the said Robert Jones his heirs and assigns against all manner of persons whatsoever In Testamony whereof the said Thomas Trundel hath hereunto set his hand and affixed his seal the day and year first within written, Signed sealed and delivered in presence of

Wm Smith Thos. Simpson   Thomas Trundle (Seal)

On the back of the aforegoing Deed are thus Endorsed to wit, Montgomery County Let Be it remembered that on the 20th day of September 1805 the within named Thomas Trundel Came before us two of the Justices of the peace for the County aforesaid and acknowledged the within Instrument of writing to be his act and deed and the land and premises therein mentioned to be the right title and estate of the within named Robert Jones his heirs and assigns forever according to the true intent and meaning thereof and act of assembly in such cases made and provided At the same time came Leah the wife of the said Thomas before us and she being privately examined apart from and out of the hearing of her said husband renounce all her right and title of dower of in and to the within mentioned land and premises to the said Robert Jones his heirs and assigns and declared she did the same freely and voluntarily without being induced thereto by fear of threats or of ill usage from her husband, or through fear of incurring his displeasure

Taken and Acknowledged before Wm Smith Thos. Simpson[10]

According to a second deed on 14 Jan. 1806 he sold 38 3/10 acres for the sum of £114.18 to James Wilson Perry. The deed was as follows:

At the request of James Wilson Perry the following Deed was Recorded the 14th January 1806 to wit, This Indenture made the twentieth day of September Eighteen hundred and five Between Thomas Trundle of Montgomery County and State of Maryland of the one part and James Wilson Perry of the County and state aforesaid of the other part Witnesseth, that the said Thomas Trundel for and in consideration of the sum of One hundred and fourteen pounds Eighteen shillings current money to him in hand paid by the said James Wilson Perry the receipt whereof he doth hereby acknowledge and himself fully paid and satisfied hath granted bargained sold released enfeoffed and confirmed, and by these presents doth grant bargain sell alien release enfeoff and confirm unto the said James Wilson Perry his heirs and assigns forever part of a tract of land called the Addition to Easy Purchase lying and being in the County aforesaid beginning at the original beginning of the said tract and running thence south twenty degrees west eleven perches north forty nine degrees west forty five and an half perches to a stone south twenty one degrees west twenty two perches to a stone south eighty three degrees west thirty perches to a stone north fifty three and an half degrees west thirty six perches to a stone standing at the end of the fourteenth line of Easy purchase north twenty three degrees west forty five perches to a stone then north fifty six and an half degrees east sixty perches to a stone standing on the given line of the Addition to Easy purchase then by a straight line to the beginning containing thirty eight and three tenths of an acre of land, To have and To hold unto the said James Wilson Perry his heirs and assigns forever the aforesaid piece or parcel of land with all and singular the rights profits benefits and priviledges thereunto belonging and all the Estate right title interest property claim and demand whatsoever whether in Law or equity of him the said Thomas Trundle his heirs executors or administrators of in and to the said tract or parcel of land or to any part or parcel thereof And the said Thomas Trundel for himself his heirs executors and administrators doth by these presents covenant promise grant and agree to and with the said James Wilson Perry his heirs and assigns that the said Thomas Trundel by his heirs executors and administrators shall and will warrant and forever defend all and singular the aforesaid and above described land and premises unto the said James Wilson Perry his heirs his heirs and assigns against all manner of persons whatsoever In Testimony whereof the said Thomas Trundel hath here unto set his hand and affixed his seal the day and year first within written

Signed Sealed and delivered in presence of
Wm Smith Thos. Simpson   Thomas Trundel   (Seal)

---

[10] Ibid., ff. 466-467, ahp.

On the back of the aforegoing Deed are thus Endorsed to wit, Montgomery County Let Be it remembered that on the 20ᵗʰ day of September 1805 the within named Thomas Trundel Came before us two of the Justices of the peace for the County aforesaid and acknowledged this Instrument of writing to be his act and deed and the land and premises therein mentioned to be the right and estate of the within named James Wilson Perry his heirs and assigns forever according to the true intent and meaning thereof and the act of Assembly in such cases made and provided, At the same time Came Leah the wife of the said Thomas and she being Examined privately and apart from her husband renounced all her right and title of dower of in and to the within mentioned land and premises unto the said James Wilson Perry his heirs and assigns and declared that she did the same freely and voluntarily without being induced thereto by fear of threats or of ill usage from her husband or through fear of incurring his displeasure

Wᵐ Smith Thoˢ Simpson[11]

In 1766, *Addition to Easy Purchase* then in Frederick Co., MD and comprised of 145 1/2 acres, was acquired by Thomas Trundle I.[12] After Thomas Trundle II, as heir of Thomas I, sold the three parts mentioned in these three deeds, he was left with only 22 1/2 acres of that parcel of land. Thomas Trundle II may have died soon after 1806. By 1810 his likely widow, Leah (?Shaw) Trundle, was head of a family in Montgomery Co., MD. In her household were: one white male under ten, one white male at least ten but under 16, two white females under ten, one white female at least ten but under 16, one white female at least 26 but under 45, seven free persons of color, and 13 slaves.[13]

Thomas Trundle II was probably born in Montgomery Co., MD on the property called *Addition to Easy Purchase*. As heir of Thomas Trundle I he seems to have lived there the rest of his short life. He and his wife, Leah, were probably members of Prince George's Parish. Apparently he was literate, having signed in full the three deeds covered here. It is possible he died by the age of 30 leaving a widow and young children.

Children of Thomas II and Leah (?Shaw) Trundle, all born in Montgomery Co., MD:

i.   Lethe⁵, b. 16 July 1797;[14] prob. m. 23 Mar. 1815 Montgomery Co., MD, **JAMES LEE**.[15]

ii. Poss. son, b. *ca.* 1798.[16]

iii. Sarah Shaw, b. 10 Mar. 1800;[17]

iv. Thomas Wood, b. 10 Mar. 1800 (twin of Sarah Shaw);[18] m. 18 Mar. 1823 Montgomery Co., MD, **HENNY ADAMS**.[19]

v.   Prob. dau. b. aft. 1800 but bef. 1810.[20]

6. THOMAS⁴ BOB TRUNDLE or **THOMAS TRUNDLE III** (John III³, John II², John I¹) (see 4), b. 16 Jan. 1746/47[21] prob. Prince George's Co., MD;[22] d. bet. 8 Oct. 1793

---

[11] Ibid., ff. 467-469, ahp.

[12] Frederick Co., MD, Deed Liber K, ff. 455-456, ahp.

[13] Montgomery Co., MD, NARA, 1810 census.

[14] Brown.

[15] Janet Thompson Manuel, comp., *Marriage Licenses Montgomery County, Maryland, 1798-1898* (Silver Spring, MD, 1987), p. 315. Her name appears as Alethea Trundle. Lethe may have been a nickname.

[16] Montgomery Co., MD, NARA, 1800 census.

[17] Brown.

[18] Ibid.

[19] Manuel, p. 316.

[20] Montgomery Co., MD, NARA, 1810 census,

[21] DAR membership papers of Anita Claire Willison #462691, descendant of Thomas III.

[22] "Old family document passed down through the Trundle/Thomas family," n. pag., copy, courtesy of Mrs Janice (Beall) Taylor, Urbanna, VA.

& 9 Feb. 1795 Montgomery Co., MD;[23] m. *ca.* 1769 prob. Frederick Co., MD, **RACHEL LEWIS**, b. 30 Mar. 1748 MD,[24] poss. Prince George's Co.; d. 1822 Bourbon Co., KY.[25] poss. d/o Daniel Lewis (see Lewis Families, Chapter Two, No. 2, ii). Rachel (Lewis) Trundle m. (2) by 8 Oct. 1813 prob. Bourbon Co., KY, James Matson.[26]

Thomas Trundle III or Thomas Bob Trundle as his name appeared in the will of his father, John III,[27] was probably a son of the first wife of John III, Alethia (---) Trundle.[28] It is possible John Trundle III had an earlier wife who was the mother of Thomas III. Other than in his father's will, his name was not found as Thomas Bob. He grew up in the home of his father, John III. He may have had no memory of his mother, but would have been cared for by his step-mother, Ann (---) Trundle.

Circa 1769 Thomas Trundle III married Rachel Lewis. On 16 May 1769 as a young man his name appeared as Thomas Trundell Jr., planter of Frederick Co., MD. In a deed of gift he received one Negro girl named Sarah from his uncle, Thomas Trundle I, whose name appeared as Thomas Trundell Sr.[29] In 1777 Thomas III as Thomas Trundell was taxed in Lower Part of Newfoundland Hundred, Montgomery Co., MD with one taxable in his household. Daniel Lewis Sr. was also living in Lower Part of Newfoundland Hundred.[30] There must have been a relationship between the wife of Thomas Trundle III who was Rachel Lewis and Daniel Lewis Sr. This was during the American Revolution and in 1777 Thomas Trundle III was a private, 7th Co., 29th (Lower) Bn., Maryland Militia.[31] In 1778 when he signed the Oath of Fidelity to the State of Maryland from Montgomery Co., the name of Thomas III appeared as Thomas Trundel.[32] That same year, 1778, he was again taxed in Lower Newfoundland Hundred, Montgomery Co.[33] He further supported the war against the British by supplying wheat and as Thomas Trunell received receipts for same 10 Apr. and 31 Oct. 1781.[34]

On 1 Jan. 1779 Thomas Trundle III as Thomas Trundell Jr. acquired a tract of land in Montgomery Co., MD called *John and Elizabeth*, being part of a tract called *Three Bealls Manor*, from Daniel Lewis who may have been his father-in-law. Thomas III paid £759 for the 108 acres and the deed was as follows:

At the Request of Thomas Trundell Junior the following Deed was Received January the 1st 1779 to wit. This Indenture made the twelfth Day of December in the year of our Lord God one thousand seven hundred and seventy eight - between Daniel Lewis of Montgomery County and State of Maryland of the one part planter and Thomas Trundell Junior of the County and State or province of the other part planter witnesseth that the said Daniel Lewis for and in consideration of the sum

[23] Montgomery Co., MD, Will Liber C, f. 150, ahp; ibid., Will Liber 1, f. 305.
[24] DAR membership papers.
[25] Ibid.
[26] Montgomery Co., MD, Deed Liber Q, ff. 442-443, ahp.
[27] Frederick Co., MD, Will Liber A-1, ff. 399-400, ahp.
[28] DAR membership papers of Florence Michele Remmele #524815, descendant of John Trundle IV or John Basel named as a son in the will of John III. Pauline Beard Cooney, comp., *History of the Beard - Bedichek - Craven and Allied Families* (1979, p. 159 has her name as Aletha and mother of John IV.
[29] Frederick Co., MD, Deed Liber M, f. 221, ahp.
[30] Eleanor M.V. Cook, "1777 Tax List of Montgomery County," *Maryland Genealogical Society Bulletin* (1990), v. 31, pp. 5-6.
[31] S. Eugene Clements & F. Edward Wright, *The Maryland Militia in the Revolutionary War* (1987), pp. 198-200.
[32] Margaret Roberts Hodges, comp., *Unpublished Revolutionary Records of Maryland* (1939), v. 3, p. 62; *Montgomery Co., Md. Oath of Fidelity & Tax Lists - 1778*, pp. 3-8, presented by Mrs. Lilly C. Stone through The Janet Montgomery Chapter, DAR (1949) has the name transcribed as Thomas Trundle.
[33] Ibid., pp. 67-69.
[34] Edward C. Papenfuse et al., *An Inventory of Maryland State Papers, Volume I, The Era of the American Revolution 1775-1789* (Hall of Records, Annapolis, 1977), pp. 380, 452.

of seven hundred and fifty nine Pounds Current Money to him in hand paid before the Sealing and delivery of these presents the receipt whereof the said Daniel Lewis doth hereby acknowledge and the said Thomas Trundell Junior his heirs Executors Administrators and Assigns thereof and of every part and parcel thereof are hereby forever exonerated requited and discharged he the said Daniel Lewis hath given granted bargained and sold aliened enfeoffed and confirmed and by these presents doth give grant bargain and sell alien enfeoff and confirm unto him the said Thomas Trundell Junior his heirs and assigns for ever all that Tract or parcel of Land called John and Elizabeth being part of a Tract of Land called "Three Bealls Manor situate lying and being in Montgomery County and State aforesaid beginning at a Stake near a bounded White Oak being the beginning Tree and of the Original Tract and standing South three perches and an half from said Tree and running thence North fifty five Degrees and an half Degree west twenty and three perches then North forty Degrees East one hundred and seventeen perches then North twenty seven Degrees East forty four perches then South forty eight Degrees East ninety perches then South twelve Degrees East one hundred and fifty perches then with a straight line to the beginning stake containing and laid out for One hundred and eight Acres of Land more or less together with all the dwelling houses out houses Orchards fences and all other the improvements advantages and appurtenances to the said Tract or parcel of Land belonging or in any manner of way appertaining and also the reversion and reversions remainder and remainders and all and singular the estate right title and interest of him the said Daniel Lewis in and to the Tract or parcel of Land and premises aforesaid to have and to hold the said Tract or parcel of Land and premises to him the said Thomas Trundell Junior his heirs and Assigns for ever to the only proper use and behoof of the said Thomas Trundell junior his heirs and Assigns for ever and to and for no other use intent or purpose whatsoever and the said Daniel Lewis for himself his heirs Executors and Administrators by these presents covenant and agree to and with the said Thomas Trundell junior his heirs and Assigns that he the said Daniel Lewis his heirs Executors and Administrators the said Tract or parcel of Land and all and singular the premises and appurtenances to the said Thomas Trundell junior his heirs and Assigns against him and his heirs and against all manner of persons whatsoever shall and will warrant and forever defend by these presents and lastly the said Daniel Lewis for himself his heirs Executors and Administrators doth covenant and agree to and with the said Thomas Trundell junior his heirs and Assigns by these presents that he the said Daniel Lewis his heirs Executors and Administrators shall and will at any time hereafter and at the proper Cost and Charges in the Law of him the said Thomas Trundell junior make and execute any further or other Deed or Deeds which may be reasonably devised advised or required for the better and more effectually conveying and assuring the Land and premises above mentioned to the said Thomas Trundell junior his heirs and Assigns for ever In Witness whereof the Said Daniel Lewis hath to these presents set his hand and Seal the Day and year first above written

Signed Sealed and Delivered
in the presence of
Charles Jones Richard Thompson

Daniel D Lewis
his

mark

(Seal)

On the Back of which Deed was thus endorsed to wit
Received the Day and Year within written of Thomas Trundell junior the Sum of Seven hundred and fifty nine pounds Current Money being the full consideration of the Land and premises within mentioned I say received by me

Daniel D Lewis
his

mark

Witness Charles Jones Richard Thompson

On the Day and year within written came before us two of the Justices of the Law for Montgomery County Daniel Lewis party to the within Deed who acknowledged the same to be his Act and Deed and the Land and premises therein mentioned to be the right property and Estate of the within named Thomas Trundell junior his heirs and Assigns forever and according to the Form of the Act of Assembly in such cases made and provided At the same time came Margaret the Wife of the said Daniel Lewis and being by us privately Examined apart and out of the hearing of her said Husband relinquished her right of Dower to the within Land and premises and declared the same to be the right property and estate of the said Thomas Trundell junior his heirs and Assigns forever and that she made this acknowledgment freely and willingly without threats from her said Husband or fear of his displeasure and according to the form of the Act of Assembly in such cases made and provided Acknowledged before us Charles Jones Richard Thompson[35]

He kept this property only a short time. On 10 Sep. 1781 Thomas III for the sum of £3,120, deeded the 108 acres known as *John and Elizabeth* to his brother, John Trundle IV (one quarter of an acre for graveyard excepted). Thomas III signed the deed as Thomas Trundle Jun[r]. The name of the wife of Thomas III, Rachel (Lewis) Trundle, does not appear in this 1781 deed.[36] This seems to have been an oversight. On 12 Apr. 1796 Rachel (Lewis) Trundle, widow of Thomas III, remedied this with a release of dower for *John and Elizabeth* to Ruth (Lewis) Trundle, widow of John IV, as follows:

At the request of Ruth Trundle the following release of Dower was recorded the 12th day of april 1796 to wit Be it known that Rachel Trundle of Montgomery county and state of Maryland widow of Thomas Trundle of the one part and Ruth Trundle of said county and state widow of John Trundle of the other part witnesseth that the said Rachel Trundle for and in consideration of a bargain and contract entered into by Thomas Trundle her late husband with John Trundle [the] Late husband of the said ruth Trundle for a certain tract or parcel of land situat lying and being in said county and known by the name of John and Elizabeth being part of a tract of Land caled three Bealls Manner which will more fully appear by a deed of conveyance from Thomas Trundle to the said John Trundle recorded among the Land records of Montgomery county in Liber B, folio 15 and 16 which will more fully appear by referrence being had thereto, & now the intent and meaning of these presents is that whereas the said Rachell Trundle never did Relinquish her right of dower in the said Land that she the said Rachell Trundle do freely willing and absolutely forever hereafter all and every her right and title of Dower in the aforesaid Land and premises and further that she conveys all her right and title in said Land to the af[d]. Ruth Trundle for the use and benefit of her the said Ruth Trundle as also for the use and benefit of the heirs of John Trundle in witness whereof the said Rachell Trundle hath hereunto set her hand and seal the twenty third day of January in the year one thousand seven hundred and ninety six
Signed Sealed and Delivered in presents of   Rachel Trundle   (seal)
An[s] Campbell Lawrence ONeale
On the back of which release of dower is the following Endorsement to wit.
Montgomery County State of Maryland the 23[d] day [of] January 1796. M[rs]. Rachell Trundle appeared before us two of the Justices of the Peace in said county and acknowledged the within Instrument of writing to be his act and deed and that all the right and title that she hath or ought to have for dower in the within named Land is the right title and estate of Ruth Trundle for herself and the heirs of John Trundle
Acknowledged before us An[s] Campbell Lawrence ONeale[37]

Thomas Trundle III seems to have moved from Montgomery Co.[38] about 1781. His name is missing from the 1783 tax assessment of Montgomery Co., MD.[39] According to the church register of King George's Parish, Prince George's Co., MD, Thomas Trundle III and his wife, Rachel, had a son, Thomas or Thomas IV, born 9 Mar. 1787.[40]

---

[35] Montgomery Co., MD, Deed Liber A, ff. 219-221, ahp.
[36] Ibid., Deed Liber B, ff. 15-16, ahp.
[37] Ibid., Deed Liber G, ff. 194-195, ahp.
[38] Ibid., Deed Liber C, ff. 530-531, ahp.
[39] Eleanor M.V. Cook, *1783 Maryland General Assessment Montgomery County, Maryland and 1782 Maryland General Assessment Upper Potomac Hundred* (1997), p. 9. The one Thomas Trundle listed would have been Thomas I rather than Thomas III.
[40] Brown, v. 1, p. 138.

On 21 May 1787 Thomas Trundle III as Thomas Trundell Jr., planter of Prince George's Co., MD, acquired two tracts of land in Montgomery Co., MD. The two tracts known as *Kent* and *Mount Pleasant* consisted of 312 acres and were deeded from William Roby Owen. This was for and in consideration of 250 acres of land in Stone Settlement, PA and the sum of £100 paid by the said Thomas Trundell, Jr. The deed was as follows:

At the Request of Thomas Trundell the following Deed was recorded with us the 21st day May 1757, (sic) To wit. This Indenture made the thirteenth day of March in the year of our Lord one Thousand seven hundred and Eighty seven. Between William Roby owen of Montgomery County & state of maryland of the one part Planter and Thomas Trundell Junior of Prince George's County and state aforesaid of the other part Planter Witnesseth that the said William Roby Owen for and in consideration & two hundred & fifty acres of Land in the Stone Settlement & state of Pennsylvania and also for and in consideration of the Sum of one hundred Pounds Current money to him in hand paid by the Said Thomas Trundell the receipt whereof the said William Robey Owen doth hereby acknowledge & the said Thomas Trundell his heirs executors adm^{rs}. & Assigns Men of authority forever exonerated righted and discharged he the said William Robey Owen hath given granted Bargained sold aliened enfeoffed and confirmed and by these presents doth fully freely clearly and absolutely give grant bargain sell alien enfeoff and confirm unto him the said Thomas Trundell his heirs and assigns forever all that parcel of Land consisting of two tracts the original known by the name of Kent and the addition by that of mount pleasant situate and being near the head of seneca in montgomery County & state aforesaid Beginning for the out lines comprehending the whole at the end of sixty four perches (?) in the third line of the original and running thence north fifty one degrees West Twenty perches North sixty two degrees west Ninety six perches north seventy degrees east forty four perches west Ninety two perches south forty eight degrees east eighty seven perches south eighty one degrees east ninety six perches south forty seven degrees west (?) (?) perches South three degrees west Forty two perches south eighty eight degrees west fifty perches south two degrees East one hundred and ten perches south sixty two degrees east eighty eight perches east eighty eight north seventeen degrees west seventy five perches North thirty five degrees east fifty perches north forty one degrees East one hundred & Twenty seven perches north twenty five degrees east one hundred & two perches north eighty one degrees west forty eight perches Then with a straight Line to the beginning containing and laid out for three hundred & twelve acres of land more or Less together with all and singular the dwelling houses out houses on hand & fences improvements of any kind advantages and appurtenances to the Land and premises above mentioned belonging or in any manner of wise appurtaining and also the revision and revisions remainder and remainders and all and singular the estate right Title and Interest of him the said William Roby Owen in and for the Land & premises above mentioned to have and to hold the said Land and premises unto the said Thomas Trundell his heirs and assigns to the only proper use of the said Thomas Trundell his heirs and assigns forever and to and for no other use intent or purpose whatsoever and the said William Roby owen doth for himself his heirs Ex^{rs} and ad^{ms}. covenant and agree to and with the said Thomas Trundell his heirs and assigns by these presents that the said Wm Roby Owen all the aforesaid Land premises with all and singular the appurtenances unto the s^d Thomas Trundell his heirs and assigns against him and his heirs and agents all manner of persons whatsoever shall and will forever warrant and defend by these presents and Lastly the said W^m. Roby Owen doth for himself his heirs ex^{rs}. Adm^{rs}. warrant (?) to and with the said Thomas Trundell his heirs & assigns by these presents that the s^d Wm Roby owen his heirs ex^{trs}. & adm^{rs}. shall and will at any time or times hereafter at the reasonable request and at the proper Cost and Charge of the said Thomas Trundle his heirs or assigns make and execute any future or other deed for the better conveying and assuring all the aforesaid land and premises to the said Thomas Trundle his heirs and assigns forever which may be reasonably advised devised or required in witness wherof the said William Roby owen hath hereunto set his hand & seal the day & year first above written

                              William Roby Owen (seal)

Signed sealed and delivered in the presence of   An^s Campbell R Wootton

On the back of which deed was written and to wit Received the day & year within written the Two hundred & fifty acres of Land in the s^d Stone Settlement as also the sum of one hundred pounds current money being the consideration of the Land & premises within mentioned William Roby Owen

Witness An⁵ Campbell R Wootton

State of Maryland Montgomery County on the day and year within written came before us two of the Justices for state county aforesaid Wᵐ. Roby Owen freely to the within said and acknowledged the same to be his act & deed & the Land & premises therein mentioned to be the right property and estate of the within named Thomas Trundell his heirs & assigns forever At the same time came Frances the wife of the said Wᵐ Roby Owen and being before privately examined apart and out of the hearing of her said husband relinquished and gave up to Thomas Trundell his heirs Assigns her right of dower to the Land & premises within mentioned & declared stated the same freely & willingly without being induced threats by (?) from her said husband or for fear of his displeasure and according to act of assembly in such cases made and provided, acknowledged before us

An⁵ Campbell R Wootton[41]

It is not clear whether Thomas Trundle III lived in Stone Settlement, PA at any time between 1781 and 1787. By 1787 he was living in Prince George's Co., MD. Just over two years later, 19 June 1789, he acquired another 200 acres of land in Montgomery Co. from Robert Beall of James. He paid £256 current money of Maryland for the land, part of two tracts of land known as *Roberts Choice* and *Kindal Meadows*. The deed was as follows:

At The request of Thomas Trundle the following deed was recorded this 19ᵗʰ. day of June 1789. To Wit,, This Indenture made this Nineteenth day of June one Thousand Seven hundred and Eighty Nine Between Robert Beall of James montgomery County in the province of maryland of The one part - and Thomas Trundle of the County and province aforesaid of the other part. Whereforth that the said Robert Beall for and in the consideration of The sum of Two hundred and fifty six pounds Current money of Maryland in hand paid by The said Thomas Trundle, the receipt Whereof is freely acknowledged and of every part Thereof acquit and fully discharge, the said Thomas Trundle, hath granted Bargained and sold by These presents. the said Robert Beall. doth give grant bargain and sell. unto The said Thomas Trundle. his heirs and assigns forever part of Two Tracts of Land called Roberts Choice, and the second resurvey in partnership Beginning at the End of the eighteenth Line of a Tract of Land called Kindal meadows and running With the said Land South Seventy nine degrees East one hundred and eight perches then North one hundred and seventy perches. then South seventy one degrees West seventy four perches then North seventy degrees. West seventy perches. then South West by south one hundred and sixty seven perches. Then With a straight line to the Beginning. containing Two hundred acres of land more or Less. To have and To hold the said Land and premises together With all and Singular the improvements conveniences and advantages to the said Land and premis Contained Within the meets and Limits afore Expressed or in any manner of Way appurtaining To the only proper use and Behoof of him The said Thomas Trundle his heirs and assigns forever and To no other use intent or purpose Whatsoever and the said Robert Beall doth for himself his heirs Executors and administrators Covenant promise grant and agree To and With the said Thomas Trundle. his heirs and assigns the aforesaid Two hundred acres of Land and Every part. and parcel Thereof against all manner of persons Whatsoever for Ever hereafter to Warrant and defend and further The said Robert Beall of James doth for himself his heirs Executors and administrators Covenant promise grant and agree To and with the said Thomas Trundle his heirs and assigns that he the said Robert Beall his heirs and assigns shall and Will from Time To time and at all Times hereafter at the a reasonable request and The proper Cost and Charges in The Law of him The said Thomas Trundle his heirs and assigns do make acknowledge suffer and Execute any further deed or instrument in Writing such as the said Thomas Trundle his heirs or assigns his or their council Learned in The law shall reasonably devise or advise for the further and Better assurance surely and suremaking the Land and premises aforesaid unto him

---

[41] Montgomery Co., MD, Deed Liber C, ff. 530-531, ahp.

The said Thomas Trundle his heirs and assigns forever In Witness Whereof the said Robert Beall of James hath hereunto set his hand and seal the day and year Above Written
Signed Sealed and Delivered in the presents of
SamlW Magruder Richard Thompson --   Robert Beall of Ja⁵. (seal)
on the Back of Which deed Were The following Endorsements. To wit.. June 19ᵗʰ 1789. Receiv⁴. of Thomas Trundle the sum of Two hundred and fifty six pounds Current money it Being full Satisfaction for the Within Land and premises
Witness   Robert Beall of Ja⁵.
SamlW Magruder Richard Thompson
Montgomery County (?) June 19ᵗʰ 1789 Then came Robert Beall of James party to the Within deed before The subscribers Two of The Justices of the peace for The County Aforesaid and acknowledged The Within deed as his act and deed and The Land and premises to be the right of The Within mentioned Thomas Trundle his heirs and assigns forever
Acknowledged Before SamlW Magruder Richard Thompson -⁴²

In 1790 Thomas Trundle III was head of a family in Montgomery Co., MD. He was the Thomas Trundle with a household composed of: two white males 16 years and upward, four white males under 16, four white females, and nine slaves.⁴³ By 1793 his health had failed and on 8 Oct. 1793 as Thomas Trundle he made his will in Montgomery Co., MD as follows:

In The Name of God Amen I Thomas Trundle of Montgomery County and State of Maryland being at this time very Sick and Weak and knowing the certainty of death to all Flesh Trusting to the Lord Jesus Christ for the Redemption of Soul through his Most precious Merrits in whom I fully put my Trust I Bless God though my Body is weak and Low I think myself in my full and proper Senses and I think myself to be properly of sound dispossing mind and Memory, Make this my Last Will or Testament disallowing all and every Will heretofore by me made and this only to be my Last Will---
First I Will my Soul to Almighty God who gave it me and my Body to the Earth to be Decently buried at the Discration of my Executrix and Executor to be hereafter Named-----
Secondly I will and Desire all my Just Debts to be paid-----
Thirdly as to what Worldley Good that god hath blessed me with I give and bequeath in the following Manner to Wit As I am siezed in a tract or parcell of Land by the Name of Trundles Inheritance and think the Land Mean for my Family to Live on, If my Executrix and Executor with the consent of my Son Evan Trundle they may Sel the said tract of Land and also with the Consent of my son Evan Lay out the money arrising from the Sale in Better Land to Live on in Order that they may be better able to Raise my small Childreen and in case the Land is sold as aforesaid Impower my Executrix and Executor to Convey it to the Purchaser in Common form but If the aforesaid Land is not sold or if it should and--- Other Land Bought with the Purchass money Should be appraised and each of my Childreen to have shar and share alike and that if any of my Childreen should Chuse to pay the appraisement the oldest one or ones having the Preferiance that it shall be Lawfull for either of my Childreen to hold the Present Land or the Land Bought by paying to the Other Childreen there share according to the Appraisement. But it is to be understood that one part of the above is to Deprive my Loving Wife Rachell Trundle of her Right of Dower during her Naturall Life of the Land I now possess or of the Land Bought with the Purchass money of the Land Sold---
And as to my Personal Estate as well as my Landed Estate after my Loving ʷⁱᶠᵉ Rachell Trundle hath her part as the Law directs The whole of the Residue to be Equally divided amongst my Childreen to wit
Basiele, Evan, Thomas and Daniel Trundle my four sons and Massey Rachell and Delilah Trundle my three Daughters share and share alike And it is my will that all my Childreen be to act and do for themself at sixteen years of Age and then to Receive there part or share of my Personall Estate And provided my Wife Continues a Widow and take proper Care of her Childreen each ones part of

⁴² Ibid., Deed Liber D, ff. 225-226, ahp.
⁴³ *Heads of Families*, p. 89.

the Landed Estate is to Remain in her hand untill the youngest Arrives at sixteen years The Reason of the share or part of my Landed Estate is to Remain in my Executrix and Executors-- hand is that they might be the better able to Educate and Raise the younger Childreen but should it be Necessary for them to Chuse Gardians from Neglect of there Education or any ill treat ment my will in that Case is that the Gardian shall Receive as well the part of the Reall Estate as the Personall Estate, it is to be Observed that all the Childreen Male and Female are free to Act and do for themselve at the Age of sixteen years and to Receive there share or part of my Estate as afore.

Lastly I constitut and appoint my Loveing Wife Rachell Trundle and Basiel Trundle my son Executrix and Executor of this my Last Will or Testament In Witness whereof I have hereunto set my hand and Seale the 8th day of October Anno Domini 1793------   Thomas Trundle

Signed Sealed and Pronounced in our hearing and the hearing
of Each of us that this Instrument of Writing Contain the Last
will or Testament of Thomas Trundle and at the same time we believe
him to be in his proper sences
An⁵ Campbell
N Stone
Samuel Edwards[44]

Thomas Trundle III died by 9 Feb. 1795[45] and there was an appraised inventory of his goods and chattels on 10 Mar. 1795 by John Williams and Thoˢ B. Beall. Creditors were Enoch J. Millard for Marsham Warring and Andrew Blair for John Laird.[46] David Trundle[47] and Evan Trundle, his mark, signed as nearest of kin. On 14 Apr. 1795 Rachel Trundle and Basil Trundle, executrix and executor, of the last will and testament of Thomas III as Thomas Trundle, made oath, "Samˡ Turner, Regʳ." The total value of the inventory, including six Negros, was £681.9.6.[48] The land referred to in his will as *Trundles Inheritance* was formerly known as *Kent* and *Mount Pleasant*.[49]

Thomas Trundle III seems to have grown to manhood in Frederick Co., MD where he probably married Rachel Lewis. By 1777 the area where they lived was in Lower Newfoundland Hundred in the new county of Montgomery. During the American Revolution he served as a private in the Maryland Militia. As a planter he acquired land in Montgomery Co. in 1779 and he sold that land in 1781 when he seems to have left Montgomery Co. In 1787 he was living in Prince George's Co., MD where he and his wife seem to have been members of King George's Parish. In 1787 he again acquired land back in Montgomery Co. where he lived the rest of his life. He was apparently literate and accumulated significant wealth in his time. By early 1795 he had died, probably at about age 50.

Rachel (Lewis) Trundle survived her husband. On 14 Apr. 1795 she served as executrix of his will in Montgomery Co., MD. His son, Basil Trundle, was executor.[50] On 12 Apr. 1796 her name appeared as Rachel Trundle in a release of dower to her sister-in-law, Ruth (Lewis) Trundle, both of Montgomery Co., MD. She signed her name in full as Rachel Trundle indicating she was literate.[51] In 1800 her name appeared as Rachel

⁴⁴ Montgomery Co., MD, Will Liber C, f. 150, author has photocopy of original.
⁴⁵ Ibid., Will Liber 1, f. 305.
⁴⁶ Ibid., Inventory Liber C, pp. 259-261, typed record, pp. 157-158, found at MCHS.
⁴⁷ Perhaps meant to be another son as the name, David Trundle, does not appear in the will (Montgomery Co., MD, Will Liber C, f. 150) and other records.
⁴⁸ Montgomery Co., MD, Inventory Liber C, pp. 259-261, typed record, pp. 157-158, found at MCHS.
⁴⁹ Ibid., Deed Liber Q, ff. 442-443, ahp.
⁵⁰ Ibid., Inventory Liber C, ff. 259-261.
⁵¹ Ibid., Deed Liber G, ff. 194-195, ahp.

Trundle when she was living in Montgomery Co. In her household were: one white male under ten, one white male at least ten but under 16, one white male at least 26 but under 45, three white females at least 16 but under 26, one white female 45 or over, and eight slaves.[52] Perhaps her son, Basil Trundle, and his young wife were living with her in 1800.[53] Her son, Evan Trundle, appeared to be living nearby.[54]

By 6 Nov. 1802 Basil Trundle had moved to Bourbon Co., KY. Perhaps his mother, Rachel (Lewis) Trundle, and her younger children moved there with him. Her son, Evan Trundle, was still in Montgomery Co., MD as of that date. This information can be noted from two partition deeds. The following deed was from Evan Trundle to Basil Trundle:

At the request of Basil Trundle the following Deed was recorded the 29th day of April 1803 to wit Know all men by these presence that I Evan Trundle of Montgomery county and state of Maryland of the one part and Basil Trundle of Burbon county and state of Kentucky of the other part Witnesseth that the said Evan Trundle for and in consideration of the sum of one hundred and fifty dollars the receipt of which the said Evan Trundle hereby confers and acknowledge and himself therewith fully satisfied and content and do exonerate and forever discharge the said Basul Trundle his heirs executors and administrators from all and every part and parcel thereof and he the said Evan Trundle therewith fully satisfied and content Hath given granted bargained sold and confirmed and conveyed in fee simple and by these presents do give grant bargain sell confirm and convey in fee Simple to Basiel Trundel all and every of my part or share undivided of a tract or parcell of land and every part of a tract of land called Trundles inheritance it being my part and share of land willed to me by my father Thomas Trundle of said County and state of maryland with all and every right title& interest in all the land and premise willed to me the said Evan Trundle by my said Father Thomas Trundle which will more fully appear by the will of my said father now the intent and meaning of the deed is that the said Evan Trundle do sell to the said Basil Trundle all and every all my right title and interest that I have or ought to have in all the landed estate of my said Father Thomas Trundle and that the said Basil Trundle shall have and hold the said land with all and every of the appurtenances thereunto belonging or in any wise appertaining forever hereafter against the said Even Trundle his heirs and all and every person claim by through or under him the Evan Trundle and he further covenants and agrees that he the said Evan Trundle his heirs executors and administrators shall and will at any time hereafter make do and execute any other instrument deed or deeds in writing that the counsell of the said Basiel Trundle larned in the law shall reasonabley advise require so it contains no more than a specialty for all the right that I the said Evan Trundle have or ought to have in all the landed property of said Father Thomas Trundel In witness whereof I the said Evan Trundle have hereinto sett his hand and seal the 6th day of November 1802

Signed sealed and delivered in presence of
AEn⁵. Campbell Lenox Martin

                            his
                     Evan X Trundle (seal)
                         mark

On the back of the aforegoing Deed are the following Endorsements To wit Montgomery County state of Maryland 6 day November, 1802 Evan Trundle appeared before use two of the Justice of the peace in said County and acknowledged the with land and premises to be the right property and estate of Basil Trundle his heirs and assigns forever and at the same time came Ann the wife of the said Evan Trundle she being taken apart and out of the hearing of her said husband and acknowled her right of dower to the said Basiel Trundle his heirs and assigns and that she doth the same freely and willing of her own free will and accord without being induced thereto by fear or threats or fear of his displeasure

     Acknowledged before   AEn⁵. Campbell Lenox Martin[55]

---

[52] Ibid., NARA, 1800 census, roll 11, p. 32 or 212.
[53] Ibid. Basil Trundle m. 20 May 1799 Montgomery Co., MD, Easter Hughes (Manuel, p. 315).
[54] Montgomery Co., MD, NARA, 1800 census, roll 11, p. 32 or 212.
[55] Ibid., Deed Liber K, ff. 471-472, ahp.

Neither Rachel (Lewis) Trundle nor heirs of Thomas Trundle III were found to be living in Maryland in 1810.[56] By then she had probably married James Matson of Bourbon Co., KY where in 1810 he was head of a family. In his household were: one white male at least ten but under 16, three white males at least 16 but under 26, one white male 45 or over, one white female 45 or over, and 31 slaves.[57] Some of the children living with James Matson may have been younger children of Rachel (Lewis) Trundle Matson. Also found as 1810 heads of families in Bourbon Co. were: sons, Evan[58] and Bazil;[59] and son-in-law, Thomas Howard.[60] They were living there on 9 Aug. 1813 when she signed her name in full as Rachel Matson in the deed which follows:

At the request of Thomas Howard the following Deed was recorded 8th October 1813 (towit) This Indenture made this seventh day of August 1813 between Bazil Trundle and Esther his wife Thomas Trundle and Daniel Trundle all of the county of Bourbon and State of Kentucky, being heirs and legal representatives of Thomas Trundle late of the county of montgomery and State of maryland now deceased of the one part and Thomas Howard of the county of Bourbon and State of Kentucky aforesaid of the other part Witnesseth that the said Bazil, Thomas and Daniel Trundle for and in consideration of the sum of three hundred dollars current money of Kentucky to them in hand paid the receipt whereof - is hereby acknowledged have granted bargained and sold and by these presents do grant bargain, sell alien and confirm unto the said Thomas Howard his heirs and assigns all their undivided parts shares and Interest in and to two tracts of land devised to us by Thomas Trundle deceased which tracts of land were known by the name of Kent and Mount Pleasant and lately by the name of Trundles Inheritance situate lying and being in the county of montgomery and State of Maryland, on the head waters of Seneca, which tracts of land contain in all three hundred and twelve acres. being the same tracts of land that were conveyed by William Roby Owen to their ancestor Thomas Trundle deceased by Deed bearing date the 13th.. day of March 1787. and devised the said heirs by his last will and testament. Together with all and singular the premises thereunto belonging or in any wise appertaining. To have and To hold the said shares of land with all its appertenances unto him the said Thomas Howard his heirs and assigns forever. And the said Bazil Trundle Thomas Trundle and Daniel Trundle for themselves their heirs executors & their shares of the land aforesaid with the appertenances unto the said Thomas Howard his heirs and assigns against the claim or claims of themselves their heirs & and all persons claiming under them but against the claim or claims of no other person or persons. do and will warrant & forever defend by these presents. In Witness whereof the said Bazil Trundle, Thomas Trundle and Daniel Trundle hath hereunto set their hands & seals the day and year first above written -

    Basil Trundle   (seal)   Thomas Trundle   (seal)   Daniel Trundle   (seal)
Know all men by these presents that we James Matson and Rachel Matson (late Rachel Trundle widow and relict of Thomas Trundle dec'd. who is named in the foregoing deed) have and by these presents do for and in consideration of the sum of one hundred dollars relinquish unto Thomas Howard his heirs & all our right title interest and claim to the tracts of land mentioned in the foregoing deed - Witness our hands and seals this ninth day of August 1813 James Matson (seal)
Attest William Jones, T.D. Watts, Thomas Berry   Rachel Matson (seal)
Bourbon County towit came before us the Subscribers two Justices of the peace in and for the county of aforesaid Basil Trundle Thomas Trundle & Daniel Trundle who acknowledged the foregoing Indenture of bargain and sale to Thomas Howard to be their act and deed for the purposes therein mentioned - also a relinquishment or Instrument of writing annexed to said deed on the part of James Matson was proved by the oaths of Wm.. Jones T.D. Watts & Thomas Berry Witnesseth thereto subscribed - and on the part of Rachel Matson wife of the said James Matson it was

56 Ronald Vern Teeples et al., *Maryland 1810 Census Index* (Bountiful, UT, 1976).
57 Bourbon Co., KY, NARA, 1810 census, roll 5, p. 250.
58 Ibid., p. 132 or 261, name appears as Ivin Trunnells.
59 Ibid., n. pag. living in Paris.
60 Ibid., p. 244.

acknowledged by the said Rachel to be her act and deed for the purposes therein mentioned. Given under our hands and seals this ninth day of August 1813. Thomas Hughes 〔seal〕

State of Kentucky (?)   Tho. Jones 〔seal〕

    I William Garrard Jr. Clerk of the County Court of Bourbon in the State of aforesaid do certify that Thomas Hughes and Thomas Jones Jr esquires before whom the within deeds of conveyance were acknowledged and whose signatures are annexed thereto, were at the time of taking and subscribing to the same and still are two of the acting Justices of the peace in and for the county aforesaid duly commissioned & sworn & that to such certificates and official acts full faith & credit is due & ought to be had & given as well in courts of Justice as thereout.

Bourbon County Court Kentucky   In Testimony whereof I have hereunto set my hand and affixed the seal of my office this ninth day of August 1813 and in the XXII year of the Commonwealth   Will Garrard Jr..

State of Kentucky (?) I, Joseph L. Stephens presiding magistrate of the County court of Bourbon in the absence of Thomas Rule who is senior magistrate in Bourbon County and in the State aforesaid, do certify that William Garrard Jr. is Clerk of our said court & that this foregoing attestation is in due form of law Given under my hand and Seal this 2nd. day of September 1813 -

        Joseph L. Stephens 〔seal〕 [61]

Rachel (Lewis) Trundle Matson died in Bourbon Co., KY in 1822 at about age 74.[62] Some Trundles in Kentucky spell the surname Trunnell.[63]

Children of Thomas III and Rachel (Lewis) Trundle:

    i.   Basil[5], b. prob. *ca.* 1771 Frederick Co., MD;[64] d. prob. KY;[65] m. 20 May 1799 Montgomery Co., MD, **ESTHER/EASTER HUGHES**,[66] d. prob. KY;[67] poss. m. (2) poss. KY, **HESTER ALLEN**.[68]

    ii.   Massey/Mary/Massian, b. poss. *ca.* 1773 Frederick Co., MD;[69] m. 27 May 1802 Montgomery Co., MD, **THOMAS HOWARD**.[70] Thomas Howard m. (1) 13 Dec. 1800 Montgomery Co., MD, Rachel Trundle.[71]

    iii. Rachel, b. poss. *ca.* 1775, Frederick Co., MD;[72] d. 16 Oct. 1801 Montgomery Co., MD;[73] m. 13 Dec. 1800 Montgomery Co., MD, **THOMAS HOWARD**.[74] Thomas Howard m. (2) 27 May 1802 Montgomery Co., MD, Massian Trundle.[75]

    iv.   Evan, b. 25 Aug. 1776[76] prob. Frederick Co., MD; m. 25? Jan. 1798 Montgomery Co., MD, **ANNA KEY**.[77]

[61] Montgomery Co., MD, Deed Liber Q, ff. 442-443, ahp.

[62] DAR membership papers of Anita Claire Willison; MSS, Trundle folder, MCHS.

[63] *History of Kentucky* (publishing info missing), pp. 754-755.

[64] *Heads of Families*, p. 89; Montgomery Co., MD, NARA, 1800 census, roll 11, p. 212.

[65] MSS, Trundle folder.

[66] Manuel, p. 315; MSS, Trundle folder.

[67] Ibid.

[68] DAR membership papers of Anita Claire Willison has his wife's name as Hester Allen.

[69] Montgomery Co., MD, Will Liber C, f. 150, author has photocopy of original; Montgomery Co., MD, NARA, 1800 census, roll 11, p. 212.

[70] "Hezikiah Wilson's Diary, Montgomery County, MD," *National Genealogical Society Quarterly* (1917), v. 6, p. 31 has her name as Massian.

[71] Manuel, p. 316.

[72] Montgomery Co., MD, Will Liber C, f. 150.

[73] "Hezekiah Wilson's Diary...," *National Genealogical Society Quarterly*, v. 6, pp. 28,30.

[74] Manuel, p. 316.

[75] "Hezekiah Wilson's Diary...," *National Genealogical Society Quarterly*, v. 6, p. 31.

[76] DAR membership papers of Anita Claire Willison.

[77] Robert Barnes, comp., *Maryland Marriages 1778-1800* (Baltimore, 1978), p. 231.

   v.   Delilah, b. poss. *ca.* 1784 Montgomery Co., MD;[78] m. poss. KY, **ROBERT BROWN**.[79]

   vi.   Thomas IV, b. 9 Mar. 1787 Prince George's Co., MD;[80] m. poss. KY, **PRISCILLA BOWMAN**.[81]

   vii.   Daniel, b. 9 July 1792[82] Montgomery Co., MD;[83] m. poss. KY, **BETSY AMOS**.[84]

7. JOHN[4] BASEL TRUNDLE or **JOHN TRUNDLE IV** (John III[3], John II[2], John I[1]) (see 4), b. *ca.* 1748[85] prob. Prince George's Co., MD;[86] d. by 26 Feb. 1795 Montgomery Co., MD,[87] bur. old family burying ground, David Trundle's, near Barnesville Dist., Dickerson Station, Montgomery Co., MD;[88] m. *ca.* 1771 prob. Frederick Co., MD, **RUTH LEWIS**,[89] b. 6 Mar. 1753[90] prob. Frederick Co., MD;[91] d. 25 Mar. 1810[92] Montgomery Co., MD,[93] bur. beside husb.;[94] d/o David & Drusilla (---) Lewis.[95]

John Trundle IV or John Basel Trundle as his name appeared in the will of his father, John III,[96] was surely a son of the first wife of John III, whose name has been given as Alethia (---) Trundle.[97] Other than in his father's will, his name was not found as John Basel. He grew up in the home of his father, John III. He probably had no memory of his mother, but would have been cared for by his step-mother, Ann (---) Trundle.

Circa 1771 John Trundle IV married Ruth Lewis. In 1776 as John Trundle, age 27, he was living in North West Hundred, Frederick Co., MD. In his household were Ruth, age 22; David, age three; John Lowos, age eight mos. In addition there were Negroes: Toney, age 24, and Tom, age three.[98]

In late 1776 the part of Frederick Co. where they lived became part of newly formed Montgomery Co. In 1777 John Trundle IV was living in North West Hundred, Montgomery Co. where his name appeared as John Trundle with two taxables in his household.[99] This was during the American Revolution and in 1777 John Trundle IV was

[78] Montgomery Co., MD, NARA, 1800 census, roll 11, p. 212.

[79] DAR membership papers of Anita Claire Willison.

[80] Brown, v. 1, p. 138; Montgomery Co., MD, Deed Liber C, ff. 530-531, ahp.

[81] DAR membership papers of Anita Claire Willison.

[82] Ibid.

[83] *Heads of Families*, p. 89; Montgomery Co., MD, NARA, 1800 census, roll 11, p. 212.

[84] DAR membership papers of Anita Claire Willison.

[85] Brumbaugh, p. 226.

[86] "Old family document..."

[87] Montgomery Co., MD, Inventory Liber C, pp. 265-267, typed record, pp. 162-163, found at MCHS.

[88] Gravestone, David Trundle's, near Barnesville Dist., Dickerson Station, Montgomery Co., MD, cited in Helen W. Ridgely, *Historic Graves of Maryland and the District of Columbia* (Baltimore, 1967), p. 181. This was at David Trundle's place where gravestone cited has mistakenly given b. & d. dates of Ruth (Lewis) Trundle to John Trundle. DAR membership papers of Margaret Wendel Jacobi #529069 gives location of cemetery as Beallsville, MD.

[89] Brumbaugh; DAR membership papers of Florence Michele Remmele.

[90] Gravestone, cited in Ridgely. Gravestone of John Trundle as cited gives him b. & d. dates of his wife, Ruth (Lewis) Trundle.

[91] Brumbaugh, p. 226.

[92] Gravestone, cited in Ridgely.

[93] Montgomery Co., MD, Will Liber G, ff. 149-151, ahp.

[94] Gravestone, cited in Ridgely.

[95] Cooney.

[96] Frederick Co., MD, Will Liber A-1, ff. 399-400, ahp.

[97] DAR membership papers of Florence Michele Remmele.

[98] Brumbaugh, p. 226.

[99] Cook, "1777 Tax List...," *Maryland Genealogical Society Bulletin*, v. 31, pp. 16-17.

a 2d Lieut., 6th Co., Middle Bn., Maryland Militia.[100] In Nov. 1777 his name appeared in a court record of Montgomery Co., MD.

> The Justices of the Court here ascertain the following Main Roads within Montgomery County and Appoint the following persons overseers thereof for the year 1778.
>
> ***
>
> 31.   From the Bladensburgh road near John Trundels to the George Town Road near John Claggetts and from Bladensburgh Road where the same turns off to George Town below Allen Bowies to Sligo Bridge near Mrs. Carrolls and from Richardsons Mill to the Main Road that leads to Andrew Heughs.
> _ _ _ Aaron Lanham[101]

In 1778 he signed the Oath of Fidelity to the State of Maryland from Montgomery Co. as John Trundel, his mark.[102] That same year, 1778, he was again taxed as John Trundle in Northwest Hundred, Montgomery Co.[103] He further supported the war against the British by supplying wheat and as John Trundle received receipts for same 9 Aug. and 14 Oct. 1780, and 6 Jan. 1781.[104]

On 10 Sep. 1781 John Trundle IV as John Trundle, planter of Montgomery Co., MD, for the sum of £3,120, acquired 108 acres known as *John and Elizabeth*. The land was purchased from his brother, Thomas Trundle III, whose name appeared as Thomas Trundle Jr. in the deed (one quarter of an acre for graveyard excepted).[105] By 1783 the area where John IV was living had become Lower Newfoundland Hundred, Montgomery Co. and he was assessed there in that year.[106] He was probably the person whose name appeared as John Trandel at the Frederick, Maryland Evangelical Lutheran Church on 15 Feb. 1785 as witness to the marriage of Archibald Browning and Margreth Louis/Lewis, Daniel Lewis' daughter.[107] In 1790 John Trundle IV was head of a family in Montgomery Co., MD. His household was composed of: two white males 16 years and upward, four white males under 16, five females and 16 slaves.[108]

John Trundle IV was very prosperous and had accumulated a lot of wealth by the time he died intestate. He had died by 26 Feb. 1795 when there was an inventory of his goods and chattels. His widow, Ruth (Lewis) Trundle, was administratrix. The total value of the inventory was £1,093.10.0. The following Negroes were included: man = Jacob; boys = Frederick, William, Harry, Isaac, Arche, and Hercules; child = Peter; women = Jenny, Rose, Flora, and Lucy; girls = Poll, Sall, and Nell; female = Nancy; small children = Milly and Jenny. Francis Deakins and Hezekiah Veatch represented Nicholas Marsteller and AEns Campbell, creditors. Basil and David Trundle were nearest kin,

---

[100] Clements, pp. 201-206.
[101] "Selections from 'November Court Minute Book,'" *Montgomery Co., Md. Oath of Fidelity...*, pp. 41, 45.
[102] *Montgomery Co., Md. Oath of Fidelity...*, p. 2.
[103] Ibid., pp. 54-56.
[104] Papenfuse, pp. 308, 326, 352.
[105] Montgomery Co., MD, Deed Liber B, ff. 15-16, ahp; ibid., Deed Liber A, ff. 219-221, ahp, published herein has description of land.
[106] Cook, *1783 Maryland General Assessment...* p. 9.
[107] Frederick Sheely Weiser, ed. & translator, *Records of Marriages and Burials in the Monocacy Church in Frederick County, Maryland and in the Evangelical Lutheran Congregation in the City of Frederick, Maryland 1743-1811* (Washington, 1972), pp. 40-41.
[108] *Heads of Families*, p. 90.

"Sam[l] Turner, Reg[r]."[109] By 12 Apr. 1797 Negro children: Rachel, ten months; and Lucy nine months had been born, both since the original inventory.[110]

John Trundle IV seems to have grown to manhood in Frederick Co., MD where he probably married Ruth Lewis. In 1776 they were living in North West Hundred, Frederick Co., MD with two children. By 1777 the area where they lived was in the new county of Montgomery. During the American Revolution he served as a 2d Lieut. in the Maryland Militia. In 1781 as a planter he acquired 108 acres in Montgomery Co. known as *John and Elizabeth.* He seems to have accumulated significant wealth. It is possible he became literate, though in 1778 he signed his name by mark. By early 1795 he had died, probably at about age 47.

Ruth (Lewis) Trundle survived her husband and was to conduct a lot of business on her own. On 26 Feb. 1795 she served as administratrix of his estate in Montgomery Co., MD. On 12 Apr. 1796 she received a release of dower from her sister-in-law, Rachel (Lewis) Trundle, for the land known as *John and Elizabeth.*[111] Ruth and Rachel must have been close kin, probably either first cousins or possibly sisters. Ruth (Lewis) Trundle acquired land after the death of her husband, John IV. On 3 Dec. 1796, for the sum of £33.6.8, she acquired from Abraham Graff, 108 3/4 acres called *Resurvey on Suburbs,* together with 247 1/2 acres from part of *Willetts Delay* and a tract called *Mount Pleasant.* The deed was as follows:

> At the request of Ruth Trundle the following Deed was recorded this 3rd day of December 1796 to wit. This Indenture made the fifteenth day of October Anno Domini one thousand seven hundred and ninety six between Abraham Graft of Montgomery County and state of Maryland of the one part and Ruth Trundle of the county and state aforesaid of the other part Witnesseth that whereas George Graft and Mary his wife had on or about the tenth day of april one thousand Seven hundred and seventy eight conveyed to them by Leonard Deakins a part of a tract of land called the resurvey on Suburbs containing about one hundred and eight acres and three quarters of an acre and whereas the said George Graft [hath] since died Intestate and his widow Mary Graft having since Inter married with Griffith Willett and they the said Griffith Willett and Mary his wife hath by their Deed bearing date with these presents conveyed the the aforesaid one hundred and eight acres and three quarters of an acre of land called part of the resurvey on Suburbs together with a part of Willetts delay and a tract called mount pleasant containing in the whole about two hundred and forty seven and a half acres unto the above mentioned Ruth Trundle as by the said Deed will more fully and at large appear and whereas there is some doubts in the purchaser Ruth Trundle that the above mentioned Abraham Graft hath some right and title to the aforesaid land called part of the resurvey on Suburbs as he being the oldest son and heir of his desceased father George Graft and in order to Satisfy those doubts in the purchaser Ruth Trundle and being at the same time willing that she should hold and enjoy the land I the said Abraham Graft have agreed and consented to give her this my deed to convey unto her all my right and title which I now may or shall hereafter have to the aforesaid land Called the resurvey on suburbs as formerly conveyed to my father and mother George and Mary Graft and which is now conveyed to Ruth Trundle by Griffith and Mary Willett as aforesaid Now this Indenture witnesseth that the said Abraham Graft for and in consideration of the above reasons as also for the sum of thirty three pounds six shillings and eight pence current money to him in hand at or before the sealing and delivering of these presents the receipt whereof is hereby acknowledged hath granted bargained and sold and by these presents doth grant bargain sell aliene confirm and make over unto her the said Ruth Trundle her heirs and assigns forever all that part of a tract or parcel of land called the resurvey on suburbs containing

---

[109] Montgomery Co., MD, Inventory Liber C, pp. 265-267, typed record, pp. 162-163, found at MCHS. Basil not found as a son in other records.
[110] Ibid., p. 567, typed record, p. 287, found at MCHS.
[111] Ibid., Deed Liber G, ff. 194-195, ahp.

about one hundred and eight acres and three quarters of an acre of land be the same more or less together with all the premises and appurtenances thereunto belonging or in any ways appertaining and also the reversion and reversions remainder and remainders rents Issues and profits of all and singular the aforesaid land and premises and every part & parcel thereof with the appurtenances and also all the right title claim Interest and demand whatsoever as well in equitty as in law of him the said Abraham Graft of in and to all the aforesaid land and premises and to every part and parcel thereof with the appertenances to have and to hold the aforesaid land and premises and every part and parcel thereof with the appurtenances unto her the said Ruth Trundle her heirs and assigns to the only proper use and behoof of her the said Ruth Trundle her heirs and assigns forever and to no other use Intention purpose whatsoever and the said Abraham Graft doth hereby for himself his heirs executors and administrators and covenant promise and agree to warrant and defend the aforesaid land and premises and every part and parcel thereof unto her the said Ruth Trundle her heirs and assigns forever as well against him the said Abraham Graft his heirs and executors and administrators as also against all manner of person or persons claiming or to claim by from or under him or them In witness whereof the said Abraham Graft hath hereunto set his hand and fixed his seal the day and year above written

Signed sealed and delivered In the presence off   Abraham Graff   ⟨seal⟩
AEn⁸ Campbell Greenbury Howard

on the back of which Deed are the following endorsments to wit on the day and date within mentioned then received of Ruth Trundle the sum of thirty three pounds six Shillings and eight pence current money

It being in full for the consideration money within Expressed

Witness present AEn⁸ Campbell Greenberry Howard   Abraham Graff

Montgomery county set on the fifteenth day of October then came Abraham Graft before us two of the Justices of the peace for the county aforesaid and acknowledged the within Instrument of writing to be his act and deed and the land and premises therein mentioned to be the right title and estate of the within mentioned Ruth Trundle her heirs and assigns forever according to the true Intent and meaning of these presents and an act of assembly in such cases made and provided

AEn⁸ Campbell
Greenberry Howard[112]

There was a second deed, also of 3 Dec. 1796, which mentions many of the same lands: *Resurvey on Suburbs, Willetts Delay*, and *Mount Pleasant*. In addition: *Merediths Hunting Quarter, Gores Adventure, Inverness*, and *Georges Delight* are mentioned. This deed seems to have been for the purpose of further settlement on the 247 1/2 acres purchased from Abraham Graff. Ruth (Lewis) Trundle was to pay an additional £928.2.6 to the grantors, Griffith Willett and his wife, Mary (---) Graff Willett. This deed was as follows:

At the request of Ruth Trundle the following Deed was recorded this 3ʳᵈ December 1796 to wit. This Indenture made the fifteenth day of October Anno Domini one thousand seven hundred and ninety six between Griffith Willett and Mary Willett both of Montgomery county and state of Maryland of the one part and Ruth Trundle of the county and State aforesaid of the other part Witnesseth that the said Griffith Willett and Mary Willett for and in consideration of the sum of nine hundred and twenty eight pounds two shillings and six pence current money to them in hand paid by the said Ruth Trundle at or before the sealing and delivering of these presents the receipt whereof the said Griffith and Mary Willett hereby acknowledge and themselves fully paid and satisfied and the said Griffith Willett and Mary Willett hath granted bargained and sold and by these presents doth give grant bargain sell alien confirm and make over unto her the said Ruth Trundle her heirs and assigns forever all that part of atract of land called the resurvey on Suburbs together with a part of the Original as also a part of atract of land called Willetts delay and a tract of land called Mount Pleasant all lying and being in Montgomery county and contiguous to each other and Included in the following courses Viz beginning for the out lines (?) of the whole at a bounded white oak the

---

¹¹² Ibid., ff. 370-371, ahp.

beginning tree of the aforesaid tract called Willetts delay and running thence by and with the out lines of said tract therein following courses Subject to and to be governed by the same calls as is expressed in the Certificate and patent thereof west one hundred perches south two perches west one perch north two degrees east sixty eight perches north seventy degrees east one perch north two degrees east thirty five perches to astone east seventeen perches and one quarter to the main road and up the road by and with it in the middle thereof the two following courses north twenty five degrees west fourteen (?) and a half perches north thirty five and a half degrees west nineteen & a half perches to the twelvth line of a tract called Meridiths hunting Quarter and with said line reversed north eighty degrees west fourteen perches to the end of the eleventh line of said land still with it reversed north seventeen and a half perches to the main Road then up said road in the middle thereof north thirty five degrees west fifty four perches to the in lines of little monocacy north fifty four and a half degrees east two perches to the tenth line of Merediths hunting Quarter and with it reversed north fifty three degrees west twenty five perches to the twenty third line of the resurvey on Suburbs and with **************** said line south seventy degrees west fifteen and a half perches to the end thereof South twenty seven degrees east two perches to the sixth line of a tract called Georges delight and with It reversed South sixty nine degrees west three and a half perches to the end of the fifth line of said lands still with said land reversed the five following courses south twenty three perches north fifty seven degrees west twenty six perches north two degrees east thirty two perches north thirty three degrees east forty perches north fifty six degrees east fourteen perches to the ninth line of Meridiths Hunting Quarter and with said line reversed north four perches to the beginning thereof north seventy two degrees west thirty eight perches to the fourth line of the Resurvey on Suburbs and with It south forty eight degrees west one hundred and twenty seven perches to the end thereof south forty four degrees east eighteen perches north fifty degrees east fifty perches to the end of the first line of the Original called Suburbs then with It South thirty five degrees west twenty perches South two degrees west twenty eight perches south twenty six degrees east twenty six perches South eight degrees west one perch to the fifteenth line of the resurvey on "Gores adventure as Established by Commission in the year one thousand seven hundred and eighty seven or eighty eight by Robert Peters then with the lines of said tract reversed with an allowance of two and a half degrees for variation South fifty seven degrees and half degree East seven perches to astone fixed at the end of the fourteenth line of said tract still with the lines of said tract reversed allowing two and a half degrees for variation being the allowance made in Executing the aforesaid commission South five and a half degrees west sixty eight perches to a stone south eighty seven and a half degrees west fifty perches south two and a half degrees west forty perches to a stone north eighty seven and a half degrees east sixty six perches to a stone then leaving said land running North seven and a half degrees east eight perches north eighty seven and a half degrees East thirty seven perches South two and a half degrees east ten perches to the ninth line of the resurvey on Gores Adventure as established as aforesaid and with It reversed north eighty seven and a half degrees East one & a half perches to a stone set up for the beginning of Robert Peters part of the resurvey on Gores adventure then with the given line of his part thereof reversed south thirty one and a half degrees East one hundred and thirteen perches to a stone fixed at the end of the forty third line of the resurvey on Gores adventure as Established by commission as aforesaid and with said land South seventy six and a half degrees East twenty six perches to a stone then north seventy seven degrees east four perches to the end of the fourth line of Inverness and with said line reversed north seventy four degrees east eighty nine perches to the given line of the original Tract called Gores adventure and then by a straight line to the first beginning containing two hundred and forty seven and a half acres of land together with all rights benefits priviledges advantages and appurtenances thereunto belonging or in any ways appertaining and also the reversion and reversions remainder and remainders and all the singular Istate right title claim Interest and demand what whatsoever as well in Equity as in law of them the said Griffith and Mary Willett of in and to all the aforesaid lands and premises and every part and parcel thereof with the appurtenances to have and to hold the aforesaid lands and premises and every part and parcel thereof with the appurtenances unto her the said Ruth Trundle her heirs and assigns to the only proper use and behoof of her the said Ruth Trundle her heirs and assigns forever and to no other use Intent or purpose whatsoever and the said Griffith Willet and Mary Willett doth hereby for themselves their heirs Executors and administrators covenant promise and agree to covenant and defend the aforesaid two hundred and forty seven acres and a half acre of land and premises and every (?) part and parcel thereof unto her the said Ruth Trundle her heirs and assigns forever as well against them the said Griffith Willett and Mary Willett their heirs executors and administrators as also against all manner of person or persons Whatsoever the rents or assesments hereafter to become due and owing to the State only fore prised and excepted) and the said Griffith Willett⁺ ᴹᵃʳʸ ᵂⁱˡˡᵉᵗᵗ doth hereby for them selves their heirs Executors and administrators covenant promise and agree to and with her the said Ruth Trundle her heirs and assigns that the said Griffith Willett and Mary Willett their heirs Executors or administrators shall and will at any time or times hereafter at the request and proper cost and charges in the law of her the said Ruth Trundle her heirs or assigns make suffer execute or acknowledge any further act or acts deed or deeds assurances or conveyances in law such as the said Ruth Trundle her heirs or assigns or her or their council learned in the law shall reasonably devise advise or require In witness whereof the said Griffith Willett and Mary Willett his wife hath hereunto set their hands and fixed their seals the day and year above written -

Signed sealed and delivered in the presence off   Griffith Willett   {seal}
AEnˢ Campbell "Greenberry Howard"   Mary Willett   {seal}

on the back of which Deed are the following endorsments to wit. on the day and date within mentioned then Received of Ruth Trundle the sum of nine hundred and twenty eight pounds two shillings and six pence current money It being in full for the Consideration money within expressed Witness AEnˢ Campbell Greenbury Howard"   Griffith Willett

Montgomery county set on the fifteenth day of October 1796 then came Griffith Willett and Mary Willett his wife before us two of the Justices of the peace for the county aforesaid and acknowledged the within Instrument of writing to be their act and deed and the land and premises therein mintioned to be the right title and estate of her the said Ruth Trundle her heirs and assigns forevere at the same time came Mary Willettᵗʰᵉ wife of Griffith Willett and being by us privately examined out of the hearing of her said husband did likewise acknowledge her right of dowery to the said tract of land to be the right title and Estate of said Ruth Trundle her heirs & assigns for ever and that she did the same freely and willingly without being Compelled thereto from her said husband of from fear of his displeasure. AEnˢ Campbell Greenberry Howard[113]

On 25 Jan. 1798, for the sum of £122.6, Ruth (Lewis) Trundle acquired in Montgomery Co., MD, 22 1/2 acres of land known as part of *Mount Carmel*. It was purchased from Francis Deakins. The deed was as follows:

At the request of Ruth Trundle the following deed was recorded this 25ᵗʰ day of January 1798 to wit. This Indenture made the sixteenth day of November seventeen hundred and ninety seven between Francis Deakins of Montgomery county and state of Maryland of the one part and Ruth Trundle of the county and state aforesaid of the other part Witnesseth that the said Francis Deakins for and in consideration of the sum of one hundred and twenty two pounds six shillings current money to him in hand paid by the said Ruth Trundle the receipt whereof is hereby acknowledged hath granted bargained and sold and by these presents doth grant bargain sell an confirm unto her the aforesaid Ruth Trundle her heirs and assigns for ever all that tract or parcel of land being part of a tract called Mount Carmel beginning at the end of the thirteenth line of said tract and running thence by and with the out lines of said tract the six following courses south two purches west one purch north two east sixty eight purches north seventy degrees east one purch north two degrees east thirty five purches east sixteen purches then leaving the out lines and running south twenty four and three quarters of a degree east sixty six purches south ten degrees west forty one purches to the aforesaid thirteenth line of the first part of Mount Carmel then by a straight line to the beginning containing twenty two and a half acres land more or less together with all the premises and appurtenances thereunto belonging or in any wise appurtaining to have and to hold the aforesaid twenty two and a half acres land and premises with all the advantages rights profits and (?) thereunto belonging unto her the said Ruth Trundle her heirs and assigns for ever and for no other use intention purpose whatsoever and the said Francis Deakins doth by these presents for himself and his heirs covenant grant and agree to warrant and for ever defend the

---

[113] Ibid., ff. 371-373, ahp.

aforesaid twenty two and a half acres land and premises aforesaid all person or persons whatsoever claiming and right or title thereto by from or under him the said Francis Deakins or his heirs unto her the said Ruth Trundle her heirs and assigns for ever according to the true intent and meaning of this deed in witness whereof the said Francis Deakins hath hereunto set his hand and seal the day and year first above written -

Signed sealed and acknowledged in presence of}   Francis Deakins {seal}

Thomas Corcoran Lloyd Beall_ _ _ _ _ _ _ _ _}

On the back of which deed is the following endorsment to wit. Montgomery County 16th Nov. 1797. Then came Francis Deakins party to the within deed and acknowledged it to be his act and deed and the land and premises therein mentioned to be the right title and estate of her the within Ruth Trundle her heirs and assigns for ever and at the same time came Eleanor Deakins wife to the said Francis Deakins and being by us the subscribers Justices of the peace for the county aforesaid privatly examined did relinquish all her right of Dower to the within land and premises and acknowledged that she did it without being induced thereto through fear or threats of her said husband and according to an act of Assembly in such cases made and provided -

Tho⁵ Corcoran   Lloyd Beall -[114]

Ruth (Lewis) Trundle continued to live in Montgomery Co., MD where she was head of her family in 1800. In her household were: one white male under ten, five white males at least 16 but under 26, two white females at least ten but under 16, one white female at least 16 but under 26, one white female 45 or over, and 19 slaves.[115] On 16 Dec. 1805, as a result of the decease of Francis Deakins, there was a settlement deed to Ruth Trundle from Leonard M. Deakins and John Hoy, executors of Francis Deakins. For the sum of £310.10, a part of *Mount Carmel* amounting to 69 acres in Montgomery Co., MD, was conveyed to Ruth Trundle. That deed was as follows:

At the request of Ruth Trundle the following Deed was recorded the 16 December 1805 to wit, This Indenture made the sixteenth day of December in the year of our Lord one thousand eight hundred and five Between Leonard M Deakins of Prince Georges County and state of Maryland and John Hoy of Washington county and District of Columbia and Executors of Colo. Francis Deakins late of Washington County and district of Columbia deceased of the one part and Ruth Trundle of Montgomery County and state of Maryland of the other part, Witnesseth that Whereas Francis Deakins did at or about the twenty fifth day of July anno Domini one thousand eight hundred and one for the consideration of thirty five hundred pounds current money pass his bond to James White of Montgomery County for the conveyance of a certain part of a tract of land called Mount Carmel lying and being in Montgomery County and containing about (blank) as by the said bond will fully appear and whereas the said James White did at or about the sixteenth day of august anno domini one thousand eight hundred and three for the consideration of three hundred and ten pounds ten shillings current money pass his bond to the said Ruth Trundle for the conveyance of sixty nine acres part of Mount Carmel and being apart of the aforesaid land which he the said James White had obtained the said Francis Deakins conveyance bond for, and whereas the said James White hath not obtained any conveyance for the aforesaid land and the said Ruth Trundle being now ready and willing to comply on her part of the contract with the said James White by making her last payment of the consideration money for the aforesaid land on her obtaining a legal deed for the same and it therefore becomes necessary to invest the legal title in the land to the said Ruth Trundle that the executors of the aforesaid Francis Deakins deceased should convey the same, This Indenture therefore further witnesseth that the said Leonard M Deakins and John Hoy Executors of the said Francis Deakins deceased for and in consideration of the above reasons and for the further consideration of three hundred and ten pounds current money to them in hand paid by the said Ruth Trundle at or before the sealing and delivering of these presents the receipt whereof the said Leonard M Deakins and John Hoy doth hereby acknowledge and themselves fully satisfied

---

[114] Ibid., Deed Liber H, f. 45, ahp.
[115] Ibid., NARA, 1800, roll 11, p. 214.

contented and paid and they the said Leonard M Deakins and John Hoy hath granted bargained and sold and by these presents doth grant bargain sell aliene confirm and make over unto her the said Ruth Trundle her heirs and assigns forever all that part of the first part of a tract of land called mount Carmel lying and being in Montgomery county and state of Maryland and bounded as follows vizt. beginning at the end of seventy perches in the third line of a tract of land called Inverness and running thence north eighty degrees west fifty perches to a stone fixed at the end thereof south seventy four degrees west forty perches to the given line of a tract of land called Gores adventure it now being about six feet south of a large stooping white oak marked with two chops to three sides then with the given line of Gores adventure north sixteen degrees east forty five perches to the beginning of the aforesaid land called Gores Adventure west sixty two perches then north ten degrees east forty one perches to the end of the seventh line of a deed for apart of the first part of mount Carmel as formerly conveyed to Ruth Trundle for about twenty two and a half acres then north twenty four degrees and three quarters of a degree west sixty six perches then east fifty perches to a stone north fifty six degrees west seven perches south eighty four degrees east five perches to the end of the tenth line of a tract called Meridiths hunting quarter then north forty degrees and a half degree east nineteen and three quarter perches to the main road leading to George Town and with it south twenty one degrees east fourteen perches and three quarters of a perch still by and with said road on the west side thereof to this first beginning containing sixty nine acres of land together with all and singular the rights benefits priviledges advantages and appurtenances thereunto belonging or in anyways appertaining and also the reversion and reversions remainder and remainders rents issues and profits thereof together with all the right title claim interest and demand whatsoever as well in equity as in Law of them the said Leonard M Deakins and John Hoye of in and to all the aforesaid land and premises To have and To hold the aforesaid land and premises and every part and parcel thereof unto her the said Ruth Trundle her heirs and assigns to the only proper use and behoof of her the said Ruth Trundle her heirs and assigns forever and to no other use intent or purpose whatsoever and the said Leonard M Deakins and John Hoy doth hereby for themselves their heirs executors and administrators covenant promise and agree to warrant and defend the aforesaid land and premises and every part and parcel thereof unto her the said Ruth Trundle her heirs and assigns forever as well against them the said Leonard M Deakins and John Hoy their heirs executors and administrators as also against all manner of persons whatsoever (the rents or assessments hereafter to become due and owing to the county or state or the united states only foreprized and excepted, In Testimony whereof the said Leonard M Deakins and John Hoy hath hereunto set their hands and seals the day and year within written, Signed sealed and delivered in the presence off - It is fully understood that Leonard M Deakins and John Hoye Ex^{rs}. and devisees of Francis Deakins only warrant and defend the above land as Executors of said Deakins and not in their individual Capacity,

	L M Deakins (Seal)
John Fleming Samuel Elgar}	John Hoye (Seal)

Be it remembered that on the 16th day of December Anno domini one thousand eight hundred and five Leonard M Deakins and John Hoy personally appeared before us two of the Justices of the peace for the county aforesaid and acknowledged the above and within instrument of writing to be their act and deed and the land and premises therein mentioned to be the right property and estate of her the said Ruth Trundle her heirs and assigns forever

   (19th Nov 1805)   John Fleming Samuel Elgar

Gentlemen, As I have passed my bond to M^{rs}. Ruth Trundle for the conveyance of 69 acres of land being a part of my purchase from Col^o. Francis Deakins and as I never had the land conveyed to me it becomes necessary, to invest the legal title of the land to Mrs Trundle the executors of Col^o Deakins should convey 69 acres of land to M^{rs}. Trundle upon her making the payments of the purchase money which is agreeable to Col^o. Francis Deakins contract you will therefore please to convey unto M^{rs}. Ruth Trundle the 69 acres of land being a part of Mount Carmel agreeable to the course and distance given and agreeable to the condition of my bond to her on her making you the full payment of the purchase money which you will please to place to my credit agreeable to the former contract between Col^o. Francis Deakins and myself

Witness Hezekiah Veatch, I am Gentlemen y^r. m^t. Obed Ser^{vt}.

                    James White

True copy John Fleming David Trundle[116]

This 1805 deed seems to have represented the last land acquired by Ruth (Lewis) Trundle. With the land from the estate of John Trundle IV, she seems to have owned 555 3/4 acres of land which she probably managed with her five older sons.

Further evidence of her business mind is exhibited in her will of 3 Feb. 1810 which she signed as Ruth Trundle, indicating she was literate. The will was as follows:

In The name of God Amen. I Ruth Trundle of montgomery County and State of Maryland being sick and weak in body But of sound disposing mind memory and understanding Thanks be to God for the same, and calling to mind the mortality of my body And knowing that it is appointed for all once to die, do Therefore make and Ordain this my last will and Testament. And principally, and first of all I recommend my soul into the hands of almighty God who first gave it me And my body to the Earth to be buried in a decent Christian like Burial at the discretion of my Executor herein after named Nothing doubting but at the General resurrection I shall receive the same again by the mighty power of God and as Touching my worldly Estate wherewith it has pleased God to bless me in this life I give devise and dispose of the same in the following manner Item: I give and bequeath To my Daughter Charlotte Belt one Negro Girl called Sophia To her and the Heirs of her body Lawfully begotten and in case of failure of such Issue Then at my daughter Charlotte's death The said Negro Sophia Together with her Increase if any to devolve into my Estate And to be Equally divided among my then surviving Children all share and share alike provided always and my will is That in case her husband should attempt to sell the said Negro Sophia with a part or all of her Increase if any for and during the life of my daughter Charlotte or otherwise That then and in that case my will is that the sale made thereof shall be null and void and the Negro Sophia and her Increase or any of (?) made sale of shall devolve into my Estate again and be Equally divided among the rest of my then surviving Children all share and share alike It being my true Intent and meaning that no sale shall be made of the said Negro Sophia nor her Increase but Kept for the use Benefit support and Maintenance of my daughter her children if any and not to be sold or Transferred out of the family-- Item. I give and bequeath to my daughter Elenor Jones one Negro Girl called Rachel to her and the heirs of her Body Lawfully begotten and in case of failure of such Issue Then at my Daughter Elenors death the said Negro Rachel Together with her Increase if any shall devolve into my Estate again and be Equally divided among the rest of my then surviving Children all share and share alike and in case her Husband should attempt to sell the said Negro Rachel Singley or with a part or all her Increase if any for and during the natural life of my daughter Elenor or otherwise Then and in that case my will is that the sale made thereof shall be null and void and the negro Rachel and her Increase or any of them so made sale of shall devolve into my Estate again and be Equally divided among the rest of my then surviving Children share and share alike-- Item. I give and bequeath to my Grandaughter Drusilla Lewis Trundle Wilcoxen The sum of five hundred dollars current money of the United States of America to be paid to her by my Executor hereinafter named at the time of her marriage and my will is that my Executor shall have the care of bringing her up and giving her Education untill she arrives at full age or day of marriage and that the Interest of the money herein bequeathed And to be paid to her by my Executor shall be applied by him toward the support maintenance and Education of her my aforesaid Grandaughter And if that should not be found sufficient for the purposes aforesaid That then and in that Case my Executor shall take in as much of my personal Estate in his hands as will make him full compensation for his Care and Trouble and for the Education he may think proper to give to my said Grandaughter--provided allways and my will is That if her father Levey Wilcoxen should be dissatisfied and should take his daughter from my Executor and take her under his care and (?) Then and in that Case my will is that no money from my Estate nor the Interest of her Legacy shall be allowed or taken for her support maintenance or Education after She is taken from the Care and (?) of my Executor-- The above Legacy of five hundred dollars being give to my Grandaughter Drusilla Lewis Trundle Wilcoxen in full for her deceased mother Letha Wilcoxens part of my Estate And further my will is that if my aforesaid Grandaughter should die before she Intermarries that

[116] Ibid., Deed Liber M, ff. 429-432, ahp.

then the five hundred dollars herein given to her shall be considered as a part of my Estate and shall be Equally divided among the then surviving Children of mine share and share alike - Item I give and bequeath to Levi Wilcoxen five shillings Current money and no more in full for any Claim or Claims he may assume for his disceased wife or his daughters part of my Estate - Item I give and Bequeath to my son Hezekiah Trundle one Gray Horse Colt about three years old next spring to be delivered to him Immediately after my decease -- And whereas all the rest of my children have arrived to full age and have received from me their share and full proportion of their deceased fathers Estate And have been paid of in a Very liberal and full proportion and to them over and above their legal share both in Negro flesh stock and Household furniture and not Confined Exactly to their Legal parts in either as by their benefits will fully appear and in order that every one may have Equal and substantial Justice Justice done them my will is that my son Hezekiah shall have his share of his fathers Estate paid to him in Negro flesh stock and Household furniture out of my Estate in the same manner as the other children have received their parts thereof and not confining him to any exact part of either of the aforesaid property but as the same may best suit him and my will is that he may be paid the same out of my Estate Immediately after my decease although he may not have arrived to the age of twenty one years. -- Item And my will is That all the remaining part of my personal Estate (?) in whatsoever Consisting or wheresoever to be found shall be set up and sold by my Executor at publick sale to the best advantage in twelve months the purchaser to give bond with approved security bearing Interest from the day of sale and the money arising from the sale thereof I give and bequeath to my Eight Children Six sons and two daughters to be Equally divided among them all share and share alike Item And all the Lands I now possess or may be siezed in fee of at the time of my decease I give and bequeath to my Eight Children that is to say David Trundle John Trundle Daniel Trundle James Trundle Otho Trundle Hezekiah Trundle Charlotte Belt and Elenor Jones To be Equally divided among them all share and share alike To them the said David Trundle John Trundle Daniel Trundle Otho Trundle James Trundle Hezekiah Trundle Charlotte Belt and Elenor Jones their Heirs and assigns forever and my will is that if it should so happen that my aforesaid eight Children should not agree in making a division of the aforesaid lands herein devised to them that then and in that Case that they or a majority of them shall nominate and appoint three of their neighbors who may be supposed to be well Experienced in such Cases and that a division made by them so chosen and appointed with their Certificate of each Childs part shall be binding to all Interests and purposes to each and every party Interested and concerned -- And Lastly I do hereby Constitute and appoint my son David Trundle my sole Executor of this my last will and Testament annulling every other and former will by me heartofore made ratifying and Confirming this and none other to be my last will and Testament In Testimony whereof I have hereunto set my hand and seal this Third day of February in the year of our Lord one thousand eight hundred and Ten

Signed sealed published declared and pronounced   }
by Ruth Trundle the within named Testatrix as and}   Ruth Trundle
for her last will and Testament in the presence of us}
who at her request and in her presence and in the}
presence of each other have subscribed our Names}
as Witnesses thereto _ _ _ _ _ _ _ _ _ _ _ _ _ _ _ _ }
Hezekiah Veatch
Hezekiah Wilson
Joseph J. W. Jones

Montgomery County Ts.t On the 7th day of June 1810 Then Came Hezekiah Veatch and Hezekiah Wilson two of the subscribing witnesses to the within last will and Testament of Ruth Trundle late of Montgomery County deceased and severally made oath on the Holy Evangels of almighty God that they did see the Testatrix herein named sign and seal this will and that they heard her publish pronounce and declare the same to be her last Will and Testament and that at the time of her so doing she was to the best of their apprehensions of sound disposing mind memory and understanding and that they respectively subscribed their names to this will as witnesses in the presence and at the request of the Testatrix and in the presence of each Other and also in the presence of Joseph J. W Jones the other subscribing witness hereto

Certified by---Solomon Holland Register[117]

Ruth (Lewis) Trundle died 25 Mar. 1810, probably before the federal census of 1810 was taken. She was 57 years of age and seems to have managed well as a widow with nine children. Some descendants of those children continue to live in Montgomery Co., MD and nearby surrounding areas.

Children of John IV and Ruth (Lewis) Trundle, all born in Frederick Co., MD or, after 1776, Montgomery Co., MD:

   i.   David[5], b. 21 June 1773; d. 8 Mar. 1846 Montgomery Co., MD, bur. his place, near Barnesville Dist., Dickerson Station, Montgomery Co., MD;[118] m. 18 Jan. 1797 Frederick Co., MD, **DRUSILLA LEWIS**[119] (see Lewis Families, Chapter Two, No. 2, viii).

   ii. John Lewis, b. 4 Jan. 1776; d. 24 Aug. 1836 Montgomery Co., MD, bur. David Trundle's, near Barnesville Dist., Dickerson Station, Montgomery Co., MD;[120] m. 26 Feb. 1799 Montgomery Co., MD, **MARY VEATCH**.[121]

   iii. Daniel, b. 13 Mar. 1778; d. 17 Mar. 1831 Montgomery Co., MD, bur. Monocacy Cem., Beallsville, Montgomery Co., MD;[122] m. 18 Nov. 1802 Montgomery Co., MD, **ESTHER BELT**.[123]

   iv. James, b. *ca.* 1779; d. 16 Aug. 1843 prob. TN; m. 14 Feb. 1806, **ELEANOR BURNS**.[124]

   v.   Otho, b. 14 Feb. 1780; d. 27 Jan. 1823 Montgomery Co., MD., bur. David Trundle's, near Barnesville Dist., Dickerson Station, Montgomery Co., MD;[125] m. 20 Jan. 1804 Montgomery Co., MD, **ELIZABETH BURNS**.[126]

   vi. Letha, b. prob. *ca.* 1782; d. by 3 Feb. 1810 prob. Montgomery Co., MD;[127] m. 3 Nov. 1801 Montgomery Co., MD, **LEVI WILCOXEN**.[128]

   vii. Charlotte, b. 6 Feb. 1787; d. 13 Apr. 1824 Montgomery Co., MD, bur. David Trundle's, near Barnesville Dist., Dickerson Station, Montgomery Co., MD;[129] m. 18 Dec. 1809 Montgomery Co., MD, **ALFRED BELT**.[130]

   viii. Elenor, b. *ca.* 1789; d. aft. 3 Feb. 1810;[131] m. 24 Dec. 1807 Montgomery Co., MD, **HENRY JONES**.[132]

---

[117] Ibid., Will Liber G, ff. 149-151, ahp; ibid., Will Liber 2, f. 240.

[118] Gravestone, cited in Ridgely.

[119] Barnes, p. 231; "Hezekiah Wilson's Diary...," *National Genealogical Society Quarterly*, v. 6, p. 29 has 19 Jan. 1797. One David Trundle living in Frederick Co., MD in 1823 (William Jarboe Grove, *History of Carrollton Manor* [Frederick, MD, 1928], pp. 251-254).

[120] Gravestone, cited in Ridgely.

[121] "Hezikiah Wilson's Diary...," *National Genealogical Society Quarterly*, v. 6, p. 29.

[122] Gravestone, cited in *Tombstone Records Monocacy Cemetery Beallsville, Montgomery County, Maryland*, p. 68.

[123] Manuel, p. 315. Daniel Trundle owned a home called *Annington*, Montgomery Co., MD in 1820's (Roger Brooke Farquhar, *Historic Montgomery County, Maryland, Old Homes and History* [Silver Spring, MD], pp. 95-97).

[124] MSS, typewritten (1901), p. 3, Trundle folder, DAR Library, Washington, DC, information mostly from Charles H. Trunnel, Georgetown, Washington, DC, has the surname as Trunnel & states they went to TN. DAR membership papers of Margaret Wendel Jacobi has m. 1810 which seems doubtful.

[125] Gravestone, cited in Ridgely, p. 182.

[126] Manuel, p. 316. Otho Trundle living in Frederick Co., MD in 1823 (Grove).

[127] Montgomery Co., MD, Will Liber G, ff. 149-151, ahp.

[128] Manuel, p. 316 has her name as Lethe, his as Levy.

[129] Gravestone, cited in Ridgely, p. 181.

[130] Manuel, p. 315.

[131] Montgomery Co., MD, Will Liber G, ff. 149-151, ahp.

[132] Manuel, p. 315.

    ix.   Hezekiah, b. 18 Jan. 1792;[133] d. 1856;[134] m. **CHRISTIANNA WHITAKER**.[135]

8. JOSIAH[4] **TRUNDLE** (*John III*[3], *John II*[2], *John I*[1]) (see 4), b. *ca.* 1752[136] Frederick Co., MD;[137] d. prob. bet. 1809 & 1820[138] *Clean Drinking,* Montgomery Co., MD;[139] m. prob. by 1772,[140] **KATHERINE WILSON**.[141]

Josiah Trundle, son of John III and Ann (---) Trundle, grew up in the home of his parents in Frederick Co., MD and was named in the 1771 will of John Trundle III. He was to receive his father's land after the death or remarriage of Ann (---) Trundle.[142] On 15 July 1768 John Trundle III had granted his son, Josiah, a special warrant to *Resurvey on the Benjamin* and on 27 Aug. 1771 shortly after the death of John III, a petition for resurvey was recorded. In the renunciation signed by Ann Trundle she stated Josiah was her son.[143]

It seems likely he had married by 1772. His wife is said to have been Katherine Wilson whose father owned land in what became Washington, DC.[144] On 29 Apr. 1773 his name appeared as Josiah Trundell when he reported stray livestock at his place in Frederick Co., MD.[145] In late 1776 the part of Frederick Co. where he lived became part of newly formed Montgomery Co. In 1778 he signed the Oath of Fidelity to the State of Maryland from Montgomery Co. as Josiah Trundel, his mark.[146] That same year, 1778, he was taxed as Josiah Trunnal in Rock Creek Hundred, Montgomery Co., MD.[147] During the American Revolution he was in the Maryland Militia just as were his two half brothers, Thomas III and John IV. By 15 July 1780 he was a private, 6th Co., Middle Bn., Maryland Militia.[148]

By 1783 the area where Josiah Trundle was living had become Lower Newfoundland Hundred, Montgomery Co. and he was assessed there in that year.[149] On 10 July 1786 as Josiah Trundell he sold property to Ann (---) Trundell, his mother, for the sum of 2,100 pounds of merchantable tobacco. The deed was signed Josiah Trundell, his mark.[150]

[133] DAR membership papers of Margaret Wendel Jacobi.

[134] *Biographical and Historical Memoirs of Pulaski, Jefferson, Lonoke, Faulkner, Grant, Saline, Perry, Garland, and Hot Spring Counties, Arkansas* (Chicago, 1889), p. 699 has a son, Hezekiah Lewis Trundle, living in Perry Co., AR in 1889.

[135] DAR membership papers of Margaret Wendel Jacobi; DAR membership papers of Florence Michele Remmele. Hezekiah Trundle owned a home called *Killmain II* , Montgomery Co., MD in 1840's (Farquhar, pp. 199-200).

[136] Montgomery Co., MD, NARA, 1800 census, roll 11, p. 247(?) indicates b. by 1755; younger sibling, Joannah, b. 1754 (Millard Milburn Rice, *This Was the Life, Excerpts from the Judgment Records of Frederick County, Maryland* [Baltimore, 1984], pp. 133-135, 146).

[137] Ibid.; Frederick Co., MD, Warrant Liber BC & GS #5, f. 157, found and transcribed by Benjamin Franklin Poinsett, MSA, 13 June 1998.

[138] Montgomery Co., MD, NARA, 1810 census, roll 14, p. 313 or 926; Gary W. Parks, comp., *Index to 1820 Census of Maryland and Washington, D.C.* (Baltimore, 1986), p. 246.

[139] MSS, typewritten, p. 11, Trundle folder, DAR Library.

[140] *Heads of Families*, p. 87.

[141] Trundle folder, Frederick Co. Historical Soc., Frederick, MD, notes on reverse side of typed certified copy of 1771 will of John Trundle Sr.; MSS, typewritten, p. 7, Trundle folder, DAR Library says he m. Miss Wilson d/o a land owner in Washington, DC.

[142] Frederick Co., MD, Will Liber A-1, ff. 399-400, ahp.

[143] MSA, Drawer 54, Land Patent Vol. BC & GS #42, f. 62-63, 479; Frederick Co., MD, copy of transcription, courtesy of Mrs. Taylor, published herein.

[144] MSS, typewritten, p. 7, Trundle folder, DAR Library.

[145] F. Edward Wright, *Early Lists of Frederick Countians 1765-1775*, p. 8.

[146] *Montgomery Co., Md. Oath of Fidelity...*, p. 2.

[147] Ibid., pp. 60-62.

[148] Clements, pp. 201-206.

[149] Cook, *1783 Maryland General Assessment...* p. 9.

[150] Montgomery Co., MD, Deed Liber C, ff. 360-361, ahp, published herein.

Later that year, on 21 Oct. 1786, for the sum of £100, Ann (---) Trundle and Josiah Trundle, sold the two parcels of land, *Resurvey on the Benjamin* and *Labrinth* to Benjamin Gittings. The deed was as follows:

At the request of Benjamin Gittings the following Deed was Recorded this 21st october 1786 (to wit) This Indenture made the twenty fifth day of April in the Year of our Lord one thousand seven hundred and eighty six Between Ann & Josaih Trundell of montgomery County and state of maryland of the one part and Benjamin Gittings of the said state and County of the other part witnesseth, That the said Ann & Josiah Trundell for and in consideration of the Sum of One hundred pounds Current money of maryland to them in hand paid by the said Benjamin Gittings the receipt whereof they do hereby acknowledge and the said Benjamin Gittings his heirs executors administrators and assigns thereof and of every part and parcel thereof all hereby forever warranted acquited and discharged they the said Ann & Josiah Trundell hath given granted bargained, sold aliened enfeoffed released and confirmed and by these presents doth fully freely clearly and absolutely give, grant bargain sell alien enfeoff release and confirm unto him the said Benjamin Gittings his heirs and assigns the following two parcells of Land being in montgomery County and state aforesd that is to free all that part of a Tract or parcel of Land being part of a Tract of Land called the Resurvey on Benjamin being at present in the Tenure and occupation of the aforesaid Josiah Trundell and the place where he dwelleth containing Sixty eight Acres and one half of an acre of Land also all that part of a tract or parcell of Land called Labrinth adjoining the part of the resurvey on the Benjamin aforesd Beginning at a stake, and running south twenty five degrees east one hundred perches then south nineteen degrees west Thirty two perches then west Thirty two perches then north eight degrees west one hundred twenty and one half perches then to the Beginning containing twenty five acres and one half of an acre of Land more or Less Together, with all and singular the dwelling houses out houses orchards fences improvements of every kind advantages and appurtenances to the two parcells of Land and premises belonging or in any manner of wise appertaining and also the reversion & reversions remainder and remainders and all and singular the estate right Title and interest of them the said Ann & Josiah Trundell in and to the parcels of Land and premises aforesaid To have and to hold the said two parcels of Land and all and singular these premises and every of their appurtenances unto the said Benjamin Gittings to the only proper use and behooff of the said Benjamin Gittings his heirs and assigns forever and to and for no other use intent or purpose whatsoever And further the said Ann & Josiah Trundell doth by these presents for themselves their, Heirs, executors, and administrators covenant and agree to and with the said Benjamin Gittings his heirs and assigns that they the said Ann & Josiah Trundell, their heirs and executors, and administrators the said two parcels of Land and all and singular these premises and every of their appurtenances to him the said Benjamin Gittings his heirs and assigns against them and their heirs, and against all persons whatsoever shall and will warrant and forever defend by these presents and Lastly the said ann & Josiah Trundell doth by these presents further, covenant and agree to and with the said Benjamin Gittings his heirs and assigns that they will at any time or times hereafter at the reasonable request and at the proper charge and cost of the said Benjamin Gittings his heirs and assigns make and execute any further or other deed or deeds for the better and more effectual conveying and assuring all and singular the aforesaid two parcels of Land & premises to the said Benjamin Gittings his heirs and assigns for ever: In witness whereof the said Ann & Josiah Trundell hath to these presents set their hands & seals the day & year first above written ---   her

Signed Sealed & Delivered}   Ann   A   Trundell (seal)
In the presence of us}   mark
AEns Campbell SamlW Magruder   his
                                        Josiah I   Trundell (seal)
                                                    mark

On which deed was the following endorsements to wit Received the day & year within written of Benjamin Gittings the sum of one hundred pounds current money being the Consideration within mentioned   his
Witness AEns Campbell SamlW Magruder   Josiah I   Trundell
                                                    mark

her
Ann   A   Trundell
mark

State of maryland montgomery County se[t] on the day and year within written came before us the subscribers two of the Justices of montgomery County Court Ann & Josiah Trundell party to the within Deed & acknowledged the same to be their act and deed and the Lands and premises therein mentioned to be the right property and estate of Benjamin Gittings his heirs and Assigns forever and according to the form of the act of assembly in such cases made & provided
AEn[s] Campbell Sam[l]W Magruder[151]

This deed does not mention a wife of Josiah Trundle. The two parcels of land, *Resurvey on the Benjamin* and *Labrinth*, had in 1767 been deeded to John Trundle III, husband of Ann and father of Josiah, by Thomas Thrasher.[152]

In 1790 Josiah Trundle was head of a family in Montgomery Co., MD. His household was composed of: one white male 16 years and upward, five white males under 16, and seven females.[153] As head of his family in 1800, his name appears to have been recorded as Josias Trundle in Montgomery Co. His household was composed of: two white males under ten, one white male at least ten but under 16, one white male at least 16 but under 26, one white male 45 or over, three white females under ten, and one white female 45 or over.[154] He was still living in Montgomery Co. in 1810. In his household were: one white male 45 or over, 13 persons of color, and 14 slaves. By then he seems to have been a widower.[155] He is missing from an 1820 census index of Maryland.[156] It seems likely he died between 1810 and 1820. He is said to have lived and died near *Clean Drinking*, Montgomery Co., MD.[157]

Josiah Trundle grew to manhood in Frederick Co., MD where he probably married Katherine Wilson. By 1777 the part of Frederick Co., where he lived became part of newly formed Montgomery Co. and in 1778 he signed the Oath of Fidelity to the State of Maryland from Montgomery Co. Also in 1778, he was taxed in Rock Creek Hundred, Montgomery Co. During the American Revolution he served as a private in the Maryland Militia. By 1783 he was living in Lower Newfoundland Hundred, Montgomery Co., likely on *Resurvey on the Benjamin* or *Labrinth,* property inherited from his father. It may be that he never learned to read or write. He continued to live in Montgomery Co. until 1810 but had probably died by 1820. His children used the surname, Trunnell.

Children of Josiah and Katherine (Wilson) Trundle, all born in Frederick Co., MD or, after 1776, Montgomery Co., MD:

    i.   John V[5], b. poss. *ca.* 1777; d. 1847 Bullitt Co., KY;[158] m. (1) --- **RIDGEWAY**;[159] m. (2) 29 Jan. 1799 Montgomery Co., MD, **ELIZABETH WELLS**.[160]

    ii.   Ann Wilson.[161]

---

[151] Ibid., ff. 403-404, ahp.

[152] Frederick Co., MD, Deed Liber K, ff. 1382-1384, ahp.

[153] *Heads of Families,* p. 87.

[154] Montgomery Co., MD, NARA, 1800 census, roll 11, p. 247(?).

[155] Ibid., 1810 census, roll 14, p. 313 or 926.

[156] Parks.

[157] MSS, typewritten, p. 11, Trundle folder, DAR Library.

[158] *History of Kentucky.*

[159] MSS, typewritten, p. 7, Trundle folder, DAR Library; Trundle folder, Frederick Co., notes.

[160] Manuel, p. 315. This family spelled the name Trunnell, settled in Bullitt Co., KY, had 13 children (*History of Kentucky*).

iii. Horatio, b. poss. *ca.* 1781;[162] d. prob. aft. 1839 Medleys Dist., Montgomery Co., MD;[163] m. 15 Jan. 1802 Montgomery Co., MD, **CATHERINE POOSE.**[164]

iv. Delilah, b. poss. *ca.* 1783; m. 21 Jan. 1807 Montgomery Co., MD, **ANDREW BARACLOIS.**[165]

v. Henry, b. poss. *ca.* 1785;[166] d. prob. aft. 1839 Georgetown, Washington, DC;[167] m. **ELIZABETH LACY.**[168]

vi. Silas, b. poss. *ca.* 1786; m. **MELINDA KNOTT.**[169]

vii. Prob. Elizabeth, b. poss. *ca.* 1788.[170]

viii. Prob. Walter, b. poss. *ca.* 1790;[171] d. aft. 1839 prob. Frederick Co., MD.[172]

ix. David, b. poss. *ca.* 1792;[173] d. prob. aft. 1839 Frederick Co., MD;[174] m. **ROSA MCMANUS.**[175]

x. Isaac, b. poss. *ca.* 1800;[176] d. aft. 1849 prob. Washington, DC;[177] m. (1) Mrs. --- (---) **WETZEL**; m. (2) **ELLEN MARTINDALE.**[178]

[161] Trundle folder, Frederick Co., notes.

[162] MSS, typewritten, p. 9, Trundle folder, DAR Library; Manuel, p. 315.

[163] Ronald Vern Jackson, ed., *District of Columbia 1810 Census Index* (1981), p. 13; District of Columbia, NARA, 1820 census, roll 5, p. 34 has surname as Trunnell; Ronald Vern Jackson & Gary Ronald Teeples, ed., *District of Columbia 1830 Index Census* (Bountiful, UT, 1977), p. 16; ibid., *District of Columbia 1840 Index Census* (Bountiful, UT, 1977); ibid., *Maryland 1840 Census Index* (Bountiful, UT, 1977), p. 148.

[164] Manuel, p. 315.

[165] William Neal Hurley Jr. *Our Maryland Heritage, Book Twenty, Trundle and Allied Families of Montgomery County, Maryland* (Bowie, MD, 2000), p. 71; Manuel, p. 315 has his surname as Barneclow.

[166] MSS, typewritten, p. 11, Trundle folder, DAR Library; District of Columbia, NARA, 1820 census, roll 5, p. 50 has surname as Trunnell.

[167] Jackson, *District of Columbia 1840 Index Census*, p. 17.

[168] MSS, typewritten, p. 11, Trundle folder, DAR Library.

[169] Ibid., p. 8, settled in Somerset, Perry Co., OH, has surname as Trunnell.

[170] Montgomery Co., MD, Inventory Liber C, pp. 556-557, typed record, p. 280, found at MCHS.

[171] Frederick Co., MD, NARA, 1820 census, roll 43, 1st Dist., p. 81 has surname as Trunnell.

[172] Ronald Vern Jackson & Gary Ronald Teeples, ed., *Maryland 1840 Census Index* (Bountiful, UT, 1977), p. 148.

[173] Frederick Co., MD, NARA, 1820 census, roll 43, 10th Dist., p. 70 has surname as Trunnel.

[174] Jackson, *Maryland 1840 Census Index* (Bountiful, UT, 1977), p. 147.

[175] MSS, typewritten, p. 9, Trundle folder, DAR Library.

[176] Ibid., p. 9; Jackson, *District of Columbia 1830 Index Census*, p. 16 has surname as Trunnell, living in Alexandria, DC.

[177] Ibid., *District of Columbia 1850 Census Index* (Bountiful, UT, 1977), p. 40 has surname as Trummel.

[178] MSS, typewritten, p. 9, Trundle folder, DAR Library.

Ill. 15 - Part of northern Kentucky showing Bourbon and Bullitt counties, from an 1814 map in M. Carey, *General Atlas of the World*. Reproduced from collections of the Library of Congress, Geography and Map Division.

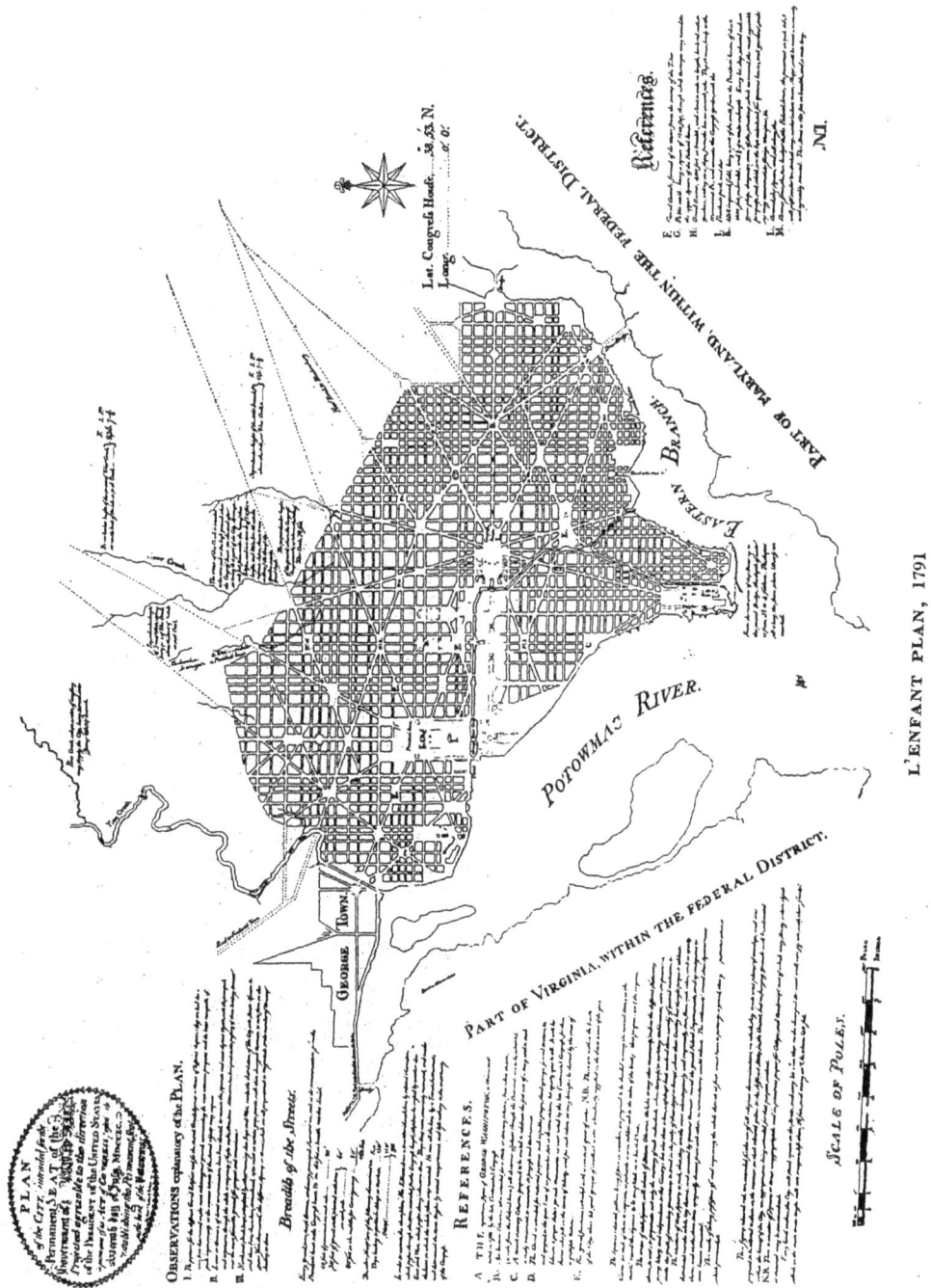

Ill. 16 - L'enfant plan for the District of Columbia, showing Georgetown, 1791. Reproduced
from Federal Writers' Project, WPA, *Washington City and Capital* (Washington, 1937), p. 100.

LEWISES AND TRUNDLES OF MONTGOMERY COUNTY IN 1778

By 1778 several Lewis and Trundle families were living in the hundreds of southeast Montgomery Co., MD.

The following appear in a List of Free Male Taxables of Lower Newfoundland Hundred from eighteen years and upward in 1778:
Daniel Lewis Sr.[1]
Daniel Lewis Jr.[2]
Thomas Trundle[3] (Jr.) (Thomas III)

The following appear in a List of Free Male Taxables of Rock Creek Hundred from eighteen years and upward in 1778:
David Lewis[4]
Jeremiah Lewis[5]
Josiah Trundle[6]

The following appear in a List of Free Male Taxables of North West Hundred from eighteen years and upward in 1778:
John Trundle[7] (John IV)
Thomas Trundle[8] (Sr.) (Thomas I)

---

[1] *Montgomery Co., Md. Oath of Fidelity & Tax Lists - 1778*, p. 68, presented by Mrs. Lilly C. Stone through The Janet Montgomery Chapter, DAR (1949).
[2] Ibid.
[3] Ibid., p. 69.
[4] Ibid., p. 61.
[5] Ibid.
[6] Ibid., p. 62.
[7] Ibid., p. 56.
[8] Ibid.

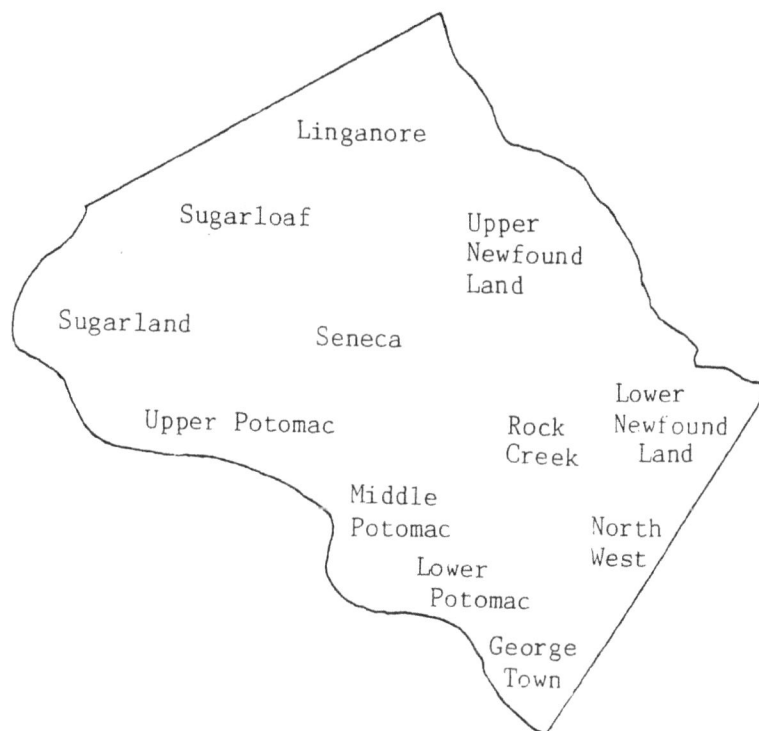

Ill. 17 - Map of hundreds in Montgomery Co., MD by 1790. Reproduced from Eleanor M.V. Cook, *Guide to the Records of Montgomery County, Maryland, Genealogical and Historical* (Westminster, MD), p. 3, by permission of Eleanor M.V. Cook.

NAME INDEX

The name index that follows includes the names of all individuals in Chapters One through Eight and the section entitled "Lewises and Trundles of Montgomery County in 1778." Those varied spellings of the surname, TRUNDLE, were given a cross-reference and placed under the surname "Trundle." Most of those born with the surname of LEWIS or TRUNDLE were indexed with a year of birth or approximate year of birth to distinguish them from others with identical names. It should be noted that a year preceded by "ca." means that person seems to have been born around that year but could have been born a number of years earlier or later.

Some other surnames with more than one spelling were placed under one surname spelling with appropriate cross-references.

Men who had the exact name for several generations may have been assigned upper case Roman numerals, as in John I, John II, John III, etc. They do not always appear that way in the text where detailed information is available. In some cases a parent is provided, as in "John s/o Robert."

Whenever possible, women were indexed under maiden surname and married surname(s). When indexed under a married surname, the surname history was reflected by including the maiden surname and any previous married surname(s) known.

Names of authors and contributors acknowledged in notes were included.

There may be more than one reference to a name on a given page though the page number appears only once.

Burgess
   Edward, 13, 45
   Elira (?), 4
Burns
   Eleanor, 123
   Elizabeth, 123
Burnside
   Joannah (Trundle) Lewis,
      33, 38, 39
   Patrick, 33, 37, 38, 39, 59,
      98
Burnsides. *See* Burnside
Butcher
   Bernard L., 12, 59, 60

—C—

Cabell
   William L., 37
Cambron
   Henry, 97, 98
Cameron
   Elisabeth, 11
Camp
   Ann (---), 56
   James M., 56
Campbell
   A., 46
   Aeneas, 105, 106, 107,
      109, 110, 114, 116,
      118, 125, 126
Cannon
   Capt., 40
Carey
   M., 128
Carroll
   Charles Jr., 85
   Ed, 73
   Mrs., 114
Cass
   Caleb, 92
Caster
   Sarah, 42
Castor
   James, 18, 20
Chappell
   Alexander, 75
   John, 65, 66, 77
Chapple. *See* Chappell
Chew
   Benjamin, 75
Christian
   John, 65, 77
   John s/o John, 65
Clagett
   Thomas, 3, 4

Claggett
   John, 114
   Sarah Jane, 52
Clark
   Benjamin, 5
   Murtie June, 9, 89
Clements
   S. Eugene, 25, 34, 45, 103,
      114, 124
Coldham
   Peter Wilson, 92
Conley
   George W., 61
   Maria (Lewis), 61
Connelly
   Elenor, 58
Connerly
   Patrick, 92
Cook
   Eleanor M.V., 7, 9, 12, 18,
      19, 20, 21, 25, 34, 39,
      55, 56, 86, 103, 105,
      113, 114, 124, 131
   Michael L., 3, 7, 46
Cooney
   Pauline Beard, 22, 89,
      103, 113
Corcoran
   Thomas, 119
Cornell
   Phebe, 39
Cotton
   Jane Baldwin, 6
Cottrill
   Elizabeth (Dawson), 43
   Luther L., 43
   Massey (Dawson), 43
Coulter
   Shirley, 46
Cramphin
   Thomas, 83, 90
Craven
   family, 22, 89, 103
Croscomb
   Ezekial, 71
Curry
   Mrs. Elmer E., 9, 23

—D—

Dallain
   Richard, 77
Darnall
   John, 84, 92
Davie(?)
   Col., 46

Davis
   Cassey (Lewis), 58
   Catherine, 39
   Eliza Timberlake, 39
   Gary L., 41
   Humphrey, 41
   Israel, 40
   James, 40
   John (b. 1788), 39, 40
   John (Sr), 39
   John David, 56
   John Jr., 56
   Joseph, 41
   Matilda, 41, 58
   Naomi, 40
   Phebe, 57
   Phebe (Cornell), 39, 40, 59
   Ruth (Lewis), 39, 40, 41,
      59
   Samuel, 37, 39, 40, 41, 59
   Samuel L., 58
   Samuel of Tenmile, 40
   Sarah, 40, 59
   William, 40
Dawson
   Bassel, 43
   David L., 43
   Delila (Lewis), 60
   Elizabeth, 43
   Ervin, 43
   George, 43
   Lemuel, 60
   Massey, 43
   Noel Kent, 11, 33, 55, 57
   Rachel (Lewis), 43
   Roanna (Lewis), 61
   Russel, 43
   Samuel, 43
   Samuel (Jr.), 43
   Texie David (Lewis), 57,
      58
   Thomas, 5
   William, 61
   Wilson, 43
Day
   Jackson H., 9, 11
Deakins
   Eleanor (---), 119
   Francis, 114, 118, 119,
      120
   Leonard, 115
   Leonard M., 119, 120
   Will Jr., 14, 15
Deaver
   John, 80
deKeyser

Doris Jean (Post) Poinsett, author of this book, was born in Buckhannon, WV and grew up on a farm a few miles northwest of the city. She is a great-granddaughter of Elmore Dow and Sarah (Post) Lewis. A graduate of West Virginia Wesleyan College, she was with Smithsonian Institution in Washington, DC for nearly 18 years. There she was employed as a computer programmer and project manager. She is author of *Valentin Pfost/Post 1740-1800 of Hardy County, (West) Virginia and Some of His Descendants,* published in 1989. In 1991 *Valentin Pfost/Post* received the American Society of Genealogists' Donald Lines Jacobus Award for excellence. She is also author of *John/Jean Poinset (- by 1739) of Burlington, New Jersey, Pierre Poinset l'aîné (- 1699) of Charles Town, South Carolina and Some of Their Descendants,* published in 1998. She is a member of the National Genealogical Society, Maryland State Society DAR, Genealogy Club of the Montgomery County (MD) Historical Society, Upshur County (WV) Historical Society, and Hacker's Creek (WV) Pioneer Descendants. She is married to Benjamin Franklin Poinsett. Since 1994 they have lived in Bethesda, MD.

About this book...

This book was written using Microsoft Word 6.0.1 as a word processor on an Apple G4 (Macintosh OS9) with 256MB of RAM and a 30 Gigabyte hard disk. The text is 12 point Century Schoolbook with quoted documents and "Name Index" ten point Century Schoolbook. Notes are eight point Century Schoolbook. "Contents," "List of Abbreviations," and "List of Illustrations" are in ten point Courier. Camera-ready copy was produced using an HP LaserJet 2100 Printer. The book is printed on pH neutral paper.